NINETEENTH-CENTURY RELIGION
AND LITERATURE

Nineteenth-Century Religion and Literature

An Introduction

MARK KNIGHT AND EMMA MASON

OXFORD
UNIVERSITY PRESS

OXFORD
UNIVERSITY PRESS

Great Clarendon Street, Oxford OX2 6DP

Oxford University Press is a department of the University of Oxford.
It furthers the University's objective of excellence in research, scholarship,
and education by publishing worldwide in

Oxford New York

Auckland Cape Town Dar es Salaam Hong Kong Karachi
Kuala Lumpur Madrid Melbourne Mexico City Nairobi
New Delhi Shanghai Taipei Toronto

With offices in

Argentina Austria Brazil Chile Czech Republic France Greece
Guatemala Hungary Italy Japan Poland Portugal Singapore
South Korea Switzerland Thailand Turkey Ukraine Vietnam

Oxford is a registered trade mark of Oxford University Press
in the UK and in certain other countries

Published in the United States
by Oxford University Press Inc., New York

© Mark Knight and Emma Mason 2006

British Library Cataloguing in Publication Data
Data available

Library of Congress Cataloging in Publication Data
Data available

Typeset by Laserwords Private Limited, Chennai, India
Printed in Great Britain
on acid-free paper by
Biddles Ltd., King's Lynn, Norfolk

ISBN 0–19–927710–9   978–0–19–927710–0
ISBN 0–19–927711–7 (Pbk.)   978–0–19–927711–7 (Pbk.)

1 3 5 7 9 10 8 6 4 2

Acknowledgements

WE wish to express our appreciation to both Roehampton University and the University of Warwick for support while working on the book. Mark would like to thank Roehampton for a HEFCE Promising Researcher Fellowship which allowed him to spend six months working on the book at the School of English and Humanities, Birkbeck College, University of London. Birkbeck were kind and generous hosts, and particular thanks are due to Sally Ledger for making the visit possible. Emma would like to thank the British Academy and Corpus Christi, Oxford, for a Postdoctoral Fellowship which granted her the time to begin the project.

Over the last couple of years a number of people have listened to ideas in this book and responded in different ways, most of which have been helpful and encouraging. Some responses have directly shaped material in the book; others have been a general source of inspiration and/or concern as we have thought about exactly what we were seeking to do in the text that follows. We wish to acknowledge all those who will find their contribution herein, and we are especially grateful to the following for their support: Isobel Armstrong, Grover J. Askins, Dinah Birch, Brian Horne, Andrew King, Jo Knight, Jon Mee, Laura Peters, Jon Roberts, Russell Rook, Chris Rowland, John Schad, Joanne Shattock, Mark Turner, and Ana Vadillo. Finally, we wish to thank the considerate young man who responded favourably to our pleas to be let into the Samuel Palmer exhibition at the British Museum, even though it was full. Our attempts to find out his name have proven unsuccessful, but given the fact that he did not charge us, it is perhaps best that we are unable to print it here.

Contents

Introduction

AT the end of his essay, 'Hebraism and Hellenism' (1869), Matthew Arnold strikes a troubled note of concern regarding his fellow Victorians, at sea without the stability of an unquestioned Christianity for support, and desperate for a new guiding force. 'Everywhere we see the beginnings of confusion', he writes:

and we want a clue to some sound order and authority. This we can only get by going back upon the actual instincts and forces which rule our life, seeing them as they really are, connecting them with other instincts and forces, and enlarging our whole view and rule of life.[1]

Arnold suggests here that society is controlled by 'actual instincts and forces', ideologies that it must seek to penetrate and then check with 'other instincts and forces'. It is on this basis that he calls for a transformation of the 'dominant idea of religion' through the re-energizing stimuli of culture and poetry.[2] Religion, however, is not abandoned, either in the essay or anywhere in the book in which it appears. Indeed, *Culture and Anarchy* is a collection of essays that is near indecipherable without at least some understanding of existing religious expressions, such as Presbyterianism, Unitarianism, Anglicanism, the Oxford Movement, and Roman Catholicism. For Arnold, religion remains 'that voice of the deepest human experience', at once directing the individual inwards into a process of self-examination and moral assessment, but also outwards to that 'one great whole' that is humanity (or in the words of Paul, the 'divine body').[3] The tension the individual experiences between a desire to turn from oneself out to others (doing) and for inner self analysis (thinking) is explicated by Arnold through the categories 'Hebraism' and 'Hellenism'. Hebraism pertains to those rules associated with Judaic Christianity, for Arnold 'self-conquest, self-devotion, the following not our own individual will, but the will of God, *obedience*', that is, laws of right conduct governed by an earnest duty to work, action.[4] Hindered by bodily desire, the Hebraic dictates a strictness of conscience tuned to receive and be aware of all manner of sin, while remaining astute to the difficulties of achieving a state of perfection before God. Hellenism, however, is entirely focused on reaching such perfection through impulsive and spontaneous thought and action, 'seeing things as they really are' by stripping them down to a core of 'beauty' and 'simplicity'.[5] Following Socrates, the Hellenic individual not only strives to perfect him- or herself, but also feels the process working, more affectively aware of the experience of life than the Hebraic individual who is forever concerned with the impact of dutiful action in the present moment. The formula constructed in the essay, then, presents Judeo-Christian Hebraism in terms of moral consciousness and right action; and Greek Hellenism as a Platonic critical intelligence productive of an 'unimpeded play of thought'.[6]

While the limited way in which Arnold demarcates the Judeo-Christian tradition is questionable, what seems to have caused concern among Arnold's Victorian readership was the premiss that the two forces he outlines are interlocked and reciprocally influential. Most readers, Arnold assumed, regarded the Hellenic as an indulgent imitation of the Hebraic, rather than the two moving along together like divergent currents of one stream. As the 'bright promise of Hellenism faded' with the advent of Christianity, so the Hebraic return to the Bible during the Reformation was eventually overshadowed by Hellenism, which in turn was checked by the Puritans. Arnold's point in mapping this uneven chronology is that the aim of both movements, whether it be sacred or secular, works to the same end: the 'salvation' or 'liberty' of humanity and the achievement of a shared feeling of 'universal order' and harmony.[7] It is from this that Arnold developed his later definition of religion in *Literature and Dogma* (1873), namely, as a guiding light fuelled alternately by human understanding of what is right in a given situation and the translation of that conclusion into action:

Religion, if we follow the intention of human thought and human language in the use of the word, is ethics heightened, enkindled, lit up by feeling; the passage from morality to religion is made, when to morality is applied emotion. And the true meaning of religion is thus not simply *morality*, but *morality touched by emotion*. And this new elevation and inspiration of morality is well marked by the word 'righteousness'. Conduct is the word of common life, morality is the word of philosophical disquisition, righteousness is the word of religion.[8]

Here is the Hellenic and the Hebraic united, right action and intuitive thought shepherded by sensibility and forging not just a design for life but a mode of reading: after all, *Literature and Dogma* was written to deepen readers' understanding of, and approach to, the Bible. As David Delaura argues in *Hebrew and Hellene in Victorian England*, Arnold sought to harmonize reason or rationalism with intuition or faith, so producing a dialectical ideal that might cancel the ongoing swing from Hebraism to Hellenism and back again.[9] Arnold's responsible citizen, then, anchored him- or herself in a state of moral emotion produced from a dialectic of rational and faithful feeling.

This dialectic might be similarly useful for modern, predominantly secular readers, who arguably tend to isolate religious questions from other apparently non-spiritual or material discourses. Theological debate was almost inseparable from philosophical, scientific, medical, historical, and political thought in the eighteenth and nineteenth centuries. To insist on rigid boundaries between the sacred and secular, as many thinkers have done from the eighteenth century onwards, is to demarcate religious space in a narrow and misleading manner. One of the central arguments of this book is that there is a continual slippage between the sacred and the secular. Religious thought and practice are present throughout nineteenth-century literature and culture, sometimes in surprising and unexpected places. Our book will actively destabilize the categories of the sacred and secular without dispensing with them altogether: despite the limitations and problems of this language, it was common currency among nineteenth-century writers. These categories also highlight the question of how to define religion in the period: modern scholars, like their nineteenth-century predecessors, must ask how religion entered public and everyday life, and what means were used to contain or define its influence. Arnold's broad definition of religion affords it a large expanse of territory, but it does so at the cost of sustaining religion as anything other than human culture. While human culture and religion overlap—the latter can only be read in terms of its relation to the former—they do not occupy precisely the same space. Tensions between religion and other cultural forces are evident throughout the nineteenth century, as between different religious belief systems: to ignore this and argue for an all-purpose definition of religion risks homogenizing and caricaturing beliefs.

We have chosen to focus our discussions in this book on British Christianity, specifically English Christianity, partly to help maintain focus amid the chronological range under discussion; and partly because, despite the import of non-Christian religions in the period, notably Judaism and Islam, Britain was predominantly a Christian culture. Describing nineteenth-century Britain in this way is not an attempt to insist on culturally uniform readings: the general understanding of what it meant to be Christian obviously changed over time and the content of any shared religious beliefs was subject to vigorous disputes. Nor, in writing freely of nineteenth-century Britain as a Christian culture, are we attempting to Christianize the past: we are simply noting that, despite a divergence of belief and practice among different denominations and traditions, the majority of people in the nineteenth century perceived British culture to be principally Christian. Acknowledging this perception is vital to study of the period, even if we rightly insist on interrogating it closely. Many nineteenth-century thinkers were similarly concerned to question what a 'Christian' Britain might look like and determine where a specifically Christian influence might be found. As the subsequent chapters of this book will show, different Christian traditions sought God in different places, from the realm of feeling to the realm of rational thought, from conservative to radical politics, and from practical action through doctrinal purity to the realm of aesthetics. For some, such as Henry Mansel, the unique contribution of Christian thought was to be found in its evocation of transcendence and/or the afterlife; while for others, like F. D. Maurice, the prominence of references to the kingdom of God in the Gospel accounts was a sign of Christianity's commitment to this world and its transformation.

Despite our own theological prejudices and preferences, many of which we have deliberately chosen to keep in this subjective introduction to nineteenth-century religion, we have tried to avoid siding with a particular denomination or expression of belief and championing it as the repository of authentic Christianity. Any suggestion that, say, the Presbyterians, the Tractarians, or anyone else, exclusively embodied true religion would be to repeat the mistake many of these organizations' most passionate supporters made when they adamantly insisted that Christian religion accorded to their definition alone. However, the problem of going to the other extreme and claiming that Christianity is to be found everywhere is that our discussion of a specific and identifiable faith risks collapsing into meaninglessness. So what do we mean when we use the term Christian? In its simplest terms, Christianity refers to a body of belief centred around the person of Jesus Christ. More broadly, to speak of the Christian faith is to make reference to a particular polyphonic narrative centred around the alleged revelation of God in the person of Christ, located in historical events and sustained by the teaching of the Church over a large expanse of space and time.

Christianity is not a closed set of rigid and obscure doctrine; it is a story, imaginatively told in the books of the Bible and interpreted over the last 2,000 years by a Church that is diverse and frequently in disagreement as to what the biblical narratives mean. The Christian narrative is evidently mediated and thus not strictly essential, but it is no less essential than other categories of thought (such as class or gender) that we commonly use as a basis for thinking about and interpreting cultural history. Like all stories, the Christian one is not predetermined, but neither is it completely open-ended. Its meaning cannot be contained and yet it is not possible to reconstitute the story in any way one wishes, primarily because each new proclamation or enactment of the narrative bears relation to the preceding part of the story, which has already been written.[10]

It is the sense of a time-bound, continuing, shared narrative that helps explain the thinking behind the Christian creeds. The writing of all the Christian creeds exposed and perpetuated considerable disagreement within the Church. Yet just because the summaries of Christian narrative provided by the creeds are highly political, it does not follow that the inherited shape of the Christian story is entirely dictated by forces alien to that story. Creeds generated controversy because their proponents believed in the public nature of the Christian story and cared about the way in which it was understood. As with the interpretation of literary texts, creeds cannot offer a reading of the text of the Christian story that is final or authoritative (hence their proliferation); this does not mean, however, that any and every reading of the Christian chronicle possesses equal validity. The ongoing deferral of doctrinal interpretation enacted through the creeds is a process that begins in the biblical narratives themselves, as St Paul recalls in 1 Corinthians 15: 3–6:

For I delivered unto you first of all that which I also received, how that Christ died for our sins according to the Scriptures; And that he was buried, and that he rose again the third day according to the Scriptures: And that he was seen of Cephas, then of the twelve: After that, he was seen of above five hundred brethren at once; of whom the greater part remain unto this present, but some are fallen asleep.

St Paul's subsequent insistence that Christ also appeared to him helps legitimate his own attempts at detailing the core of the Christian narrative in his letters. The incompleteness of any gloss, however, ensured that the Early Church would continue Paul's interpretative work, offering more detailed summaries of what they believed to be the intrinsic 'gospel' message. The best known of these early summaries is probably the Apostles' Creed:

> I believe in God, the Father almighty,
>   creator of heaven and earth.
> I believe in Jesus Christ, his only Son, our Lord.
>   He was conceived by the power of the Holy Spirit
>   and born of the Virgin Mary.
>   He suffered under Pontius Pilate,
>   was crucified, died, and was buried.
>   He descended to the dead.
>   On the third day he rose again.
>   He ascended into heaven,
>   and is seated at the right hand of the Father.
>   He will come again to judge the living and the dead.
> I believe in the Holy Spirit,
>   the holy Catholic Church,
>   the communion of saints,
>   the forgiveness of sins,
>   the Resurrection of the body,
>   and the life everlasting. Amen.

While the Apostles' Creed has been used extensively in western Christendom since its development by the Early Church, some felt that it lacked the detail necessary to resolve certain key theological debates, such as the Trinity, with its belief in a God consisting of three persons in perfect and eternal communion; and the Incarnation, with its reading of Jesus as fully God, fully man, and fully both. These subjects were addressed in both the Nicene Creed, issued by the Council of Nicaea in AD 325, and in the Athanasian Creed, originally attributed to St Athanasius but now thought to have been formulated in the fifth century.[11]

Beyond the creeds mentioned, the most recognized statement of faith in the nineteenth century was the Thirty-nine Articles. This collection of doctrinal statements had been adopted by the Church of England in the sixteenth century and was used throughout the nineteenth century as a test of theological orthodoxy, despite containing more ambiguity than some were prepared to admit. Clergy were required to affirm (and, before 1865, subscribe to) the Articles, and the dominance of the Church of England as the arbiter of religious thought was evident in the fact that, up until 1871, those wishing to enter Oxford and Cambridge universities were also expected to subscribe to them. This factor at least reveals how central the Established Church was for nineteenth-century

Christianity.[12] While many of our chapters concentrate on dissenting groups and counter-movements, expressions of faith outside the Church of England remained highly contingent on the Established Church. In many respects, the so-called secularization of religion in the latter part of the nineteenth century is best understood as a diminution of the power and reach of the Established Church rather than the decline of Christian ideas and culture.

For the majority of people in the nineteenth century, the doctrinal intricacies of the Church were experienced through texts that were unlikely to appear in a course of formal theology: hymns, tracts, poetry, and fiction. Many nineteenth-century households, for instance, owned a copy, not just of the Bible, but also of the Book of Common Prayer, the official service book of the Church of England. The version used in the nineteenth century had been revised in 1662 to accommodate Puritan grievances, and it mediated a variety of religious material through diverse literary forms. Arnold's notion of literature as a mode of religious thought opposed to the constraints of doctrinal consideration, and his aim to 'free "literature" from the "dogma" surrounding it' have been an unfortunate catalyst of the division of literature and theology in the modern university.[13] It is, however, a division that falls apart on closer investigation, as a number of critics have successfully shown.[14] The evolving relationship between Scripture and literature, for example, spurred hermeneutical innovations which impressed upon both modern linguistic and critical theory, as John Schad's work illuminates.[15] And as David Jasper suggests in *The Sacred and Secular Canon in Romanticism*, while poets like Wordsworth and Coleridge claimed an authority once held solely by the Bible, critics like Ruskin, Newman, and Carlyle began to recognize the playful, contradictory, and sometimes immoral messages inherent to Scripture.[16] Christianity in particular interrogated and reconstructed itself over and over as the chapters in this book demonstrate, stirred by new approaches to Scripture, doctrine, and the structure of the Church and its community. The critical hermeneutics that emerged from religious innovators such as John Wesley, John Keble, and G. K. Chesterton served at once to revitalize Christian thinking while also unmasking the use of both Scripture and other key religious texts as they had been employed for social manipulation or control. For all the harm Christianity had affected on women, Mary Wollstonecraft noted, it had also provided the terms of their liberation. As the theologian Christopher Rowland declares in *Radical Christianity*, Christianity offers people a powerful language of hope rooted in the idea of revelation and apocalypse, unveiling social and cultural conditions and offering an 'eschatological expectation of how society might be in the future'.[17] Many of the writers we address here use religion to the same end, employing or reinscribing Christian ideas and doctrines to comment on contemporary issues. The dissenting impact on the hymn, for example, sought to emotionalize a seemingly dry genre not only to reshape it in accordance with a new, mutinous theology, but also to draw more apathetic believers back into an active, communal faith. So successful was Dissent in this objective, that the Tractarians, moved by Romantic poetics, countered Dissent's popularizing move by reformulating the hymn as a private, meditative lyric that would serve as an antidote to a rapidly changing and anxiety-inducing Victorian era.

Even those writers who seem to stand against Christianity in the long nineteenth century are locked into an engagement with it, many grounded in a particular belief-system in their youths. George Eliot and John Ruskin, for example, both oscillate in their relationships to the Evangelicalism that coloured their childhoods, while Wordsworth and Coleridge move between varying religious systems as their social and domestic politics shifted according to circumstance. The unbelieving utilitarian, John Stuart Mill, for example, recognized that Christianity enabled a particular approach to the project of amending the material world, one shaped by moral responsibility and public duty. In addition to affecting even apparently secular debates in the period, Christianity was also built into the foundations of governance, Britain's Christian identity sustained by the unique bond that had been forged between Church and State. In England specifically, the State's approval of Anglicanism meant that any significant change in doctrine, liturgy, or Church structure had to be overseen and sanctioned by parliament while the monarchy were entrusted as defenders of the faith. No wonder Louis Althusser deemed religion a state apparatus, an ideological institution whose influence seeped into all aspects of the social fabric by framing life itself from birth through to marriage and finally death.[18] At the same time, Foucault's theory of reverse discourse seems applicable here, Christianity's focus on who should or should not be included in the Church drawing attention to many fraught issues concerning sexuality, class, gender, and race as our chapters show.[19] Yet there is something in Christianity's creedal foundation that enables writers as diverse as Christopher Smart, William Blake, and Christina Rossetti consciously to enact and then overturn religious law in creative and often radical terms. It is this capacity of the Christian faith for renewal, reform, and even revolution, which we hope to draw out in this book.

The diversity of perspectives among nineteenth-century writers who engaged with Christianity offers considerable challenges for those interested in the relation between religion and literature in the period. In the context of this book, we are profoundly aware how much has been left out. There are a host of important writers who receive little or no attention in the ensuing chapters, including, among others, Jane Austen, Alfred Tennyson, George MacDonald, Mark Rutherford, and Mrs Humphrey Ward. Further, it is not only important writers that are missing from the chapters that follow. Several important issues, such as the debates surrounding (non)observance of the Sabbath day and the textual legitimacy of the Revised Version of the Bible (1881–4), have been excluded from our introduction to nineteenth-century religion and literature.[20] No 'introduction' can ever live up to the comprehensiveness promised by such a title, and the problem is particularly acute with regard to nineteenth-century religion. Religion was not just another aspect of the nineteenth century: it found its way into every area of life, from family to politics, sport to work, church architecture to philanthropy. The list of topics that we might reasonably have considered in this book is endless. What we have sought to do, therefore, is to offer a way into some of the nineteenth-century's main texts, beliefs, and religious events, rather than provide a fully comprehensive guide. Moreover, our commitment to literature as a distinct textual mode has influenced our decision to explore the religious life of the period through a range of close readings. Rather than pack the book with as many references and examples as possible, we have chosen to exemplify a number of specific religious ideas in relation to select literary texts. This enables, we think, a forum in which different ways of reading the religious aspects of texts might be developed. Given our concern not to foreclose further discussion nor assert *a specific* way in which study of nineteenth-century religion and literature should be pursued, our joint authorship might be seen as something of an advantage. Certainly our experience of writing the book together has afforded us continual reminders that there is more than one way of imagining and thinking nineteenth-century religion and literature.

Instead of structuring this book according to a strict chronology, we have built each chapter around a particular religious movement or tradition. The difficulty with this arrangement is that it implies, quite wrongly,

that certain religious movements were exclusive to certain periods—
Evangelicalism and the mid-nineteenth century, for instance—when
this is blatantly not the case. All structures provide a narrative, whether
they like it or not, and our decision to order our focus on different
religious movements according to the broad chronology of the long-
nineteenth century will almost certainly encourage readings that we
readily acknowledge as problematic. We do not wish, for example, to
suggest that Catholicism is the epitome of religious development, nor
to imply that Dissent is a movement that one grows out of over time.
Our hope is that, in spite of these pitfalls, the decision to combine a
thematic and chronological structure facilitates the clear introduction of
complex theological ideas while simultaneously pointing to constructive and suggestive threads that cross over localized Christian traditions.
We have no wish to lock any writer, or his or her work, into a particular belief-system or religious ideology, nor are we concerned to shut
down what Christianity signifies, either doctrinally or culturally. Our
approach to William Blake provides a case in point. A writer fiercely
struggled over by critics intent on claiming him as the standard bear-
er of a Christian, humanist, or secular politics, his work refuses to be
categorized even as it is steeped in biblical rhetoric, Pauline theology,
and social radicalism. Our discussion of Blake in Chapter 1 alludes to
several religious lenses that might be used to view his work: Moravian,
Swedenborgian, Anabaptist, and Antinomian. We also stress, however,
that read outside of these movements, Blake's work remains prophetic,
apocalyptic, homiletic, and poetic, assuming an art form which consistently makes reference to, and is invested in, a body of belief represented
by Jesus Christ. Jesus is an artist for Blake because he creatively imagines
ways of compassionately responding to human suffering: debates which
lie outside of the redemption of humanity are simply not 'Christian' for
him. As Blake declares at the start of *A Vision of the Last Judgment* (1810):
'The Last Judgment when all those are Cast away who trouble Religion
with Questions concerning Good & Evil or Eating of the Tree of those
Knowledges or Reasonings which hinder the Vision of God.'[21] Those
who seek to muddy God's redemptive Christian vision by reducing it to
moral dichotomies or fixed laws, Blake suggests, are guilty of reasoning
it away or paralysing its meaning.

    Endeavouring to find a way into the fluidity of Christianity in this peri-
od, however, necessarily involves some contextual work and we position
many writers in relation to religious traditions they at once acknowledged and resisted. In recognition of the fact that nineteenth-century

religious belief and culture did not emerge from a vacuum in 1800, our two opening chapters make extensive reference to eighteenth-century religious debates. Chapter 1 outlines the influence of dissenting culture in the eighteenth century, asking what it might have meant to be a Dissenter or nonconformist. We establish what the Dissenters sought to move away from, outlining their rejection of ceremonial ritual and orderly worship for a public and spontaneous form of communal prayer marked by express intimacy with God. Differentiating 'old Dissent' from 'new', the chapter explores the development of the three main nonconformist bodies in the period, Presbyterianism, Congregationalism, and the Baptists, identifying those areas where they overlap and break from each other. In understanding the significance of these movements, the chapter also considers the profound impact of the Evangelical Revival, both on the development of Christianity and on the emergence of a new, private lyric later reworked by the Romantics. Discussing the hymnal innovations of Isaac Watts and John Wesley, for example, the chapter addresses the more unorthodox writing of Smart and Blake, both accused of a religious mania or 'enthusiasm', as well as the equally animated religious writing of Hannah More and Emily Brontë. We also turn to the influence of dissenting academies on writers like Anna Barbauld and Joseph Priestley, who both related to Dissent as a movement able to re-sensitize the emergent Enlightenment Christian, in order that he or she approach God with his or her heart, rather than head. Similarly, Dissent also allowed for psychological and scientific inquiry hitherto regarded as dangerous by an increasingly outdated orthodoxy forced to confront the Christian element in previously 'heretical' discoveries. Our second chapter follows on directly by turning to Unitarianism, a branch of Dissent that embraced late eighteenth-century rationalism, liberal capitalism, and Enlightenment culture within the terms of its beliefs. Preaching to middle-class believers in comfortable, elegant chapels, the Unitarians denied the divinity of Christ, the existence of 'mythical' realms like heaven and hell, and those doctrines difficult to discuss empirically, such as the Immaculate Conception and the Resurrection. The immense importance of the Trinity to Christianity, however, isolated the Unitarians who became increasingly secular in the way that they focused on education, women's rights, and the poor. As well as exploring the work of Mary Wollstonecraft, Wordsworth and Coleridge, Richard Price, Felicia Hemans, and Elizabeth Gaskell in relation to their individual interests in Unitarianism, the chapter sketches the relationship of this branch of Dissent both to the discourse of sensibility and also to its sister religion, Quakerism. We also cast light on a central debate within Unitarianism regarding the loss of mysterious or revelatory elements of faith, an event championed by William Johnson Fox and his literary circle; but mourned by those associated with the pioneering James Martineau.

The third chapter moves into the Victorian period to examine a religious and literary group known as the Oxford Movement, or Tractarianism, headed by preacher-poets whose doctrines and aesthetics alike enchanted writers from Wordsworth to Christina Rossetti and Gerard Manley Hopkins. Defined by its investment in restoring a High Anglican Catholic law to the Church, the Tractarians publicly discussed reserve, the Eucharist, confession, the Incarnation, and analogy, while also proscribing those literary methodologies they regarded as most suitable for communicating with God. Keble's *Lectures on Poetry* (1832–41) read like a manifesto designed to educate the reader in religious poetics while teaching him or her how to respond to it correctly. Yet Keble, like his fellow poets Isaac Williams and Frederick Faber, also sought to teach Christians how to write poetry, a genre which for him was capable of relieving readers from the troubles of an anxious world and leading them back to God. We close this chapter by noting the aesthetic impact of Tractarianism on secular writers like Walter Pater, who saw in the movement a sentimentalism compatible with both paganism and hedonism. Chapter 4 examines a group that was often deeply hostile to the Oxford Movement. Evangelicalism crossed denominational boundaries (including those between the Established Church and Dissent), and was marked by its emphasis on Christian beliefs such as the Cross, conversion, and the idea that the Bible was the supreme source of revelation. The permeable and invisible boundaries of Evangelicalism made it almost impossible to classify, a factor that led to distorting caricatures among some commentators. Outsiders were not alone in struggling to identify Evangelicalism accurately: Evangelicals expended considerable energy in trying to clarify what they were about, and they often answered the question by noting what they were not (for example, Catholic or Broad Church). There was more to Evangelicalism than its hostility to others, however. Our chapter explores the complex (dis)engagement of Evangelicalism with its surrounding culture, with reference to mid-century novels such as *Jane Eyre*, *David Copperfield*, *The Moonstone*, and *Bleak House*. Although the latter two texts are notable for their use of caricatured religious figures, they nevertheless manage to capture accurately Evangelical unease about the Bible and its interpretation in the mid-nineteenth century, a concern stirred up by the publication of *Essays and Reviews*. Part of the Evangelical response to the hermeneutic uncertainty of the period was to take refuge in rhetorical preaching, dramatic revivalism, and sensational tales of conversion. After considering the treatment of Evangelical discourse by novelists, the final part of the chapter reflects on questions of judgement, exploring the treatment of temptation and the trope of the fallen woman in *Middlemarch* and *Tess of the D'Urbervilles* respectively. The chapter ends by tracing a vociferous debate among Evangelicals over hell, one that exposed the narrowness of doctrine and the diversity of theological perspective that characterized the movement.

Our attempt in Chapter 4 to appreciate the complexity of Evangelicalism is followed in Chapter 5 by an attempt to rethink the meaning of secularization. The dramatic development of modernity in the second half of the nineteenth century had a visible and sizeable impact on religious belief in Britain, but we take issue with the common assumption that Christianity experienced a linear and fatal haemorrhage in the latter part of the nineteenth century. Beginning with a close reading of Dickens's *A Christmas Carol*, we suggest other ways in which secularization might be read. The consequences for religion of the cultural ascendancy of materialism are considered with the help of several short ghost stories. Parallels are then made between the way in which this genre sought to come to terms with the unknown, and an important debate among theologians in the mid-Victorian period over the relative merits of transcendence and immanence as the starting-point for theology. Such theological differences, between those who sought God in the world beyond, and those who sought him in the here and now, help explain the different attitudes towards the city that one finds among Christian groups of the period. Some Christians viewed the city negatively, but others found in it the means of refiguring the relation between Christianity and culture. Using George Gissing's novels, and material relating to the work of the Salvation Army, the chapter argues that one of the effects of nineteenth-century urbanization was to restore a prophetic role to the Church, one that took seriously the call found in the Sermon on the Mount (Matthew 5–7) for the people of God to be salt and light. Dissenting Christians found it easier than their counterparts in the Established Church to accommodate the role of prophet: the latter were more likely to occupy positions of socio-political power and this investment in the establishment made it harder for them to criticize their surrounding culture. Inevitably, the decline of Christianity's privileged position in society undermined both the status of the Church of England and also the idea of a state religion, but this is not evidence of a decline in Christianity per se. Late nineteenth-century contestations of faith expressed themselves in debates about blasphemy and freethinking, as *Jude the Obscure* reveals, and yet such challenges, seemingly detrimental to religion, in fact created a new platform for continued discussion. The chapter concludes by suggesting that, despite its author's antagonism to Christianity, Hardy's novel reminds us of the rewriting that is intrinsic to the Christian tradition.

The final chapter shows the extent to which the religious map of Britain was redrawn at the end of the century. It explores the interest among many late nineteenth-century writers in both Catholicism and the religious ideas with which it was, albeit problematically, associated, such as Mysticism. We begin with the work of J. K. Huysmans, a writer, like Oscar Wilde, whose turn to Catholicism has been treated sceptically by many critics. The chapter argues that some of this scepticism stems from a long tradition of British anti-Catholicism, manifest throughout the nineteenth century and exemplified in Bram Stoker's *Dracula*. Protestant readers were often blinded to the diversity, nuance, and intellectual vitality of Catholic writers, but, as recent critics such as Frederick Roden and Marion Thain have pointed out, the poetry of writers such as Michael Field (the pseudonym of Edith Cooper and Katherine Bradley) was profoundly influenced by Catholic theology. After reflecting on the important role of Catholic publishers in the period, the chapter examines the treatment of nature and creation in the work of Alice Meynell and Oscar Wilde, both of whom utilized different forms of sacramentalism to see religion in the material world. While sacramentalism offered a means of linking together religion and aesthetics, it also brought with it the possibility of slipping into increasingly heterodox interpretations, as the work of Marie Corelli exemplifies. Our last chapter closes with a discussion of Meynell's distinction between mysticism and religion as a means of structuring a comparison between two important but different writers at the turn of the century: W. B. Yeats and G. K. Chesterton.

NOTES

1. M. Arnold, 'Hebraism and Hellenism', in *Culture and Anarchy* (1869), ed. J. D. Wilson (Cambridge: Cambridge University Press, 1990), 129–44 (144).

2. Arnold, 'Sweetness and Light', in *Culture and Anarchy*, 43–71 (54).

3. Ibid. 47–8.

4. Arnold, 'Hebraism and Hellenism', 132.

5. Ibid. 131, 134.

6. Ibid. 132.

7. Ibid. 131.

8. M. Arnold, *Literature and Dogma; an essay towards a better apprehension of the Bible* (London: Smith, Elder and Co., 1873), 20–1.

9. See D. J. Delaura, *Hebrew and Hellene in Victorian England: Newman, Arnold, Pater* (Austin, Tex.: University of Texas Press, 1969).

10. For a helpful account of the way in which writers seeking to rewrite the Bible are faced with a text that is not entirely malleable, see H. Fisch, *New Stories for Old: Biblical Patterns in the Novel* (New York: Macmillan Press, 1988).

11. See J. N. D. Kelly, *The Athanasian Creed* (London: A. & C. Black, 1964); and J. N. D. Kelly, *Early Christian Creeds*, 3rd edn. (Harlow: Longman, 1972).

12. In his recent study, *Contested Christianity: The Political and Social Contexts of Victorian Theology* (Waco, Tex.: Baylor University Press, 2004), Timothy Larsen justifiably complains of the comparative neglect of dissenting religion among historians working on the nineteenth century, a neglect that is especially apparent in Owen Chadwick's nevertheless magisterial and indispensable work, *The Victorian Church*, 2 vols. (London: A. & C. Black, 1966).

13. P. Davis, *The Oxford English Literary History*, viii. *1830–1880: The Victorians* (Oxford: Oxford University Press, 2002), 134.

14. It is worth noting that a number of contemporary academic journals explore the relationship between literature and theology—see, for example, *Literature and Theology*, *Religion and Literature*, and *Christianity and Literature*.

15. See A. C. Thiselton, *New Horizons in Hermeneutics: The Theory and Practice of Transforming Biblical Reading* (Grand Rapids, Mich.: Zondervan, 1992); and J. Schad, *Queer Fish: Christian Unreason from Darwin to Derrida* (Brighton: Sussex Academic Press, 2004).

16. See D. Jasper, *The Sacred and Secular Canon in Romanticism: Preserving the Sacred Truths* (Basingstoke: Macmillan, 2000).

17. C. Rowland, *Radical Christianity: A Reading of Recovery* (Oxford: Polity Press, 1988), 11.

18. See L. Althusser, 'Ideology and Ideological State Apparatuses: Notes Towards an Investigation' (1970), in *Lenin and Philosophy* (London: New Left Books, 1971), 127–86.

19. See M. Foucault, *The History of Sexuality: An Introduction* (1976), trans. R. Hurley (London: Penguin, 1990), 101.

20. For a useful account of nineteenth-century Sabbatarianism, see J. Wigley, *The Rise and Fall of the Victorian Sunday* (Manchester: Manchester University Press, 1980); and for a thoughtful analysis of the impact of the Revised Version of the Bible, see J. Marsh, *Word Crimes: Blasphemy, Culture, and Literature in Nineteenth-Century England* (Chicago: Chicago University Press, 1998), 255–9.

21. W. Blake, *[A Vision of the Last Judgment]*, *For the Year 1810*, in *The Poetry and Prose of William Blake*, ed. D. V. Erdman (New York: Doubleday, 1965), 544.

1

Dissent: Wesley to Blake

On 14 July 1791, the Constitutional Society of Birmingham arranged a dinner to celebrate the anniversary of the storming of the Bastille. Anti-revolutionary fervour was already high, and the celebration provoked an organized mob to attack the homes of several Dissenters, including the scientist, Joseph Priestley. His chapel, house, library, and laboratory were all burned down. Commenting on the events, Priestley wrote:

In all the newspapers and most of the periodical publications I was represented as an unbeliever in Revelation and no better than an atheist... On the walls of houses, etc., and especially where I usually went, were to be seen, in large characters, '... DAMN PRIESTLEY; NO PRESBYTERIANISM; DAMN THE PRESBYTERIANS' etc., etc.[1]

While Priestley had publicly defended Presbyterianism, he was himself at first an Arian and then a Socinian, religious positions which confused his graffiti-scrawling opponents as much as they do many twenty-first-century readers.[2] To understand what upset the rioters, as well as those within the Established Church of England, we must unpack what it meant to be a 'Dissenter' or a 'nonconformist'. In its literal sense, Dissent defines religious positions that refused to conform to the Tudor model of Anglicanism implemented by the Church of England. In this sense, Roman Catholicism and Judaism are also nonconformist religions, but this chapter is concerned to map Protestant nonconformism and how it separated itself from the dominant authority of Anglicanism. Anglicanism founded such authority not only on the Bible but also on Church Tradition as it was demarcated by the Patristic Fathers, the three Creeds (Nicene, Apostolic, and Athanasian), the Thirty-nine Articles, and the Book of Common Prayer (1662).[3] Nonconformists, or Dissenters, however, considered such tradition a distraction from what they believed was the sole source for Christian authority: the Bible. As the Evangelical clergyman, Charles Simeon declared: 'God has not revealed his truth in a system: the Bible has no system as such. Lay aside system and flee to the Bible ... Be Bible Christians and not system Christians.'⁴

The differing foundations upon which Anglicans and Dissenters built their beliefs had a significant impact on the way they practised such faith. Anglicans invested in a form of ceremonial rooted in ritualism and a medieval liturgical tradition; a conception of the Church as a national institution with state power; and a form of worship characterized by reserve, dignity, order, and comprehensiveness. Nonconformists, however, favoured plain scriptural readings rather than what they regarded as mysterious ceremonials; considered worship to be specific to local, gathered churches; and privileged a form of public prayer that was intimate, spontaneous, particular, and direct. Yet the difference in emphasis on these elements within various forms of nonconformism consists of more than pedantic doctrinal preferences. Divergent opinions in dissenting belief affected the individual's everyday life: his or her politics, moral prerogatives, aesthetic inclinations, and literary tastes. Literature much elevated by late eighteenth-century nonconformists (the 'new' Dissenters), such as Milton's religious works, had been more anxiously considered by their predecessors (the 'old' Dissenters). This chapter will identify what defined old and new dissenting outlooks, exploring the significance of the main three nonconformist bodies—the Presbyterians, Congregationalists, and Baptists—for the development of religious poetry, prose, and pulpit oratory in the late eighteenth century and Romantic period. Such positions will often appear to overlap because they in themselves change during the eighteenth century: it only makes sense to consider Anna Barbauld, for example, as a *late*, rather than early eighteenth-century Presbyterian, as we shall see. As the period became increasingly latitudinarian, that is, tolerant of varying belief-systems, many individuals shifted their religious allegiance: the first Presbyterian, then Baptist, and finally Unitarian minister, Joshua Toulmin, even requested that, on his death, his pall should be carried by six ministers of different denominations.⁵ Liberal, oppositional, and dedicated to reform, Dissent inevitably overlapped with radical politics in the period, especially the Unitarians and Quakers who are discussed in Chapter 2. In this chapter, however, we will turn first to old Dissent, then to the Evangelical revival and its impact on the hymn and religious lyric, and subsequently to the dissenting academies that educated believers in nonconformist tradition. Our aim here is to contextualize the later chapters by detailing some essential eighteenth-century religious and literary debates without which nineteenth-century religion makes little sense. A brief discussion of perhaps the most radical of all 'Dissenters', William Blake a prophetic poet whose faith has laid the foundations for much modern debate over what constitutes a Christian dissenting position, brings us to the turn of the century and the end of the chapter.

OLD DISSENT

Early eighteenth-century nonconformism, or 'old Dissent', had two main concerns: the relationship between God and the believer; and the organization of the Christian Church. Both had been under-mined, thought the nonconformists, by Charles II's reformed Church of England, imposing as it had an Act of Uniformity (1662) which required the use of all the rites and ceremonies in the Book of Common Prayer within church services. The Act also demanded that every minis-ter be episcopally ordained, a move that forced almost 2,000 clergymen to leave the Established Church, barring them from the universities of Oxford and Cambridge, and preventing them from holding civil or military office. While the Act of Toleration (1689) offered some compromise, the ascendancy of the zealous conformist, Queen Anne, in 1702, led to a series of attacks on Dissenters and their properties which were textually supported by reactionary Anglican sermons such as those given by the Bishop of Oxford, Henry Sacheverell. While the lofty hypocrisy Sacheverell represented was considered distasteful by many, and notoriously satirized by Daniel Defoe in *The Shortest Way with Dissenters* (1702), full rights to all believers were not reinstated until legislation implemented by the Duke of Wellington in 1828. At the same time as liberal ministers were forced into orders with which they disagreed, the clergy holding up the Established Church were perceived by many as corrupt and 'immoral'. Thomas Coke insisted to the Bishop of London that these immoral ministers set a terrible example by frequenting 'cardtables, balls, horse-racing, theatres and all other places of fashionable amusement', only preaching a message of humility and discipline on a Sunday.[6] As John Clare lamented in 'The Parish':

> Too high religion looks her flocks to watch,
> Or stoop from pride to dwell in cots of thatch,
> Scenes too important constant business brings
> That lends no time to look on humbler things.[7]

Certainly those rural communities to which Clare sought to give a voice felt under attack from a middle-class clergy as much as the enclosure movement, and revivalism and Dissent offered both escape from clerical control and also a way of securing some power in society. Eighteenth-century nonconformists came to consider themselves radical reformers, protecting the relationship between God and individuals from all social backgrounds by stressing that God's grace and human responsibility were at the heart of faith. Grace signifies God's benevolence towards humanity, a supernatural free gift which individuals do not earn or deserve but which nevertheless allows for their redemption from sin through Christ's crucifixion. It is almost like a fuel which everyone possesses but which must be stimulated by the individual in order to spark the energy that grants moments of divine illumination regarding both how to live in the mortal world and develop a meaningful relationship with God. Since Aquinas, Christians believed that God could be reached through both 'natural' or intellectual knowledge (reason); and also an affective or supernatural knowledge (faith). At the end of the seventeenth century, a movement known as Deism began to stress the former approach, rejecting revelation, providence, and divine intervention for the idea that God created the world for rationalist humans to do with what they will. For the Deists, Christianity comprised ethical action, morals, and charitable works, yet, for many Dissenters, this viewpoint rendered belief an icy experience devoid of feeling or experience of the divine. Even though the dominant dissenting positions in the period—Presbyterianism, Congregationalism (or Independence), Baptism, and Quakerism—seemed to hold very different theological opinions, they all agreed that feeling was essential to sincere belief in God.

All of the dissenting positions occupied by believers in the early eighteenth century placed value on an emotive *and* rational relationship with God, even though the expression of the two factors varied. While the Presbyterians and Independents alike both invested in a Calvinist theology practised within some sort of national Church, the two religious groups were regarded as sharply opposed during this period. The first derives its name from the word *presbyteros*, or 'elder', hinting at the pyramidical organization of its members and its stress on clerical leadership. Presbyterianism had been brought into Scotland by the Calvinist John Knox in 1560, and then secretly introduced into England in 1572. When Civil War broke out in 1642, however, Parliament looked around for allies from all camps, securing the support of Presbyterians by pledging to adopt their rigid, hierarchical, and clerically dominated 'church order'. A few years later, the Presbyterians had put in place a religious system that became their main constitutional document: the Confession of Faith passed by the Westminster Assembly of Divines in 1646. Written in part as a response to High Church Anglicanism, which seemed to the Presbyterians to be overly interested in the pleasures of ornate ritual, the document underlined the importance of recognizing God as the sovereign and scripture as law. Elders were to be ordained as responsible for the discipline and mission of local congregations, who in turn were accountable for their own religious education by a constant study of Scripture and recommended theological writings. Yet the body of clergy who had debated the Westminster Confession included some who found Presbyterianism too rigorous in its theology, and stressed instead the necessity for a greater tolerance of belief. The decisive break came at a meeting known as the Salter's Hall Synod in 1719, where many Presbyterians refused to subscribe to a belief in the Trinity. While most Presbyterians were Trinitarians (they believed in the three-personed God), the younger, more tolerant generation of believers thought it morally wrong to require subscription to a much debated creed and so split from old Presbyterianism.[8] Divorced as they were from the Synod and the Confession, then, this group became known as the Independents (sometimes called Separatists), including as it did a number of smaller sects who considered Presbyterianism too orthodox and Puritan.

Independent believers were often referred to as Congregationalists, because, unlike the Presbyterians, they favoured a system of church governance in which the laity held a kind of communal power allowing every local congregation to be self-regulating. The 'Church', then, only signified as far as it identified a living, gathered group of believers who had to take responsibility for their own faith by studying the Bible, acting charitably, and supporting their community. Theoretically, Congregationalist ministers had little authority within their parish, acting on behalf of a laity who had previously approved and elected them. The Independents claimed further that no power was to be concentrated in any kind of ruling body, and that the individual believer was relatively free to speak his or her mind on matters of faith without fear of correction or derision. All of these ideas were also advocated by the Baptists, who pushed the centrality of biblical authority, local church independence, and the priesthood of all believers even further. Baptists also insisted on the separation of the Church from the State, fearing that monarchical or governmental interference in religious matters would prevent believers trusting solely in scriptural leadership. Christ had not died on the Cross so that mortal officials could rule social life, argued the Baptists, and they insisted on making law the idea of 'justification by faith' to ensure that personal belief was valued over external actions or influences. No wonder the Baptists, like the Independents, split from the Presbyterians when the monarchy regained power and seduced the latter into an acceptance of a conforming High Anglican Church order. Some Presbyterians, however, were frustrated by their newly compromised position and sought to forge an allegiance with the Independents that became known as the 'Happy Union' of 1691. What divisions and reunions such as this tell us is that there was always an ongoing process of merging between different dissenting Churches at play in the eighteenth century, even though we can still usefully draw a line between those (like the old Presbyterians), who longed for re-inclusion in the Established Church, and those (like the Baptists), who felt safer outside of conformity.

EVANGELICAL DISSENT

Some considered this line a superficial one, however, as well as being potentially threatening to the degree of power Dissent as a united movement might hold in relation to its battle against rationalism, Deism, and orthodox conformism. Old Dissent always worked to accommodate other religious positions, but as it splintered into multiple sects and churches, the rationalists removed themselves from the Evangelicals only to threaten the core of Dissent itself. As Isabel Rivers argues, by disavowing feeling in its religious politics where affectionate beliefs had once held great sway, rational Dissent became a threat to Dissent itself.[9] Feeling had always been part of Evangelical Dissent, a pietistic religion that invested deeply in the primacy of the believer's own experience of religion and in the variety of the experiences of others. Referring to the belief that Christ is a saviour figure sent to spread the 'good news' as it appears in the Gospels, Evangelicalism had initially been associated with seventeenth-century Puritanism. Evangelicals certainly considered the heart and affections as the guides of the will and understanding, one of the few Puritan traditions accepted by rational and Evangelical Dissent alike. Rationalists, however, moulded the knowledge of the heart into both a kind of religious psychology and a philosophical exploration of what constitutes human nature; whereas Evangelicals tended to elevate such knowledge as a way of subverting an increasingly rational and intellectual climate in religious debate.

Isaac Watts and Philip Doddridge were ideally placed to stage-manage such a debate, the former raised as an orthodox Calvinist but settling as an Independent; the latter siding with a strain of low Calvinism which opposed both orthodoxy and rational Dissent as cold and dry belief-systems. Both feared that Dissent had lost its identity, and so agreed on the revival of a vital and practical religion that stressed the role of feeling in producing moral action. Reason was still valued, in that it provided the individual with the means to receive, test, and accept revelation, but, without feeling, it was a 'poor, dark bewildered thing', wrote Watts, unable to grasp knowledge or provide an impetus for good works.[10] The two preachers used the word 'affection' to describe the relationship between reason and feeling, one that connoted devotional feeling itself as Anna Barbauld would pick up in her essay, *Thoughts on the Devotional Taste, on Sects, and on Establishments* (1775), to which we return below. Watts was careful to define affection against stronger feelings like passion, claiming in *The Doctrine of the Passions Explained and Improved* (1729) that the latter feeling was primarily felt in 'the Flesh and Blood'.[11] Affection, on the other hand, signified a balanced emotion able to excite and move the individual, incline him or her to '*Benevolence* or *Good-will*', but always dependent on reason as its anchor point.[12] Affection was also considered important as that which obliged the believer to unite with others, whether this be God or fellow human beings, thus causing 'a mutual Communication of good offices between the Lover and the Person beloved' which ultimately leads to '*Devotion* to God, which is the highest Love'.[13]

Driving and enabling strong relationships, affection formed the foundation for the body of the Church and that public devotion which Deists most feared: the very essence of much Dissent lay in the relationship between the minister's close, affectionate relationship with his congregation. He was thus expected to apply general doctrine to the special circumstances of individuals, just as poets of the period began to use the genre as a way of communicating events and feelings particular to him-or herself. In this sense, Watts is a pre-Romantic in that he valued poetry as a way of both expressing the self, and also transmitting religious ideas, investing in an affectionate and gentle lyricism which would become a model for eighteenth-century dissenting hymns. This gentle lyricism is not passive, however. Watts's hymns suggest that he considered solid, unquestioning faith to stem only from a personal upheaval in which one is internally disturbed by a heartfelt experience of the divine. As J. R. Watson argues, hymns are 'hermeneutical acts', condensed reinterpretations of scripture and theology that serve as a platform on which to celebrate the importance of revealed religion and the glory of God in the created world.[14] In 'Eternal Wisdom! thee we praise', for example, anthologized by Wesley in *A Collection of Hymns selected for the people called Methodists* (1780), Watts intimates that God's presence only feels real in the world when the believer becomes fearful of it, entering into a religious state which triggers the imaginative power necessary to begin comprehending the divine:

> Thy glories blaze all nature round,
> And strike the wond'ring sight,
> Through skies, and seas, and solid ground
> With terror and delight.
>
> Infinite strength and equal skill
> Shine through thy works abroad.
> Our souls with vast amazement fill.
> And speak the builder God.

Watts follows these verses, however, by concluding the hymn with a more tender reminder that after the believer's fear has subsided, affectionate 'softer passions' will be stirred moving him or her closer to a loving, rather than terrifying God:

> But the mild glories of Thy grace
> Our softer passions move;
> Pity divine in Jesu's face
> We see, adore, and love.

The simplicity of such verses to communicate a complex relationship made the hymn an ideal vehicle to carry religious messages, a far remove from the dreary chants Watts supposed were alienating congregations from God in the period. He sought instead to compose clear and pious verses that might impart the truth of the Gospels in both the simplest and also most compelling terms. 'Come, let me Love' stages this by enacting a sexual encounter between the believer and God through a plain and yet passionate language:

> O 'tis a Thought would melt a Rock,
> And make a Heart of Iron move,

> That those sweet Lips, that heavenly Look
> Should seek and wish a mortal Love!

For the worshipper singing in church, the hymn enables a feeling of physical interaction with God, as he or she is embraced by Christ's 'naked arms' in the communal setting of the chapel or church.

For the Wesleys, the hymn was doubly important as both the best mode of spreading an Evangelical message to the greatest number of people; and also as a way of illuminating the personal relationship the believer was free to forge with God. The Wesleyan, or Methodist hymn used language that was clear, precise, and accessible, offering a place for the worshipper to meditate on, as well as learn by heart, brief phrases from the Scriptures.[15] While many literary critics regard these hymns as devoid of aesthetic merit, they were nonetheless hugely successful in their aim to versify tenets of scriptural law in an available and memorable manner; the tune and metre of such hymns spiritually and emotionally uplifted the believer, a far cry from the turgid homiletic rhetoric many clergy preached.[16] As D. W. Bebbington argues, poetry proved the most popular literary genre of the Evangelical revival, a factor Wesley attributed to poetry's capacity to express 'perspicuity and purity, propriety, strength' rather than the esoteric lyricism of a poet like Christopher Smart.[17] All the same, the Wesleys concurred with Smart's aim to whip up the believer into a state receptive to God's word, achieved in part by the rousing strains of those texts selected for their *A Collection of Hymns*. Charles Wesley's 'I Want a Principle Within' (1749) is suggestive of the importance Methodism placed both on the believer's own emotional relationship with God, and also on the strength religion had to control or 'quench' such passion:

> I want a principle within
> of watchful, godly fear,
> a sensibility of sin,
> a pain to feel it near.
> I want the first approach to feel
> of pride or wrong desire,
> to catch the wandering of my will,
> and quench the kindling fire.
>
> .   .   .   .   .
>
> Almighty God of truth and love,
> to me thy power impart;
> the mountain from my soul remove,
> the hardness from my heart.

> O may the least omission pain
> my reawakened soul,
> and drive me to that blood again,
> which makes the wounded whole.

Hymns such as this are sometimes referred to as 'conversion hymns', religious poems that capture the range of feelings the believer encounters on the Christian journey. Charles Wesley was regarded as a particularly skilled proponent of such verse, in part because of his successful employment of rhetorical questioning to reveal the joy he experienced during and as a result of his own conversion:

> And can it be, that I should gain
> An interest in the Saviour's blood?
> Died he for me, who caused his pain?
> For me? Who him to death pursued?
> Amazing love! How can it be
> That thou, my God, shouldst die for me?[18]

The profound popularity of Charles's hymns can be attributed to more than just their depiction of personal religious joy. Many had a political element which Charles achieved by rewriting scriptural passages to reflect the social conditions of his age: 'Sinners my gracious Lord receives', for example, draws on Mark 2: 17 to speak to those who feel undeserving before God, but Charles lists such sinners, not simply as the weak or unbelieving, but more specifically as 'Harlots, and publicans, and thieves'.[19] The Methodist hymn was thus able to highlight a number of social issues present in the public conscience—prostitution, petty crime, and financial exploitation—and secure their resolution in moral passages from the Bible.[20]

The politically subversive side of the Wesleyan hymn was often attacked under a different guise, however, that of enthusiasm, an arousing internal affective experience associated with both poetry and religion that, as William Hazlitt put it, melted and then kindled the heart.[21] For the religious critic John Dennis, enthusiasm differed from mere sensation in that it could only be generated by meditative concentration on complex theological issues, self-regulating rather than unruly.[22] Dennis argued that enthusiastic passion of this kind could transform both poetry and humanity, shaping the mind through religion. Thus poetry emerges from an enthusiasm 'moved by the ideas in contemplation', rather than a 'vulgar passion' which arises from 'the objects themselves': a potentially intellectual endeavour, then, rather than a purely instinctive one.[23] Many did see enthusiasm as vulgar, however, considering it to be a dangerous check to 'progressive' Enlightenment values: as the third Earl of Shaftesbury noted, enthusiasm was like a 'growing mischief' or a 'disease' which inflamed the individual like a contagious itch.[24] For others, enthusiasm was a code word for Roman Catholic superstition, although David Hume was careful to separate the two in his essay 'Of Superstition and Enthusiasm' (1741). Where enthusiasm allowed 'raptures, transports, and surprising flights of fancy', superstition depresses the individual's spirits to such an extent that he or she cannot approach God, distressed by his or her unworthiness and forced to use a priest as mediator.[25] Enthusiasts are more 'free from the yoke of ecclesiastics', experiencing a 'fury' like 'that of thunder and tempest, which exhaust themselves in a little time, and leave the air more calm and serene than before'.[26] Yet even Hume's more sympathetic assessment of enthusiasm's liberatory potential was marked by a worry that it functioned like a virus to which the morally weak were especially prone. An upstanding Anglican clergyman such as the poet Edward Young, then, was able to regulate his presentation of enthusiasm, where an ostensibly deranged street preacher like Christopher Smart was not.

Young's success was rooted in his poem *Night Thoughts on Life, Death, and Immortality* (1742–5), popular because of its lyrical blend of epic, universe poetry and quiet, elegiac reflection on mortality and faith. Its 10,000 lines follow nine sleepless 'nights' in which the narrator attempts to console the believing reader by defending Christianity to an unpredictable reprobate called Lorenzo, now an atheist now a Deist, but always unable to express himself or his beliefs with any sincerity or emotion. For Lorenzo, the poem is 'too turbulent' and 'too warm', and yet it is this strength of feeling that allows the narrator to find solace in a universe where the human seems small and insignificant:

> The planets of each system represent
> Kind neighbours; mutual amity prevails;
> Sweet interchange of rays, receiv'd, return'd;
> Enlightening, and enlighten'd! All, at once
> Attracting, and attracted! Patriot-like,
> None sins against the welfare of the whole,
> But their reciprocal, unselfish aid,
> Affords an emblem of millenial love.[27]

Passages such as this one cast Young as a Newtonian, that is, a believer who sought to release the question of God's existence from empirical debate and into the realm of human experience. Isaac Newton argued that the world and that which lay beyond it worked together as one scientifically forged and theologically controlled space designed to strike awe into the humble believer.[28] This too was the thinking behind *Night Thoughts*, drowning the reader in endless commentaries on faith and its trials, but always spurring him or her on with moments of incredible feeling that demanded an emotional and rational engagement. In contrast Smart's problem was that he was perceived as a poet lacking a rational framework for his presentation of fervent religious faith, having been incarcerated at St Luke's asylum after a period of impulsively praying aloud in public and forcing passers-by to join him. His contemporaries regarded him as a brilliant Cambridge poet ruined by religious mania, an opinion seemingly reinforced by the work Smart produced while confined: the *Song to David* (1763) and the posthumously published *Jubilate Agno* (1758–63; 1939) were both regarded as ostensible proof of his mental illness. Yet the two poems offer revolutionary paraphrases of Scripture, offering a dissenting alternative to the standard Anglican liturgy and making an implicit criticism of self-regarding, effusive meditations such as *Night Thoughts*. Smart updates conventional biblical techniques such as parallelism by blending Scripture with personal detail to produce a curious text that might tempt all readers, not just pious believers.[29] The antiphonal structure of *Jubilate Agno*, for example (each line begins with either 'Let' or 'For'), creates a humorous interpersonal dialogue packed with punnable morphemes that allow for linguistic games rather than didactic instruction.[30] As Geoffrey Hartman suggests, by choosing to write genial if strange poems about comforting subjects such as domestic pets, Smart offers reassurance to even the most tormented doubter:

For I will consider my Cat Jeoffry.
For he is the servant of the Living God duly and daily serving him.
For at the first glance of the glory of God in the East he worships in his way.
For this is done by wreathing his body seven times round with elegant
    quickness.
For then he leaps up to catch the musk, which is the blessing of God upon his
    prayer.
For he rolls upon prank to work it in.
For having done duty and received blessing he begins to consider himself.

For having consider'd God and himself he will consider his neighbour.
For if he meets another cat he will kiss her in kindness.
For when he takes his prey he plays with it to give it chance.
For one mouse in seven escapes by his dallying.

(ll. 695–701; 713–16)

The believer should not look up towards heaven, thought Smart, but around him or her to focus on everyday manifestations of God's creative power and mercy, such as a cat allowing a mouse to escape. This sentiment is hardly enthusiastic, but critics were as suspicious of Smart's poetry as his belief, a fate to which the Evangelical poet and hymnist William Cowper was also destined. Where Smart's poetry stays cheerful, however, Cowper's, considered quite miserable by the rather cool Elinor in Jane Austen's *Sense and Sensibility* (1811), threatened always to disclose an anxious and precarious faith. 'The Castaway' (1799) perhaps exemplifies such disquiet, the narrator seeking, but unable to find, God's support: 'No voice divine the storm allay'd, | No light propitious shone; | When, snatch'd from all effectual aid, | We perish'd, each alone' (ll. 61–4).

Enthusiasm and its varying effects marked sermons, religious pamphlets, and, in the case of Dennis, literary criticism, as much as it did poetry. Even the sometimes chilly George Eliot, who famously despised the fervent tones of *Night Thoughts* for being too wordy and abstract, claimed to have been moved by writing out the sermons for her fictional Methodist preacher in *Adam Bede* (1859).[31] Based on Eliot's aunt, Elizabeth Evans, Dinah Morris preaches in a typically enthusiastic style, sincere and emotive and focused on the believer's personal relationship to Christ rather than issues of doctrine. As Eliot insisted: 'How curious it seems to me that people should think Dinah's sermons, prayers and speeches were *copied*—when they were written with hot tears, as they surged up in my own mind!'[32] Certainly Wesley's sermons seem to have effected a similar impact on most of his listeners, although Horace Walpole confessed that he found Wesley's preaching pitch enactive of a 'very ugly enthusiasm'. The commentary of the Methodist John Nelson is perhaps more representative of general opinion at the time, however:

As soon as he got upon his stand, he stroked back his hair, and turned his face towards me where I stood, and I thought fixed his eyes upon me. His countenance struck such an awful dread upon me, before I heard him speak, that it made my heart beat like the pendulum of a clock; and when he did speak, I thought his whole discourse was aimed at me.[33]

For believers like Nelson, Wesley was able to conjure an experience of enthusiasm specifically within him, but since most of Wesley's converts felt the same, he was successful with both individuals and field-preaching to larger crowds. Wesley learned the technique of open-air preaching, or 'mass evangelism', from George Whitefield, and the two men were both aware of enthusiasm's power to create an abnormally highly charged atmosphere in which converts would fall to the ground crying out their feelings of faith. This 'religion of the heart', established by Wesley and Whitefield, was Methodism, the belief-system that would finally divide Evangelical from rational Dissent and push many of the latter into Unitarianism.

METHODISM

Passionate feeling of a simple and vital nature was central to Methodist belief, although Wesley ultimately disavowed enthusiastic feeling, claiming that nothing in his religion's blueprint dissented from the Church of England. Methodism has an ambivalent relationship with Dissent because it occupies the seemingly contradictory role of both rejuvenating orthodox Anglicanism (the Evangelical or Protestant revival) as well as firing up the religious fervour often associated with nonconformity. Yet in the eighteenth and nineteenth centuries, it was often confused with Evangelicalism until Wesley made clear that Methodists were more interested in personal conversion and the Atonement of Christ (the reconciliation of the world with God through Christ).[34] Its driving message was that of justification by faith, which, as we noted above, insisted that Christ had done all that was needed for men and women to achieve salvation, belief, and, therefore, holiness, through the crucifixion and its consequent message of forgiveness. A resolute commitment to the reality of faith was seen as the sole condition of acceptance by God: sincerity in the performance of good works was not enough. This zealous promotion of faith looked like fanaticism to its opponents, but we can link its direct and adamant nature to both the Presbyterians, and also the Church of England Calvinists, whose unwavering tenet of the sovereignty of God ruled that humanity was always under the jurisdiction of a ruling power beyond itself.

Calvin's endorsement of the doctrine of predestination, that only the elect shall be saved, influenced the eighteenth-century Evangelical revival to the extent that some of its many strands took on this systematic dogmatism, notably the Calvinist-Methodists in Wales. Yet convictions were inherited from both the anti-Calvinist Arminians, who directly opposed predestination in believing that salvation is open to all; and also the Moravians, discussed further below, whose emphasis on individual religious experience was, for Wesley at least, an assertion of faith's singular importance.[35] Wesley himself began as a High Churchman who forged his religious constancy as a counter to the worldliness of university life at Christ Church, Oxford, where he studied in the 1720s. Frustrated with the frivolity of Oxford and all he encountered there, including his brother Charles, Wesley rushed to be ordained in 1725 so that he could serve for a while as his father's curate. He returned to Oxford three years later to find his brother a changed man, attending church regularly and committed to intense routinized prayer, that methodical worship that was said to have inspired the name 'Methodist'.[36] The two brothers joined with their friends William Morgan and Robert Kirkham to form the 'Holy Club', attended also by Whitefield (then an Anglican deacon) and dedicated to promoting the importance of personal religious faith and feeling.

Wesley's own conversion on 24 May 1738 was a momentous event in the preacher's life, described by him as an experience in which religious disillusionment was replaced by a vivid belief and strong conviction in the love of a personal Saviour.[37] His first impulse was to spread news of his experience, one which inspired him to engage in a huge conversion project impacting on over half a million people in Britain between 1740 and 1840.[38] As we have seen from Nelson's testimony, one of Wesley's key assets in winning individuals over was his own fervent faith: as a preacher he was a charismatic example to those who felt driven to spread the Word of God. Preaching was more than a theatrical activity performed by the likes of poets and preachers for Wesley, and he argued that all believers had the right to preach, moving that Methodist leaders should be licensed in accordance with the 1689 Act of Toleration (that is, without ordination or institutionalized theological training). Methodist services were deemed devotional exercises wherein participants could commune directly with God, and they were warned not to call preachers 'ministers' to avoid all allusion to ecclesiastical authority. For many clergy unable to break from the ways of the Established Church, Wesley's lay preachers seemed infuriatingly wholesome, nobly poor, committed to their faith, and prone to taking themselves extremely seriously.[39] As Paul Langford argues: 'Part of the magic of Methodism was that it not only held out the assurance of redemption to men of modest birth and education, but permitted them to offer the same assurance to others.'[40] The clerical profession was generally an impoverished one throughout the period, but the Methodists made a virtue of such poverty, undermining the message of texts like Oliver Goldsmith's *The Vicar of Wakefield* (1766) and Evan Lloyd's *The Curate* (1766) to end the exploitation of the unfortunate clergyman. As Lloyd declared in *The Curate*, critiquing the hierarchy inherent to the Established Church:

> 'Mong all the wretches found on *Proxy*'s list,
> That crawl 'twixt heav'n and earth, and scarce subsist;
> 'Mong all the lots to which the poor is heir,
> The hardest portion is the *Curate*'s share.

(ll. 189–92)

In its overhauling of power within organized religion, then, Methodism was glaringly nonconformist, and in 1808 *The Edinburgh Review* claimed that Evangelists, Wesleyans, and Calvinists should be all classed under 'the general term of Methodism'.[41] Wesley admitted to the confusion stemming from Methodism's sometimes ambivalent relationship to the Established Church, confessing: 'It is not easy to reckon up the various accounts which have been given of the People called Methodists. Very many of them as far remote from the truth as that given by the good gentleman in Ireland, "*Methodists*! Ay, they are the people who place all religion in *wearing long beards*".'[42] Yet Wesley held fast to the idea that Methodism was neither Church nor sect, and he preferred the title 'Society' to describe the public forum in which believers were encouraged to personally relate to God.[43] While the lack of unification within Methodism was a concern, it also excused it from having to form a coherent and rigid set of doctrines and Wesley was proud of the absence of any distinctive orthodoxy. He required only that the believer express a vehement desire to save his or her soul and a wish to flee from the 'wrath to come'.[44]

Freed from the rigid, unbending orthodoxy of a male-dominated Anglicanism, early Methodism readily embraced female believers, some of whom were encouraged to preach themselves as a marker of the unbounded availability of God's grace. Wesley's own mother, Susanna, was a remarkably liberated Christian, the daughter of a dissenting minister who had allowed her a full education in theology and classics.

Much to the horror of Wesley's high Tory father, Susanna even led religious services at their parish in Epworth while her husband was away.[45] Later in his ministry, Wesley seems to have sided with his father's conservative religious position, but as a young preacher, he demanded:

But may not *women*, as well as men, bear a part in this honourable service? Undoubtedly they may; nay, they ought; it is meet, right, and their bounden duty. [Indeed] there is neither male nor female in Christ Jesus ... You, as well as men, are rational creatures. You, like them, were made in the image of God; you are equally candidates for immortality; you too are called of God, as you have time, to 'do good unto all men'. Be 'not disobedient to the heavenly calling'.[46]

Part of Methodism's mass recruitment was reliant on an open acceptance of women and over half of Britain's Methodists were female in the eighteenth century, many of them unmarried, choosing a personal commitment to Christ over a potential husband.[47] Towards the end of the period, Methodist societies in Lancashire and Cheshire averaged a 55 per cent female membership and in urban centres like Manchester, Stockport, and London, the figure rose to 70 per cent.[48] Methodism fostered a new image of woman that emphasized her role as a guardian of moral standards and piety, rather than as a licentious Eve.[49] She was granted opportunities for self-expression, equality with men, female solidarity, and even economic power: one of Wesley's most important patrons was the lay preacher Mary Bosanquet. Even Wesley's system of 'classes', containing twelve people who supported each other's faith, educational progress, and personal well-being, was formed on the basis of group compatibility rather than gender, making official the role of female religious leadership.[50] Women's importance as class-leaders, Sunday School teachers and local preachers endured within Methodism, foretelling the centrality of women to moral, as well as religious education in the Victorian period and beyond.

Two women who benefited from Methodism's feminist agenda were the conservative, Hannah More, and the radical, Emily Brontë. Aspiring and middle-class, More is representative of the Christian philanthropist, embodying the steady piety of the Evangelical 'good woman' so fashionable at the time.[51] Born of a Presbyterian family who had shifted their allegiance to the Established Church, More underwent a religious conversion to 'vital religion', influenced in her decision by Doddridge and William Wilberforce. Wilberforce had a profound effect on many attracted to Evangelicalism, including the Prime Minister, William Pitt, and his own conversion in 1785 forged his professional status as a Member of Parliament in a strictly Christian cast. Founder of the Bible Society and the Society for Bettering the Condition of the Poor, his *A Practical view of the Prevailing Religious System of Professed Christians* (1797) encouraged readers to reform themselves spiritually and then turn to the improvement of society, its education, public health, prison systems, and so on. Like Wilberforce, More found in her faith a foundation for her relentless forwarding of a moral agenda she believed would improve the position of the poor. Intervening in parliamentary discussions on poverty and publishing several nutrition and recipe books for those on meagre incomes, More nevertheless insisted that the underprivileged should rely primarily on the virtues of sobriety, humility, and industry. She communicated this message in countless publications, *Coelebs in Search of a Wife* (1808), *Practical Piety* (1811), *Christian Morals* (1813), and *Essay on the Character and Practical Writings of St Paul* (1815), so successfully that even Wesley expressed some envy at the ease with which she excelled in her Evangelical mission. Her series of *Cheap Repository Tracts* (1795–8) comprised of Bible stories, allegorical tales, religious poetry, and instructional stories, and echoing Wesley's insistence that theological learning was best achieved through thinking about human experience, sold an astounding two million copies by the end of their first year of publication. Their immense popularity derived in part from More's strategic marketing of the booklets, which she designed to look like seditious pamphlets complete with riveting titles and illustrated with woodcuts. While considered conservative and moralizing by modern criticism, the tracts do at the least promote education for the labouring classes: 'The Sunday School', for example, tells of a cynical farmer who is eventually won over by one Mrs Jones's argument that the poor learn to read and write in order to rise in society.

More's role as an educator of the poor even moved her critics to stigmatize her as an enthusiast, a fear she had already fuelled in her fervent support of abolitionism.[52] As a influential member of the Society for Effecting the Abolition of the African Slave Trade, More wrote fervently on the subject of slavery, demanding that enthusiastic rhetoric be used to comment upon the issue to secure the attention of the public. What use is the 'strange pow'r of song! the strain that warms the heart' (l. 43), More wrote in 'Slavery: a poem' (1788), if it does not remind us that God granted all humans the capacity to feel deeply and with dignity:

Does then th' immortal principle within
Change with the casual colour of a skin?
Does matter govern spirit? or is mind
Degraded by the form to which 'tis join'd?
No: they have heads to think, and hearts to feel,
And souls to act, with firm, tho' erring, zeal;
For they have keen affections, kind desires,
Love strong as death, and active patriot fires;
All the rude energy, the fervid flame,
Of high-soul'd passion, and ingenuous shame:
Strong, but luxuriant virtues boldly shoot
From the wild vigour of a savage root.

(ll. 63–74)

Like her religious tracts, More's poem struck a chord with an increasingly politicized public already receptive to the abolitionist literature of Wilberforce and Thomas Clarkson, and slavery was finally outlawed in Britain in 1807. Like Wesley, More sought to remove herself from associations with enthusiasm, denouncing 'frantic enthusiasts' as enemies of 'active virtue' in *Practical Piety*.[53] Yet she still drew on its religious and poetic associations to enforce both evangelism and abolitionism, keeping within the Church of England but all the time pushing, and dissenting from, its limits.

Emily Brontë, on the other hand, found in enthusiasm a model for the fervent feeling which so marks her poetry and passionate novel, *Wuthering Heights*.[54] Brontë was surrounded by Methodist history growing up in Haworth, her clergyman father succeeding the notoriously fiery preacher, William Grimshaw, whose 'ecstatic devotions, his robust preaching, and his swashbuckling spiritual discipline formed an important component in the background of the Brontë children'.[55] The charismatic Grimshaw may even have stood as a prototype for Heathcliff, his ardent, if not obsessive, romance with Cathy exemplary of the kind of feeling associated with Methodist conversion experiences. Brontë's poetry also owes a debt to Methodism, as Ken Burrows suggests, infused as it is with the 'long, short, and common measures of Watts and the Wesleys and Cowper'.[56] For Burrows, however, Brontë uses these measures to broach an attack on Methodism, which for her was the same as all forms of organized religion: stultifying and repressive. He argues that she creates an 'anti-hymn' to effect this assault, subverting an ostensibly controlled use of hymnal diction, syntax, stanza, and rhetoric with a nervous 'energy' that casts scorn upon religious ideals. In this light, we might read Brontë's poem, 'There let thy bleeding branch atone' (n.d.), as a mimicry of the Wesleyan hymn beginning, 'See streeming [*sic*] from the accursed Tree | His all atoning Blood!'[57] For Burrows, Brontë's poem parodies choric communal worship by constructing the narrator as isolated and alone, a solitary being that deems God's name 'cursed' (l. 5).[58] The predominant 'icon of the crucifix' is thus transformed from an image of forgiveness to one of vindictiveness.[59] God becomes an angry tyrant, his wrath a 'wildering maze' the narrator spends many useless and 'mad hours' trapped within, so highlighting what Burrows calls the 'constraint and madness of pietistic Evangelical worship' (ll. 9, 10).[60]

DISSENTING ACADEMIES

For many thinking believers, then, Methodism was so full of feeling it threatened forever to explode into an experience from which a homecoming was moot: as Jon Mee comments, no return ticket could be promised for those setting out on an enthusiastic journey.[61] Where Watts and Doddridge feared that rational Dissent had sapped belief of its energy and heart, many intellectual Dissenters were eager to stress the thoughtful nature of their beliefs, a factor which underlined the establishment of 'dissenting academies'. Education was central to all Dissenters, regarded as the best way to reform religious culture and considered an ideal location in which to shape human affection and thus social relations: sermons were as concerned with manners, ethics, conduct and virtue, as scriptural law. Dissenting academies arose after the Restoration of Charles II in 1660 in response to those restrictions placed on worship that prevented the education of nonconformist ministers. These academies grew in the eighteenth century, offering a number of different subjects deemed suitable for the training of dissenting ministers and other men preparing for professional and commercial life. The most influential academy was established by Presbyterians at Warrington in 1757, running as an independent academic institution until 1786 and funded privately by dissenting sympathizers and affluent professionals invested in subjects related to the improvement of business and commerce. Oxford and Cambridge were considered outdated and overly elitist by the new middle classes who sought a liberal education that might prepare men for the law, medicine, or trade as much as for the ministry. In this respect, the academies correspond to the red-brick universities of 1960s Britain, seeking to educate freed from the shackles of politically and pedagogically backward traditions. As Barbauld's niece, Lucy Aikin, reminisced:

I have often thought with envy of that society. Neither Oxford nor Cambridge could boast of brighter names in literature or science than several of these dissenting tutors—humbly content in an obscure town, on a scanty pittance to cultivate in themselves, and communicate to a rising generation, those mental requirements and moral habits which are their own exceeding reward. They and theirs lived together like one large family, and in the facility of their intercourse they found large compensation for its deficiency in luxury and splendour.[62]

Certainly Warrington's syllabus was revolutionary, offering a wide range of subjects, from languages, classics, astronomy, civil law, philosophy, and history, through to pneumatics, astronomy, magnetism, and accounting. Some considered Warrington a little too progressive, the liberal Calvinist minister, Job Orton, noting that the sermons of Warrington divinity students tended to be overly intellectual and obscure: 'they are too dry and philosophical in their composition, and do not come home to men's consciences, as every minister should do'.[63] All the same, the seminars of tutors like the Nottingham minister and local politician, George Walker, confirmed the positive links that could be forged between 'secular' subjects and divinity; politics, like religion, Walker claimed, being 'a branch of morals, it involves the character and happiness of a people, and to think and act aright in it must forever be a serious duty of man'.[64] Students concerned more specifically with theology were even able to study the history of Judaism at Warrington, as well as more conventional subjects like church history and divinity, and were themselves a diverse group including Presbyterians, Baptists, Independents, and some conforming Anglicans.

By instructing men of varying religious affiliations in a group-learning process, Warrington's educational system was part of a general shift in the mid- to late eighteenth century in which Dissent's dividing lines became increasingly blurred. Barbauld, for example, grew up within a branch of Presbyterianism that had developed into a free, liberal, rational, and tolerant belief-system, and in her later life found herself theologically torn between old Dissent and Unitarianism. Barbauld was descended from a family of Independents and Presbyterians, allowing her to engage with the doctrinal and cultural heritage of both, as did many late eighteenth-century Dissenters. As Daniel E. White argues, her grandfather, John Jennings, and his brother, David Jennings, had trained many members of the dissenting elite, including Philip Doddridge, Joshua Toulmin, and Abraham Rees.[65] Even before she married the Presbyterian minister, Rochemont Barbauld, Barbauld (then Anna Aikin) was an Arian Presbyterian, and considered the Socinian position, later so influential on Unitarianism, to be 'Christianity in the Frigid Zone'.[66] She worshipped at Rochemont's parishes in Hampstead and Newington Green, was reviewed in the periodical press as a Presbyterian, and indirectly received her education at the Warrington Academy.

What mattered to Barbauld, however, was less her denominational affiliation than the devotional theory and practice behind individual faith. Old Presbyterianism was objectionable to her precisely because it constructed such faith as a gruelling experience pursued within a dark, Calvinist framework. Later Presbyterianism, however, touched by Watts and Doddridge's affectionate ideas, emphasized a gentler belief constituted by benevolent actions between humans and a loving relationship with God. As Barbauld declared:

The age which has demolished dungeons, rejected torture, and given so fair a prospect of abolishing the iniquity of the slave trade, cannot long retain among its articles of belief the gloomy perplexities of Calvinism, and the heart-withering perspective of cruel and never-ending punishments.[67]

For Barbauld, Christianity was not about human worthlessness and sin, but about communities bound by social affections inspired by God's love. Where personal or private faith isolated the believer, laying him or her open to 'languor on one side, and enthusiasm on the other', public or communal worship accommodates only good feeling, 'admiration, love, and joy [which] swell the bosom with emotions which seek for fellowship and communication'.[68] Popular Evangelicalism might endorse a passionate relationship with God, but such zeal in fact served to block the believer's relation to God as a living sovereign, locked as it was into endless theological debates such as those on enthusiasm outlined above. Barbauld was more concerned with how the human physically experienced Christian life, claiming in *Pastoral Lessons* (1803) that God constructed us specifically to feel:

Who can behold the wonderful construction of man, the number of veins, of arteries and of nerves, which compose his frame, and forget to admire, to adore the Power that formed him?[69]

This sense of the believer's emotional familiarity with God as a friend or parental companion is more immediate still in 'An Address to the Deity'

(1773), visionary experience deriving not from spontaneous moments of insight, but from a mindful habit of associating God with everyday life:

> God of my life! and author of my days!
> Permit my feeble voice to lisp thy praise;
>
> .   .   .   .   .   .
>
> If friendless, in a vale of tears I stray,
> Where briars wound, and thorns perplex my way,
> Still let my steady soul thy goodness see,
> And with strong confidence lay hold on thee;
>
> .   .   .   .   .   .
>
> With thee in shady solitudes I walk,
> With thee in busy crowded cities talk,
> In every creature own thy forming power,
> In each event thy providence adore.
>
> (ll. 1–2, 49–52, 63–6)

The believer could only develop this kind of steady faith, Barbauld argued, by a process of thoughtful meditation enabled both by the community in which one lived and also by the books which one read.

Thoughts on the Devotional Taste, for example, betrays her worry that many Dissenters were unable to distinguish between those hymns, prayers, and sermons designed to instruct and improve the believer and simple polite literature marketed for a less discerning readership. For Barbauld, the litmus test of whether or not a text was appropriate was whether it conjured the right kind of religious feeling, one that wavered between enthusiasm and cold rationalism and paralleled sensibility in its make-up. This authentic religious feeling Barbauld referred to as 'devotion', a term she used to describe 'a taste, an affair of sentiment and feeling':

Its seat is in the imagination and the passions, and it has its source in that relish for the sublime, the vast, and the beautiful, by which we taste the charms of poetry and other compositions that address our finer feelings.[70]

Devotion signifies a spiritually refined constitution, then, a state of being or selfhood that is fuelled by Wattsian 'religious affections'.[71] The 'strange excesses' of enthusiasm on the one hand and disillusionment on the other have plagued the late eighteenth century, Barbauld argues, weakening devotion in believers so that their spirits are drained of inner feeling. As a consequence, believers have become overly reliant on external structures, referred to in the essay as 'sects' (dissenting groups) and 'establishments' (state-supported churches). Sects begin as 'persecuted' groups and so thrive only by the 'entire affection of its followers, the sacrifices they make to principle, the force of novelty, and the amazing power of sympathy', all of which 'contribute to cherish devotion'.[72] Bound by love and friendship, these sociable communities stand firm against their critics, but when their fervour burns low they necessarily fall into 'reasoning and examination'.[73] After a period of debate, these followers become 'tired of a controversy which becomes insipid from being exhausted', and they thus turn back to the church for support, only to be entirely sucked back into its 'vortex'.[74] Barbauld then suggests that these 'established' churches invoke emotion in the believer, not through community, but by the 'mysterious pomp of antient [sic] ceremonies; by the sacredness of peculiar orders, habits, and titles' and by connecting themselves to 'antiquity'.[75] Possessing a grandeur and stability derived from history, establishments are forced to seek to understand the past in obsessive detail, causing them ultimately to descend into 'superstition'.[76] Both sects and establishments are flawed for Barbauld because they fixate the believer's attention on big picture philosophies of religion, rather than guiding him or her to work out what faith specifically means for them. Only the believer who allows devotion to lead his or her religious belief can uncover that 'warmth and beauty' in the world reflective of God: 'the devout man' alone, Barbauld writes, 'on the altar of his heart, presents his own sighs, his own thanksgivings, his own earnest desires'.[77]

Devotion, then, serves as a safety-valve to temper any enthusiastic feelings to which the believer might become prey, while still allowing a fully emotional relationship with God to develop. Her critics, however, considered Barbauld's theorization of devotion restricted by the very category of taste that she believed worked as its anchor. As Jon Mee argues, her friend Joseph Priestley thought that 'taste' dampened religious feeling, while Barbauld worried that Priestley held an impetuous and risky position in relation to his faith that bordered both on enthusiasm and, worse, impoliteness.[78] His beliefs were almost too nonconformist for Barbauld, an amalgamation of Cambridge Platonism and Dutch Arminianism founded upon the English Presbyterianism into which he was born.[79] Priestley claimed to see 'reason to embrace what is generally called the heterodox side of almost every question', an outlook which seems to have enabled his innumerable scientific discoveries, as well as his unusual innovations into theological discussions. It was

Priestley, for example, that revived interest in David Hartley's *Observations on Man* (1749), republishing it in 1775 as a work that allowed Christianity to engage with the emergent disciplines of physiology, neurology, psychology, and metaphysics without falling into Deism or atheism. Hartley had also attended a dissenting academy at Daventry and his ideas stimulated Priestley's own unwillingness to adjust his view on the importance of religious feeling. Reading the *Observations*, Priestley wrote, 'produced the greatest, and in my opinion, the most favourable effect on my general turn of thinking through life':[80]

it greatley [*sic*] improved that disposition to piety which I brought to the academy and freed it from the rigour with which it had been tinctured. Indeed, I do not know whether the consideration of Dr Hartley's theory, contributes more to enlighten the mind, or improve the heart; it effects both in so super-eminent a degree.[81]

The crucial claim by which Priestley was so affected was Hartley's sense that human mental phenomena are produced by 'association'. As humans, we feel by receiving signals that vibrate along the nervous system, giving us either pleasure or pain; we make sense of such sensations by associating or connecting together what we see, hear, touch, and smell in the world; these connections allow us to think and act within the world; and we then express these thoughts in language, a system which reveals what we like and do not like—our values.[82] For Hartley, however, the process goes further in that these values are monitored by 'theopathy', or the human's relationship with the divine. Individuals might choose not to develop this relationship and to become unbelievers, but this simply means that the divine lies dormant within them, their theopathic mode untriggered until they decide to activate it.[83] As an affective experience, then, God became a scientific 'fact', an idea that placed the bodily and the physical at one with the rational and mindful: as Priestley affirmed, 'man does not consist of two principles, so essentially different from one another as *matter* and *spirit*'.[84] Our senses, and not empirical evidence, are what 'prove' God's existence for Hartley, able as they are to pick up the vibrating energies of which the universe is comprised, and to draw them inside the individual body that grants personal identity. No wonder Hartley was such an influence on Blake, who engraved a portrait for the 1791 edition of *Observations*, and whose notion of human existence as divine energy takes Hartley, and the nonconformist position, to its furthest extreme.

BLAKE

While Blake's religious position is extreme, it is an essentially Christian one, based as it is on centralizing the figure of Christ at the heart of what it means to be a human being. His elevation of the experiential element of religion derives from his interest in a number of dissenting ideas: the Moravian emphasis on love; the Anabaptist elevation of Christ; and the Swedenborgian investment in mysticism. The Moravians, who numbered Blake's mother among their members during her first marriage, emerged from the work of the fifteenth-century priest, John Hus, who sought to return the predominantly Roman Catholic Bohemia and Moravia to an early form of Christianity. His agenda was to highlight the radical aspect of the Early Church, encouraging believers to read the liturgy in their own language and to free themselves from the clerical hierarchies imposed by Catholicism. Some of these 'Hussites' compromised with the Roman Church to form a separate group called the Utraquists; those who remained with Hus became known as the Unity of the Brethren who, after much persecution (Hus was burned at the stake as a heretic), relocated to Germany in the early eighteenth century. In 1722, these emigrants set up a village on the estate of Count Nicholas Zinzendorf, who assembled their beliefs into the Moravianism which was so successfully exported to Georgia at the time of John Wesley's visit. The Moravian love feast exemplified their basic belief in the affective power of the Gospel over that of dogma or doctrine, and it was the personal, vital faith practised at these communal events which so affected Methodism.

The Moravian focus on living humbly and spreading the word of Christ to the poor connects them to the Anabaptists, who themselves began as a radical wing of the Protestant Reformation in 1525. The Anabaptists believed that individuals should choose baptism as adults (rather than having it imposed on them as infants), giving everyone access to a 'born again' experience in which they are inspired to live by a system of ethics and morals based on the scriptures. Claiming that their strength lay in their marginalized and notably pacifist position of powerlessness and poverty, rendering them heirs of the failed Peasants' Revolt (1524–6), the Anabaptists spurned private property, and met not in ornate church spaces, but instead in fields, woods, or in the houses of their community. Like the Moravians, the Anabaptists privileged the words of Christ as they are recorded in the Gospels and suggested that by continuously reading these texts the believer would be filled with a guiding spirit: certainly Blake's work endlessly interprets and paraphrases Scripture, placing Christ at the centre of all understanding. How Blake constructs the figure of Christ is a more complex issue, and grounded in his ultimately defiant reading of the writings of Emanuel Swedenborg.

Blake read almost everything he engaged with defiantly, and this is what marks him as a Dissenter, or, as E. P. Thompson puts it, an 'antinomian', one who stands 'against the law', especially those legislated by hypocritical authoritarians.[85] Antinomianism, for example, is traditionally associated with Paul's polemics against Mosaic Law in his epistles to the Romans and to the Galatians, wherein he bemoans the failure of his fellow believers to follow Christ's moral commandments. Like Paul, Blake's religion was Christological rather than ecclesiological, and the poet was primarily concerned with Christ's curative responses to authority, poverty, suffering, and injustice. Blake's work is also polemical in that it overturns any system that seeks to limit these responses, provoking many sharp parodies of theological texts such as Swedenborg's *Heaven and Hell* (1758). Swedenborg helps us read Blake partly by way of contrast: only the former claimed to have experienced profound revelations in which he penetrated the spirit world and saw spirits, angels, and even Christ. The son of a clergyman and professor of theology, Swedenborg initially became an engineer for the Swedish government, driven by his conviction that all matter in the universe was infused with a divine force. Echoing Hartley, and more directly influenced by Jacob Boehme, he wrote long tracts on the relationship between matter and energy, God and the human, and the brain and psychology, 'converting' in 1743. His religion impacted in Britain in 1787 through Robert Hindmarsh's foundation of the first Church of the New Jerusalem in London, where Swedenborg's *Heaven and Hell* and *The Last Judgement* (1758) were distributed. These books suggested both that everyone is capable of entering the spirit world through faith, and also that there is an internal message in the scriptures that can be accessed through privileging its emotional content. For Swedenborg, it is this revelation—that we understand Christ only through love and feeling—that constitutes the Second Coming, ushering in a new age of Christianity built on love, friendship, and a spiritual perception of what lies beyond mortality.

That Blake privileged the love Christ represents in the Gospels is without question and yet he departs from Swedenborg by focusing on the Incarnation of this love in the lived world, rather than in a removed spirit realm. In *The Marriage of Heaven and Hell* (1790), for example, Blake rewrites Swedenborg's text by replacing his moral 'Memorable Relations' with mock-anecdotal 'Memorable Fancies' in which he discusses theological ideas with angels and devils, and has dinner with the prophets Isaiah and Ezekiel. The emergent message of the poem is that humans, like Christ, consist of contradictions and opposites and that without this we become imprisoned within false systems or institutions:

Without contraries there is no progression. Attraction and Repulsion, Reason and Energy, Love and Hate, are necessary to Human existence. From these contraries spring what the religious call Good & Evil.[86]

Swedenborg's writings, Blake declares disapprovingly in plate 3, are like 'linen clothes folded up', neat and methodical analyses of religious ideas—love, compassion, virtue, and so on—that should instead be read spontaneously, oppositionally, and with 'eternal delight'.[87] If we follow Blake's oppositional logic, the 'bad' voices in the poem, such as that of the Devil, suddenly become worth listening to, and even Christ is constructed as a heretic and rebel in order that we pay attention to his actions. As the Devil reminds us, Christ broke all of the ten commandments in the Gospels, but was at the same time 'all virtue, and acted from impulse: not from rules'.[88]

Impulse and desire are the driving forces behind Blake's concept of Christianity, one that is only operational through the gathered and animated presence of feeling and thinking individuals. As Jonathan Roberts argues, Blake forwards a gospel of personal and political liberation enacted by individuals who have woken up both to their own emotions and senses and also to the recognition that they are part of a larger, divine body. This divine body is the imagination, 'not something that individuals utilize or possess, but something in which they may participate'.[89] As Blake writes in *The Laocoön* (1826–7):

The Eternal Body of Man is the Imagination, that is, God himself, the Divine Body
Jesus: we are his Members.
It manifests itself in his Works of Art (In Eternity All is Vision).

Art redeems the imagination by 'melting apparent surfaces away, and displaying the infinite which was hid', emancipating individuals from materialism and a narcissistic focus on selfhood that inevitably produces alienation, hostility between people, and war ('Art Degraded,

Imagination Denied, War Governed the Nations', Blake writes in *The Laocoön*).⁹⁰ Christians, then, are artists for Blake, able to free society from tension and conflict by investing in the eternal human over temporal states of error or wrongdoing. This locates the forgiveness of sins as '*the* defining feature of Christianity' for Blake, and his reception in the late Victorian period was as a radical, philanthropic visionary and Dissenter who sought to rebuild a nation broken by capitalism as the New Jerusalem.⁹¹ The gradual secularization of Blake's art of protest ironically begins with the political movements which emerge from dissenting religion, and the struggle to retain a link between Christianity and radicalism is nowhere better exemplified than in Unitarianism, to which we turn in Chapter 2.

NOTES

1. Quoted in T. H. Huxley, 'Joseph Priestley' (1874), in *Science and Education: Essays by Thomas H. Huxley* (London: Macmillan and Co., 1899), 1–37 (22 n. 1)
2. Arianism, named after the fourth-century Christian priest, Arius, held that God had 'created' Christ thus making him a superior, but non-divine, being; Socinianism, discussed further in the next chapter, similarly argued that Christ was completely human, a mortal man chosen by God to fulfil a divine mission. Those who believe Christ's divinity *is* essential to the Christian understanding of salvation are said to hold 'soteriologist' beliefs, a viewpoint famously forwarded by Athanasius in response to Arius.
3. The Nicene Creed or the Niceno-Constantioplian Creed stated that Christ was 'of the same substance' as the Father and stressed the reality of the Holy Spirit; the Apostolic and Athanasian Creeds both argue for Christ's divinity and the centrality of the Trinity to salvation.
4. A. W. Brown, *Recollections of the Conversation Parties of the Rev. Charles Simeon* (London, 1862), 269, in W. R. Ward, *Religion and Society in England 1790–1850* (London: B. T. Batsford, 1972), 18.
5. D. E. White, 'Anna Barbauld and Dissenting Devotion: Extempore, Particular, Experimental', *Enlightenment, Gender and Religion Colloquium*, University of London (2004).
6. Quoted in S. Drew, *The Life of Thomas Coke* (London, 1817), 289, 293; and see Ward, *Religion and Society*, 11.
7. 'The Parish' was not published during Clare's lifetime, but the poet's modern editors estimate that it was written 1812–31; see *John Clare: A Critical Edition of the Major Works*, ed. E. Robinson and D. Powell (Oxford: Oxford University Press, 1984).

8. R. E. Schofield, *The Enlightenment of Joseph Priestley: A Study of his Life and Work from 1733 to 1773* (University Park, Pa.: Pennsylvania State University Press, 1997), 167.

9. I. Rivers, *Reason, Grace and Sentiment: A Study of the Language of Religion and Ethics in England 1660–1780*, i. *Whichcote to Wesley* (Cambridge: Cambridge University Press, 1991), 167.

10. I. Watts, 'Rational Defence of the Gospel', in *The Works of the Rev. Isaac Watts D. D.*, ed. E. Parsons, 7 vols. (Leeds: Edward Bains, 1800), i. 192; and see Rivers, *Reason, Grace and Sentiment*, i. 187.

11. I. Watts, *The Doctrine of the Passions Explained and Improved, Or, A Brief and comprehensive scheme of the Natural Affections of Mankind, Attempted in a plain and easy Method. With an Account of their Names, Nature, Appearances, Effects and Different Uses in Human Life to which are subjoined Moral and Divine Rules for the Regulation or Government of them* (1729), 5th edn. (London: J. Buckland and T. Longman, 1770), 7.

12. Watts, *Doctrine of the Passions*, 35.

13. Ibid.

14. J. R. Watson, *The English Hymn: A Critical and Historical Study* (Oxford: Clarendon Press, 1997), 19–20.

15. D. W. Bebbington, *Evangelicalism in Modern Britain: A History from the 1730s to the 1980s* (London: Unwin Hyman, 1989), 67–9.

16. Wesley claimed that the hymn was designed to persuade 'the critic to turn Christian rather than the Christian to turn critic', J. Wesley, letter to L. Tyerman (n.d.), in G. R. Balleine, *A History of the Evangelical Party in the Church of England* (London: Church Book Room Press, 1908), 29.

17. J. Wesley, letter to S. Furley, 15 July 1764, in Bebbington, *Evangelicalism*, 67.

18. C. Wesley, 'And can it be, that I should gain?', *A Collection of Psalms and Hymns* (London: W. Strahan, 1744).

19. See C. Wesley, *Hymns for those that Seek, and those that have Redemption in The Blood of Jesus Christ* (Bristol: Felix Farley, 1747).

20. Hogarth had highlighted the problem of prostitution in M. Hackabout's *The Harlot's Progress* (1732); D. Defoe's *Moll Flanders* (1724) betrayed the network of petty criminals riddling eighteenth-century London; and J. Gay's *The Beggar's Opera* (1728) betrayed the middle-class thieves who thrived in the City. See Watson's reading of the hymn's social conscience in *English Hymn*, 227–8.

21. '[W]herever any object takes such a hold of the mind as to make us dwell upon it, and brood over it, melting the heart in tenderness, or kindling it to a sentiment of enthusiasm … this is poetry', in W. Hazlitt, 'On Poetry in General', *Lectures on the English Poets* (1802), in S. Tucker, *Enthusiasm: A Study of Semantic Change* (Cambridge: Cambridge University Press, 1972), 92.

22. J. Dennis, 'The Advancement and Reformation of Modern Poetry' (1701), in A. Ashfield and P. de Bolla (eds.), *The Sublime: A Reader in British Eighteenth-Century Aesthetic Theory* (Cambridge: Cambridge University Press, 1996), 32–4 (33); D. B. Morris, *The Religious Sublime: Christian Poetry and Critical Tradition in Eighteenth-Century England* (Kentucky: The University Press of Kentucky, 1972), 50.

23. J. Dennis, 'The Grounds of Criticism in Poetry' (1704), in Ashfield and de Bolla (eds.) *Sublime*, 35–9 (35).

24. Earl of Shaftesbury, 'On Enthusiasm', in *Characteristics of Men, Manners, Opinions, Times, etc.* (1699), in I. Kramnick (ed.), *The Portable Enlightenment Reader* (London: Penguin, 1995), 90–6 (92–4).

25. D. Hume, 'Of Superstition and Enthusiasm', in *Essays: Moral and Political* (1741), in Antony Flew (ed.), *David Hume: Writings on Religion* (Chicago: Open Court, 1992), 3–9 (4–5).

26. Ibid. 7.

27. E. Young, *The Complaint: or Night Thoughts on Life, Death, and Immortality* (1742–5); E. Young, *The Poetical Works of Edward Young*, 2 vols. (London: George Bell, 1906), IV. 631, IX. 698–705.

28. Morris, *Religious Sublime*, 2.

29. D. Norton, *A History of the English Bible as Literature* (Cambridge: Cambridge University Press, 2000), 273.

30. G. Hartman, 'Christopher Smart's "Magnificat": Toward a Theory of Representation', in *The Geoffrey Hartman Reader*, ed. Geoffrey Hartman and Daniel T. O'Hara (Edinburgh: Edinburgh University Press, 2004), 29–49 (41).

31. For Eliot, the poet is so general in his invocation of emotion that all feeling expressed means nothing at all, lines such as 'His hand the good man fixes on the skies, | And bids earth roll, nor feels her idle whirl' being offensive in their contempt for physical, human life: 'the monstrous absurdity', she railed, 'of a man's grasping the skies, and hanging habitually suspended there, while he contemptuously bids the earth roll, warns you that no genuine feeling could have suggested so unnatural a conception'; in G. Eliot, 'Worldliness and Otherworldliness', in the *Westminster Review*, 67 (Jan. 1857), 27.

32. G. S. Haight (ed.), *The George Eliot Letters*, 7 vols. (New Haven: Yale University Press,1954–6), iii. 176.

33. H. Walpole, letter to J. Chute, 10 Oct. 1766; J. Nelson, *An Extract from the Journal of Mr John Nelson: To Which is Added, A Brief Memoir of His Life and Death* (Liverpool, 1807), in R. A. Knox, *Enthusiasm: A Chapter in the History of Religion* (Oxford: Clarendon Press, 1950), 513.

34. E. Jay, *The Evangelical and Oxford Movements* (Cambridge: Cambridge University Press, 1983), 3; S. L. Ollard (ed.), *A Dictionary of English Church History* (1912) (London and Oxford: A. R. Mowbray, 1948), 215.

35. Bebbington, *Evangelicalism*, 22, 27.

36. S. Andrews, *Methodism and Society* (London: Seminar Studies in History, Longman, 1970), 25; see also V. H. H. Green's *The Young Mr Wesley: A Study of John Wesley and Oxford* (London: Edward Arnold, 1961), 148; and *John Wesley* (London: Thomas Nelson and Sons, 1964), 28.

37. Jay, *Evangelical*, 3.

38. D. Hempton, *Methodism and Politics in British Society 1750–1850* (London: Hutchinson, 1984), 12.

39. P. Langford, *A Polite and Commercial People: England 1727–1783* (Oxford: Oxford University Press, 1989), 266, 272.

40. Ibid. 273.

41. R. P. Heitzenrater, *Wesley and the People called Methodists* (Nashville, Tenn.: Abingdon Press), 208, 64; the situation was provoked further by the many breakaway groups that claimed affiliation with Methodism; E. P. Thompson lists some of the many 'breakaway [*sic*] groups of "Ranters"—the Welsh "Jumpers" (cousins to the American "Shakers"), the Primitive Methodists, the "Tent Methodists," the "Magic Methodists" of Delemere Forest, who fell into "trances" or "visions", the Bryanites or Bible Christians, the "Quaker Methodists" of Warrington and the "Independent Methodists" of Macclesfield', *The Making of the English Working Class* (New York: Pantheon, 1963), 388.

42. J. Wesley, 'A Short History of Methodism' (1765), in *The Works of John Wesley*, ix. *The Methodist Societies, History, Nature and Design*, ed. Rupert E. Davies, gen. ed. A. C. Outler, 26 vols. (Nashville, Tenn.: Abingdon Press; Oxford: Clarendon Press, 1989), ix. 367–72 (367).

43. F. Dreyer, 'A "Religious Society Under Heaven": John Wesley and the Identity of Methodism', *Journal of British Studies*, 25 (1986), 62–83 (65, 66).

44. Ibid. 66.

45. C. Cupples, 'Pious Ladies and Methodist Madams: Sex and Gender in Anti-Methodist Writings of Eighteenth-Century England', *Critical Matrix*, 5 (1990), 30–60 (37).

46. J. Wesley, 'Sermon 98: On Visiting the Sick' (1786), in *The Works of John Wesley*, iii. *Sermons III: 71–114*, gen. ed. A. C. Outler, 26 vols. (Nashville, Tenn.: Abingdon Press; Oxford: Clarendon Press, 1986), 384–97 (396); see also D. A. Johnson (ed.), *Women in English Religion* (New York and Toronto: The Edwin Mellen Press, 1983), 71.

47. See L. Davidoff and C. Hall, *Family Fortunes: Men and Women of the English Middle Class, 1780–1850* (London: Hutchinson, 1987), 107 ff.

48. Hempton, *Methodism and Politics*, 13.

49. Cupples, 'Pious Ladies', 36 n. 14, 31.

50. Johnson, *Women in English Religion*, 63.

51. M. G. Jones, *Hannah More* (Cambridge: Cambridge University Press, 1952), 77–81.

52. J. Saunders, 'Putting the Reader Right: Reassessing Hannah More's *Cheap Repository Tracts*', *Romanticism on the Net*, 16 (Nov. 1999); and see J. Mee, *Romanticism, Enthusiasm and Regulation: Poetics and the Policing of Culture in the Romantic Period* (Oxford: Oxford University Press, 2003), 62.

53. H. More, *Practical Piety; or, The Influence of the Religion of the Heart on the Conduct of Life*, 2 vols. (1811), i. 13.

54. See E. Mason, ' "Some god of wild enthusiast's dreams": Methodist Enthusiasm and the Poetry of Emily Brontë', *Victorian Literature and Culture*, 31: 1 (2003), 263–77.

55. F. Baker, *William Grimshaw: 1708–1763* (London: The Epworth Press, 1963), 267.

56. K. C. Burrows, 'Some Remembered Strain: Methodism and the Anti-Hymns of Emily Brontë', *West Virginia University Philological Papers*, 24 (1977), 48–61 (49); Burrows notes that ' "common measure" classically consists of a quatrain of alternating eight- and six-syllable lines; "short measure" is a quatrain of three six-syllable lines and one—the third—eight-syllable line; "long measure" traditionally has a quatrain of eight-syllable lines. All of the stanzas may be doubled'; on hymn-metre, see also D. Davie, *The Eighteenth-Century Hymn in England* (Cambridge: Cambridge University Press, 1993), 107 ff.

57. S. Wesley, Jr., *John Wesley's First Hymn-Book: A Collection of Psalms and Hymns* (1737), ed. F. Baker and G. W. Williams (Charleston, SC: Dalcho Historical Society, 1964), 44, in Burrows, 'Some Remembered Strain', 52.

58. Burrows, 'Some Remembered Strain', 53.

59. Ibid. 52.

60. Ibid. 57.

61. See Mee, *Romanticism, Enthusiasm and Regulation*.

62. L. Aikin, *Memoir of Mrs Barbauld including Letters and Notices of her Family and Friends* (London: George Bell and Sons, 1874), 33.

63. 'Original letter from the Rev. Job Orton', *Protestant Dissenter's Magazine*, 6 (1799), 53, in J. Seed, 'Gentlemen Dissenters: The Social and Political Meanings of Rational Dissent in the 1770s and 1780s', *The Historical Journal*, 28: 2 (1985), 299–325 (313).

64. G. Walker, 'The Duty and Character of a National Soldier', in *Sermons* (London, 1790), ii. 437.

65. White, 'Anna Barbauld and Dissenting Devotion'.

66. Quoted in White, 'Anna Barbauld and Dissenting Devotion'; and see Andrew Fuller, *The Calvinistic and Socinian Systems Examined and Compared, as to their Moral Tendency* (London, 1802), 42.

67. A. L. Barbauld, *Remarks on Mr Gilbert Wakefield's Enquiry into the Expediency and Propriety of Public or Social Worship* (London: Johnson, 1792), 75–6.

68. Ibid. 76.

69. A. L. Barbauld, *Pastoral Lessons and Parental Conversations, intended as a Companion to Hymns in Prose*, 3rd edn. (London: Darton and Harvey, 1803), lesson xv, 86–7.

70. A. L. Barbauld, *Devotional Pieces, compiled from the Psalms and the Book of Job: to which are prefixed, Thoughts on the Devotional Taste, on Sects, and on Establishments* (London: J. Johnson, 1775); full text reprinted in *Anna Letitia Barbauld: Selected Poetry and Prose*, ed. W. McCarthy and E. Kraft (Peterborough, Ontario: Broadview, 2002), 209–234 (211).

71. Barbauld, *Thoughts on the Devotional Taste*, 212.

72. Ibid. 223.

73. Ibid. 224.

74. Ibid. 224–5.

75. Ibid. 226.

76. Ibid. 227.

77. Ibid. 217.

78. Mee, *Romanticism, Enthusiasm and Regulation*, 180, 182.

79. Schofield, *Enlightenment of Joseph Priestley*, 50.

80. J. Priestley, *Autobiography of Joseph Priestley. Contains Memoirs of Dr Joseph Priestley, written by himself* (1806), introd. J. Lindsay (Bath: Adams and Dart, 1970), 76.

81. J. Priestley, *An Examination of Dr Reid's Inquiry into the Human Mind on the Principles of Common Sense, Dr Beattie's Essay on the Nature and Immutability of Truth, and Dr Oswald's Appeal to Common Sense in Behalf of Religion* (London: J. Johnson, 1774), p. xix.

82. R. C. Allen, *David Hartley on Human Nature* (New York: State University of New York, 1999), 6.

83. Ibid. 8–9.

84. Quoted in Mee, *Romanticism, Enthusiasm and Regulation*, 284; it is also worth comparing Priestley's comment to plate 4 of Blake's *The Marriage of Heaven and Hell* (1790): 'All Bibles or sacred codes. have been the causes of the following Errors. i. That Man has two real existing principles Viz: a Body & a Soul', in *The Poetry and Prose of William Blake*, ed. D. V. Erdman (New York: Doubleday, 1965).

85. See E. P. Thompson, *Witness Against the Beast: William Blake and Moral Law* (Cambridge: Cambridge University Press, 1993), 10.

86. Blake, *Marriage*, plate 3.

87. Ibid., plates 3–4.

88. Ibid., plates 23–4.

89. J. Roberts, 'St Paul's Gifts to Blake's Aesthetic: "O Human Imagination, O Divine Body"', *The Glass*, 15 (2003), 8–18 (10).

90. Blake, *Marriage*, plate 14; Blake, *The Laocoön*, in *Poetry and Prose*, ed. Erdman.

91. Roberts, 'St Paul's Gifts', 15; C. Rowland, *Radical Christianity: A Reading of Recovery* (Oxford: Polity Press, 1988), 113.

2

Unitarianism: Priestley to Gaskell

Towards the end of the eighteenth century, the Unitarian minister Richard Price expressed his fear that 'the most valuable part of the dissenting interest is likely to be ground to death between enthusiasm on the one hand, and luxury and fashion on the other'.[1] As the last chapter suggested, enthusiasts threatened to render religion nothing more than a mystical experience of heightened emotion; while the late Presbyterians seemed preoccupied with only a 'tasteful' faith sanitized as it was for a chic, urban, and bourgeois middle class. In stark opposition to the modest Methodist or Anglican clergyman, rational Dissenters were concerned with luxury, legitimizing the accumulation of capital and the enjoyment of what this could buy. Even their chapels were elegant and comfortable, and dancing, cards, the theatre, and literature were all considered acceptable, the congregation literate, intellectual, opulent, and socially prosperous.[2] Not everyone was at ease with the new Dissenters, however, one Calvinist preacher despairing that 'in general they are of a loose dissipated turn of mind assembling in the gay circles of pleasure, and following the customs and manners of the world'.[3] Certainly new Dissent, particularly Unitarianism, was founded on a liberal capitalist politics that encouraged a faith compatible with genteel professionalism rather than unworldly devotion, recruiting in commercial centres rather than the rural areas in which Wesley had excelled. This shift, from a Calvinist-based Presbyterianism through to a more rational Dissent and finally Unitarianism, was notably dependent on the overthrow of many orthodox Christian ideas. As John Seed argues, 'the divinity of Christ, the existence of hell and the devil, the doctrines of original sin and the immaculate conception and other tenets were abandoned as irrational superstitions'.[4] Nevertheless, the Trinity remained *the* central doctrine of Christianity during this period, the refusal to believe Jesus was the son of God remaining a criminal offence until 1813: if Jesus was a mortal, albeit one with a divine mission, then he could not have volunteered to take human sin away by atoning for it through his crucifixion.[5] This logic outraged many believers, Wesley's hymn, 'For the Mahometans', testifying to such fury: 'Stretch out Thine arm, Thou Triune God | The Unitarian fiend expel, | And chase his doctrine back to hell.'[6]

For others, like William Paley, God was not interested in chasing anyone anywhere and instead stood as an ethical anchor securing human happiness. In *Natural Theology; or, Evidences of the Existence and Attributes of the Deity* (1802), Paley insisted that God had given human beings the capacity to undergo pleasure in order that they experience their own and that of others, morally obligating us both to each other and also to feel good. What remained important for Unitarians was the freedom to debate such questions, underlining as they did the right of the individual to employ rational inquiry in order to arrive at a set of personal conclusions. Education remained key, the Unitarians piloting a new approach to secondary education in the early nineteenth century that was made manifest in the Hazlewood and Bruce Castle schools to which Charles Dickens referred as 'the only recognition of education as a broad system of moral and intellectual philosophy, that I have ever seen in practice'.[7] This chapter will offer an outline of 'new Dissent' with a focus on Unitarianism, mapping its beginnings in the eighteenth century, through to its impact on Romanticism and the early Victorians. Many writers who sought to experiment with religious ideas, Coleridge, Mary Wollstonecraft, and Hemans, for example, were attracted to Unitarianism, especially as their radical publisher, Joseph Johnson, belonged to its ranks. Many at the fringes of Dissent, including some Quakers, also discussed below, turned to Unitarianism as a reasoned response to an increasingly fragmented religious culture. Yet, as we shall see, the more reasoned the Unitarians became, the more some believers mourned the loss of mysterious or revelatory elements of faith, provoking a debate between the role of reason and mystery in religion staged between two key leaders of the movement: William Johnson Fox and James Martineau. The chapter closes by turning to Elizabeth Gaskell, whose presentation of Dissent in her novels is always tempered by her sympathy towards any religious position expressed with conviction, itself a defining characteristic of the Unitarian Christian.

'ANTI-TRINITARIANISM'

If old Dissent had drawn up religious systems grounded in individual beliefs and politics, then new Dissent forged a politics from religious systems. The dissenting academies had radicalized many Christians to the point where their religious beliefs had become a platform on which they could discuss political and ethical matters including slavery, rights for women, and the status of the labouring classes. Many liberal Dissenters gradually accepted humanitarian principles into their religion, notably freedom of conscience, and it was common for a Dissenter to remain within his or her 'old' nonconformist congregation while also attending a Unitarian meeting house. Price and Joshua Toulmin even ministered to their respectively Presbyterian and Baptist congregations while holding Unitarian positions elsewhere, and it was only in the nineteenth century that one could be 'born into' the Unitarian faith, rendering it at this time a society of converts. Theophilus Lindsey, John Disney, William Frend, Robert Southey, and Coleridge left the Church of England directly for Unitarianism and those who were more uncertain about their faith, such as Wollstonecraft, Godwin, and Hemans, found it an accommodating and tolerant branch of latitudinarianism. It was not tolerant to all belief-systems, however, and, like Arminianism, was built on an adamant rejection of Calvinism, 'a very wrong, bad scheme' wrote the preacher Philip Gibbs as early as 1737, 'I know not of anything that has more defaced the beauty of the Christian religion'.[8] By the late eighteenth century, this kind of feeling had developed into 'Calvinophobia', a primarily Unitarian prejudice fuelled by various accounts of the part Calvin had played in the execution of the radical anti-Trinitarian, Michael Servetus, burned at the stake in 1546. Servetus had refused to acknowledge that the Bible in any way advocated a belief in the Trinity and insisted that Jesus was the son of an eternal God, rather than being himself eternal or divine. The Unitarians regarded him as their first martyr, and many followed Servetus on to the scaffold, including Edward Wightman, who famously burned at the stake twice after his executioners mistook the angry profanities he shouted through the flames as a recantation of heresy.

In 1648, an ordinance was passed rendering such heretical denial of the Trinity a capital offence, but the force of this law was partly counteracted by the increased popularity of the ideas of Laelius and Faustus Socinus, whose rejection of the divinity of Christ a century before had founded the Socinian movement. Faustus, Laelius's nephew, developed his uncle's anti-Trinitarianism into a system which asserted that the only way to know God is through the revealed word of Scripture: reaching God through contemplation of innate ideas or nature, for example, was misguided. The argument behind 'Socianism' was that faith had to be the most essential aspect of Christianity: if all religions were simply 'true', then how could one differentiate between the good and the bad ones? Christianity is moral and good, Faustus claimed, not because it is empirically indisputable but because the promises behind it are 'true', redemptive, and consolatory. The works of the Socinuses were reprinted and translated during the early-modern period, chiefly by John Biddle who was assisted by the Sabellian, Thomas Firmin, renowned for supervising the first use of the word 'Unitarian' in 1687.[9] At this point, Unitarianism included both Socinians and Arians under its rubric, one outlined by both the London preacher, Thomas Emlyn, in his *Vindication of the Worship of the Lord Jesus Christ on Unitarian Principles* (1706); and more notably by the Arian chaplain to Queen Anne, Samuel Clarke, in *Scripture Doctrine of the Trinity* (1712). As a Newtonian (he translated the *Optics* in 1706), Clarke opposed the materialism of Thomas Hobbes, the pantheism of Spinoza, and the empiricism of Locke, and argued that God was an eternal, independent, and immutable sovereign, impossible for a mortal mind to comprehend. All the same, humanity should trust, Clarke argued, that God was a single, intelligent, and wise power whose being comprises time and space: everything is an attribute of God, then, including Christ, disabling any argument for the latter's divinity. As Clarke argued in *Scripture Doctrine*, only God is self-existent, an argument hotly debated, and finally denied, at Salters' Hall in 1719. Here, Dissenters were mostly concerned to argue against Calvin's teaching that only the elect could be saved, an idea supported by statement seventeen of the Thirty-nine Articles, 'Of Predestination and Election'.[10] The problem for Dissenters was that all of the Thirty-nine Articles, including this one, were unquestioningly Trinitarian, provoking them to challenge the Church's ruling that all believers 'subscribe' to them.[11] This campaign intensified in the 1770s under the leadership of Theophilus Lindsey, who gathered a group of Cambridge men, including Wilberforce and Simeon, along with many Anglican clergy, in order to seek legal relief from subscription.[12] Lindsey organized their views into the Feathers Tavern Petition to Parliament in 1772 and, when this was rejected, the preacher resigned his Anglican living to open a Unitarian Christian Chapel in Essex Street, London, in 1774.

Lindsey escaped prosecution for using the name 'Unitarian' at his chapel, despite the fact that such behaviour contravened both the Toleration (1689) and Blasphemy (1698) Acts. With newfound bravado, Lindsey felt encouraged to develop a fresh Christological theology which declared that Christianity had to be the true religion because of what was known about Christ: what other belief-system had allowed a mortal man to unite communities, enact miracles, and be resurrected? For Lindsey's friend, Priestley, this underlined Christianity's benevolent and loving aspect, one only a Unitarian-based belief could shape, joining 'all persons and all things' in 'an immense glorious and happy system'. He declared:

the great author of this system, makes us regard every person and every thing in a friendly and pleasing light. The whole is but one family. We have all one God and Father, whose affection for us is intense, impartial and everlasting. He despises nothing that he has made, and, by ways unknown to us, and often by methods the most unpromising, he provides for our greatest good. We are all training up in the same school of moral discipline, and are likewise joint heirs of eternal life, revealed to us in the gospel.[13]

This essentially humanitarian view was shared by many at Essex Street, including both John Disney, the first secretary of the Unitarian Society for Promoting Christian Knowledge, and his successor, Thomas Belsham, who had been a divinity tutor at both Daventry and Hackney dissenting academies. For these men, the material, benevolent, and ethical aspect of humanist Christianity was forever threatened by Trinitarianism because it had emerged, not from the scriptures, but from the spiritual philosophy of Plato. Plato's system of metaphysics asserted that the world can be divided into 'things' and 'ideas': what we see around us ('things') are imitations of bigger, unchangeable concepts ('ideas'). Add into this dualistic philosophy a creator God, and Platonism becomes Trinitarianism, both adding up to nothing more than a branch of black magic, thought Priestley, in which souls, sons of God, doctrines, and so on, were randomly deemed 'divine':

Austin, speaking of the principles of *Plato*, *says*, that 'by changing a few words and sentences, the Platonists would have become Christians, as many of those of later times have done' ... But, unhappily, these admirers of Plato carried their admiration, much too far; and ... were more particularly struck with that very part of this system, namely, that concerning the doctrine of *ideas*, and the divine intellect.[14]

Ideas were not actions, argued Priestley, implying that the ethical teachings of Jesus of Nazareth encouraged material, not speculative, good works, a conviction that would come to underline modern 'liberation' or 'practical' theology.[15] Christian orthodoxy, then, was a mere imitation of Platonism, the Church Fathers flattered into its philosophical pretensions and preferring it to the other, less intellectually led options: a too harsh Stoicism; or a too worldly Aristotelianism or Epicureanism.[16] Trinitarianism was Platonism in disguise.

Despite Priestley's varying dissenting views, Coleridge, like many Dissenters, recognized him as 'the author of the modern Unitarianism', although, as a philosopher-poet, he was himself led back to Trinitarianism through his interests in Platonism.[17] Initially in training for the Anglican priesthood under the direction of his father, John Coleridge, a biblical scholar and vicar of Ottery St Mary, Coleridge was drawn to Priestley's Unitarianism at Cambridge under the influence of William Frend and Robert Southey. Frend's Unitarianism was distinctly political, and his opposition to the war against republicanism in France, coupled with his nonconformist beliefs, led to his trial before the university Senate, disrupted by a group of protestors organized by Coleridge. With Southey, Coleridge devised the idea of a Pantisocracy, a utopian model of community the men planned to establish in Pennsylvania, where Priestley had emigrated after the Birmingham riots (and which had been founded by the Quaker William Penn in 1681). Such a community was built on the idea that everyone, men and women alike, would commit equal time to both work and intellectual pursuits, ushering in a new way of living modelled on that of Jesus and his disciples. As a prototypical society, Pantisocracy would be fuelled by a communal affection that would eventually spill over into the rest of the world as a kind of regenerative tonic.[18] This rendered Pantisocracy an apocalyptic project for Coleridge, serving to announce, he wrote to Southey, a 'miraculous Millennium' that would shake up orthodoxy and those associated prejudices that had driven Priestley from his home.[19] Even after the project was abandoned for financial reasons, Coleridge continued to forward the idea of a social apocalypse figured through the believer's closeness to Christ, one in which the self is entirely subordinated to divine authority. As he stated in 'Religious Musings' (1794):

> GOD only to behold, and know, and feel,
> Till by exclusive Consciousness of God

> All self-annihilated it shall make
> GOD its Identity: God all in all!
> We and our Father ONE!
>
> (ll. 41–5)

Presenting this as a prophecy, wherein the reader is encouraged to rid him- or herself of the individual imagination to join in a larger sense of universal benevolence, Coleridge disavowed the enthusiastic strains of some Dissenters for a politicized kind of religious feeling.[20] For in 'annihilating' selfhood and then investing in this loss, the believer is liberated into a space free of egoistic desires where affection is turned outwards, at first to God, then to one's personal circle and finally to the whole of society:

The ardour of private Attachments makes Philanthropy a necessary *habit* of the Soul. I love my *Friend*—such as *he* is, all mankind are or *might be*! The deduction is evident—. Philanthropy (and indeed every other Virtue) is a thing of *Concretion*—Some home-born Feeling is the centre of the Ball, that, rolling on thro' Life collects and assimilates every congenial Affection.[21]

'Home-born' feeling also infuses that domesticated attachment to Christ Coleridge invokes at the end of 'The Aeolian Harp' (1795), a 'Faith that inly *feels*' (ll. 61, 54) and connects all to the 'Family of Christ' through a kind of Hartleyan association. Hartley argued for a divine sovereign that dwells within the believer, a 'God | Diffused through all', wrote Coleridge in 'Religious Musings' (ll. 130–1), asserting a fundamental principle of Unitarianism that echoes through 'Frost at Midnight' (1798) and more ominously so in 'The Ancient Mariner' (1797). As he commented in his notebook, the 'strongest argument for [Chri]stianity [is] the weak Argument that do yet persuade so many to believe—i.e. it fits the human heart'.[22]

Unitarianism also allowed Coleridge to Christianize his politics and understand his faith as materially useful. 'Fears in Solitude' (1798), for example, begins by attacking those who dogmatically recite rules and laws without thinking about their content or impact on human life. The 'sweet words | Of Christian promise' are muttered either by those 'too indolent | To deem them falsehoods or to know their truth'; or by sanctimonious moralizers who 'gabble o'er the oaths' they 'mean to break' (ll. 63–72):

> the very name of God
> Sounds like a juggler's charm; and bold, with joy,
> Forth from his dark and lonely hiding-place,

(Portentous sight!) the owlet Atheism,
Sailing on obscene wings athwart the noon,
Drops his blue-fringéd lids, and holds them close,
And hooting at the glorious sun in Heaven,
Cries out, 'Where is it?'

(ll. 79–86)

Such vain questioning is answered later in the poem as the narrator appeals not to a dictatorial God, but to a benevolent being able to unite warring communities and soothe the individual's anxieties: 'all my heart | Is softened, and made worthy to indulge | Love, and the thoughts that yearn for human kind' (ll. 196–7; 230–2). For Coleridge, Christ too taught believers to perceive the world through love rather than mystery, and, like Priestley, the poet blamed the Gnostics for introducing a false Trinitarianism, producing as they did 'all the Mysteries, Impostures, and Persecutions, that have disgraced the Christian Community'.[23]

Coleridge finally entered the Unitarian ministry in 1798 with the support of William Hazlitt and Josiah Wedgwood. His position was short lived, however, the poet finding Unitarianism emotionally paralysing ('O for some Sun to unite heat & Light!' he wrote) and Coleridge converted back to a Trinitarian understanding of God through his reading of German Idealist philosophy.[24] Unitarianism suddenly appeared hollow and without meaning for the poet, its members like 'naked Philosophers' trapped in a 'musaeum of cut & dried Faith | —The English Unitarians = the Hermit Crab'.[25] By 1805, the entire movement seemed nothing more than 'idolatry' to Coleridge, who now thought of its public supporters as treacherously unfaithful to even their own concept of God: he accused Priestley of atheism, and Barbauld of secular coolness.[26] Coleridge had met Barbauld at the home of their mutual friend, John Prior Estlin, a Warrington Academy educated Unitarian preacher and philosopher. At first Coleridge was enchanted by Barbauld, writing to Estlin: 'The more I see of Mrs Barbauld the more I admire her—that wonderful *Propriety* of Mind! ... how steadily she keeps it within the bounds of practical Reason.' In the same letter, however, he lamented that his own 'Subtleties too often lead me into strange (tho' God be praised) transient Out-of-the-way-nesses. Oft like a winged Spider, I am entangled in a new Spun web', a foreshadow of his future restlessness with what he came to perceive as a chilly Unitarianism.[27] Indeed, Coleridge later attacked Barbauld for being as personable as 'an icicle', while her poem, 'To Mr C[olerid]ge' (1799), accused him of becoming stuck in a 'maze of metaphysic lore'.[28] Certainly his Trinitarian *Aids to Reflection* (1825) attacks Belsham, Paley, and Priestley for depersonalizing the divine to such an extent that it erases it altogether, forcing the believer to turn outside of him- or herself to imitate Christ's actions, rather than look inward to reflect upon what these actions signify and imply. What Rousseau called *sentiment intérieur*, innate good feeling or sensibility, was significant for Coleridge's faith because it enforced the idea of the individual as conscious and sensate of those feelings that unfold the divine within.[29] This neo-Platonic dimension of religious experience is founded on love, if not of the erotic kind favoured by Wollstonecraft (to whom we turn shortly), of a kind that resembled what Coleridge called a profound 'joy and tenderness' for others; his faith, even in its more orthodox moments, seems always Platonic because it regards actions inducive of human love to function as mirrors of God's higher love and divinity.[30]

A SOCIETY OF FRIENDS

Coleridge's fascination with the metaphysical significance of friendship and interpersonal relationships was also shared by another socially radical dissenting sect, the Quakers, or the Society of Friends. His personal acquaintance with the Society is corroborated through his public defence of the Quaker, Edward Fox, widely praised for his gentle treatment of the mentally ill and whom Coleridge heralded for 'his spirited exertions in favour of the oppressed'.[31] In selected ways, the Quakers shared much with the early Romantics, stressing the importance of individual feeling (they argued for the immediacy of Christ's teaching within each person); supporting radical reform (they instigated the abolitionist movement and refused to implement any kind of hierarchical system in their meetings); and rejecting old orthodoxies as intolerant and restrictive. As Michael Mullett argues, as early as the seventeenth century 'Quakerism was the most radical organized religious movement to appear', presenting a huge threat to orthodoxy and other nonconformist movements and amassing almost 60,000 members in the 1650s alone.[32] The Quakers' promotion of equality between men and women was more remarkable still, asserting as they did that the Holy Spirit recognized no difference between the sexes. Women were granted their own meetings and ministry, as well as their full consent in marriage, and in this period, where only 11 per cent of women were able to sign their names, almost 66 per cent of Quaker women were literate.[33] From its inception, the Quakers sought to work against the prejudices they regarded in other religions, such as the subordinate role allocated to women, support for war or conflict, and the fear caused by predestination and the imputation of sins. Sin itself was even regarded, not as bad or immoral behaviour that trespassed outside a self-righteous code of laws, but as a personal burden imposed on the individual by corrupt ideology from which they might escape through quiet faith.[34] Both their founder, George Fox, and also their only 'theologian', Robert Barclay, constantly underlined the belief that religious truth is reached individually, the inner voice of God speaking directly to the soul rather than through ordained ministers in consecrated buildings. This emphasis on the individual relationship the believer fosters with God also demoted the Bible as of inferior import to the emotional experience of faith, one which the individual was encouraged to spontaneously express as a 'testimony' during otherwise silent weekly meetings. For the reformer and Quaker, John Woolman, this experience served to illuminate:

a Principle which is pure, placed in the human Mind, which in different Places and Ages hath had different Names; it is, however, pure, and proceeds from God. It is deep, and inward, confined to no Forms of Religion, nor excluded from any, where the Heart stands in perfect Sincerity. In whomsoever this takes Root and grows, of what Nation soever, they become Brethren.[35]

Like the Romantics, the Quakers sought to destroy any definition that might fix their agenda, Woolman suggesting here that any formal encoding of his religious practice would render it false before a God indifferent to denominational preference. So too did they seek to articulate their beliefs in a 'natural', unadorned manner, Penn demanding that Friends should: 'Speak properly, and in as few words as you can, but always plainly; for the end of speech is not ostentation but to be understood.'[36] We might profitably compare this to Wordsworth's justification of the subject-matter of those poems included in the *Lyrical Ballads*; as he writes in the 'Preface' (1802):

Low and rustic life was generally chosen, because in that condition, the essential passions of the heart find a better soil in which they can attain their maturity, are less under restraint, and speak a plainer and more emphatic language; because in that condition of life our elementary feelings co-exist in a state of greater simplicity, and, consequently, may be more accurately contemplated, and more forcibly communicated.[37]

Penn and Wordsworth alike sought to disseminate a religio-political message through simple language, and the Quakers established a library of pamphlets to win converts and reinforce the values of existing members. While the Quakers often distrusted the arts, especially the theatre (considered a capricious and artificial genre), they were often themselves presented favourably in literature, notably Elizabeth Gaskell's *Sylvia's Lovers* (1863) and Anthony Trollope's *Marion Fay* (1871–2). Overseas, John Greenleaf Whittier's *Legends of New England* (1831) and Harriet Beecher Stowe's *Uncle Tom's Cabin* (1852) had fast become popular texts in the American Quaker tradition. Many writers remained suspicious, however, perhaps sensing in Quaker testimonies that dangerous enthusiasm discussed in the last chapter. Charles Lamb, for example, confessed to Coleridge that 'I have had thoughts of turning Quaker', but on attending a meeting

saw a man under all the agitations and workings of a fanatic, who believed himself under the influence of some 'inevitable presence'. This cured me of Quakerism. I love it in the books of Penn and Woolman; but I detest the vanity of a man thinking he speaks by the Spirit, when what he says an ordinary man might say without all that quaking and trembling.[38]

In a later essay, Lamb admitted the attraction of 'the Foxian orgasm', but this surely contrasts heavily with the plainness of religious experience Penn insisted believers should communicate in a bare and clear-cut language.[39]

Simplicity of feeling and expression is central to the 'religious' element of Wordsworth's verse, whether this is pantheistic, as sections of 'Tintern Abbey' (1798) attest; expressive of a Unitarian investment in one God, exemplified in parts of *The Prelude* (1805); or appears as a more orthodox commentary on Christianity itself, exemplified in the *Ecclesiastical Sonnets* (1822). Wordsworth and Coleridge were both briefly attracted by pantheism—the idea that the material universe is the only divine being and that its every aspect, living or otherwise, is part of God ('pan'—all; 'theos'—God).[40] The word pantheist was first used by the Deist John Toland in *Socinianism Truly Stated* (1705), indicating not only Toland's rejection of religious orthodoxy, but also his opposition to all forms of authority, including the monarchy.[41] The radicalism, religious and political, associated with pantheism in the late eighteenth century, appealed to the young Wordsworth, who pledged himself to the democratic cause of the French Revolution after witnessing devastating scenes of poverty in Paris and Blois. Yet as democratic support for an increasingly corrupt and terrifying Revolution faded, so Wordsworth's trust in unified religious systems dwindled, whether pantheism or Unitarianism, as 'Tintern Abbey' (1798) evinces. At first, the poem reads as a celebrated illustration of the personal relationship pantheism encourages the believer to develop with his or her surroundings, as well as his or her emotional reaction to it.[42] God appears as a

> sense sublime
> Of something far more deeply interfused,
> Whose dwelling is the light of setting suns,
> And the round ocean and the living air,
> And the blue sky, and in the mind of man;
> A motion and a spirit, that impels
> All thinking things, all objects of all thought,
> And rolls through all things.
>
> (ll. 95–102)

In this extract spiritual experience binds the viewer with the world, thus making it easier for him or her to find, as Coleridge wrote in 'Fears in Solitude', 'Religious meanings in the forms of Nature!' (l. 24). For Coleridge, nature offered the believer a key to momentarily unlock God's mystery, an epiphany the city-dweller might only experience through careful study of the Bible, trapped in urban artifice and needing Christ to enable revelation of God.[43] Wordsworth, however, asserts a 'chearful [*sic*] faith' that is dependent, not on where the individual is situated, but on interpersonal feeling, whether this is experienced with God or with a fellow human being. Nicholas Roe reminds us that the poem is riddled with an uncertainty and reservation that qualifies the poet's 'repeated claims to faith', as it signals that nature, like the situation in France, inevitably corrodes and changes.[44] Yet Wordsworth sustains his faith in a religion grounded in human feeling in two ways. First, the poem is situated at the end of the *Lyrical Ballads* (1798), and as such makes a striking contrast with the preceding sketches of human suffering, grief, and poverty. Having encountered these startling and sometimes spooky tales of mad mothers, crippled wanderers, betrayed lovers, and desolate beggars, the reader is necessarily plunged into a state of alienation redeemed by the consolatory experience of reading 'Tintern Abbey'. From alienation comes affection, Wordsworth argues. Second, the poem is articulated in the presence of the poet's sister, Dorothy, who represents a human sympathy that is immediately healing, the entire memory on which the narrative is based 'More dear,' Wordsworth writes, 'for thy sake' (l. 160). Feeling between people is what materializes faith, the poem implies, regardless of how one perceives the physical or spiritual world.

A COMMON GOOD

Wordsworth and Coleridge's investment in simple human interaction and friendship as a way of practising religious faith was rooted in an eighteenth-century preoccupation with community and the common good, many philosophers were captivated by humanity's relationship to benevolence, sensibility, and affection. Paul, and after him Aquinas, had both stressed the profound importance of the believer's relationship to his or her community. Aquinas directly invokes 1 Corinthians 12: 24–6 when he insists that:

All who are contained in any community are related to it as parts to a whole. The part is what it is in virtue of the whole; therefore every good of the part is to be directed towards the good of the whole ... Since every man is part of a state, it is impossible for any man to be good unless he is well adapted to the common good.[45]

As Peter N. Miller reminds us, eighteenth-century religious toleration and diversity challenged the post-Reformation sense of a national, state-driven religious uniformity, especially when so many Dissenters took up causes outside of the state in Europe and America alike.[46] Community was no longer a conforming body of like-minded people; instead it was a disparate but welcoming society of liberated individuals all seeking representation and civil rights.[47] An important intervention into these debates was Adam Smith's *The Theory of Moral Sentiments* (1759), which argued that human sympathy and compassion derived, not from an innate moral sense (as Shaftesbury and Hume asserted), but from a moral nature or sentiment made up of propriety, prudence, and benevolence. Smith's theory implied that we are all acts of a creative imagination in that we adjust our behaviour according to how we think others will assess us: our internal self strives to conform to the expectations of the external spectator. While Smith contends that benevolent or dutiful actions consequently stem from a fear of social disapproval, the implication of his thesis is that individuals strive to identify with and understand the emotional dispositions of others to maintain good relations with them. The motive for such moral sympathy is 'religion', Smith argues, our 'natural sense of duty' and charitable 'love of mankind' driven by 'a sense that God has commanded us to perform' this way.[48] Furthermore, 'universal benevolence' can 'be the source of no solid happiness to any man' unless it is 'under the immediate care and protection of that great, benevolent and all-wise Being, who directs all movements of nature; and who is determined, by his own unalterable perfections, to maintain in it, at all times, the greatest possible quantity of happiness'.[49]

Smith's views were particularly well received by the Unitarian community based in Newington Green, London, a centre of religious and political radicalism and ministered over by Richard Price. Price was a model political Dissenter, the son of a Welsh nonconformist minister and writer of countless cheap sociological tracts on how to improve daily life for the poor, the national debt, and the American War of Independence. So influential were his pamphlets on the war with America that he became intimate with Benjamin Franklin, whose invitation to attend Congress abroad in 1778 was only refused because of his staunch loyalty to his congregation at home.[50] Price could not go as far as his friend Priestley in advocating Socinianism, and preferred instead the security of Arianism as it allowed him to recognize Christ as both divine and human. Like Priestley, however, Price's key concerns regarded the subject of ethics and the free agency of human will. In his *Review of the Principal Questions in Morals* (1757), Price suggested that right and wrong belong to actions that individuals must learn to judge through reason and understanding. One's ability to enact such judgement correctly, however, is dependent on a rational sense carefully shaped by the emotions: happiness, for example, derives not from divine providence, but from right action, decency, and rectitude. It is in this sense that Price preached a religion, not of the heart, but of moral sentiment, regulated tenderness, and the common good, one close in kind to Blake's human-centred theology. This is perhaps why many non-Unitarians felt welcome in Price's chapel, Benjamin Franklin and Adam Smith both visiting him there and Mary Wollstonecraft regularly attending his Sunday meetings after moving to Newington Green to establish a girls' school. As John Brewer suggests, Price's community appeared to be a 'small, snug, dissenting coterie', and its members were quick to defend one another against orthodox attack.[51]

Price certainly found himself under fire from the establishment when he openly defended the French National Assembly in a hugely controversial sermon preached to the London Revolution Society at the Old Jewry meeting house in 1789. 'On the Love of our Country' heralded the French Revolution as a rational, rather than hysterical, response to a corrupt monarchy, the French Assembly's 'Declaration of the Rights of Man and of the Citizen' directly inspired by the American 'Declaration of Independence' (1776) Price had already vehemently supported. The sermon provoked a bitter attack from the conservative Whig, Edmund Burke, who declared in *Reflections on the Revolution in France* (1790) that Price had exploited the pulpit for political crusading. The preacher's 'flippant, vain discourse', demanded Burke, threatened always to explode into a 'full blaze' of enthusiasm, Price being nothing more than a modern 'Hugh Peters', the Puritan minister who had presided over the execution of Charles I.[52] Burke stormed further that any 'good moral and religious sentiments' Price may have intended were 'mixed up in a sort of porridge of various political opinions', his imprudent espousal of the French Revolution being 'the grand ingredient in the cauldron'.[53] Worse still were Price's connections with literary radicalism:

I looked on that sermon as the public declaration of a man much connected with literary caballers, and intriguing philosophers; with political theologians, and theological politicians, both at home and abroad. I know they set him up as a sort of oracle; because, with the best intentions in the world, he naturally *philippizes*, and chants his prophetic song in exact unison with their designs.[54]

While Price held that he was always tempered by reason in the pulpit, Burke considered him a zealous prophet who had privileged his own fiery views over any responsibility to his congregation or the common good. As Jon Mee argues, not only did Burke think Price's sermon rendered dissenting religion irresponsible and careless, arrogantly dividing the Church from the State, but he also argued that it proved how easily those unchecked by the discipline of orthodoxy could be swept into 'unhallowed transports', religious, political, and sexual.[55]

Equally prey to such transports, Burke believed, were Tom Paine and Mary Wollstonecraft, both of whom made clear their commitment as Pricean 'caballers' in their respective responses to the statesman: *The Rights of Man* (1791) and *A Vindication of the Rights of Men* (1790). Paine supported the Revolution because it pledged to grant free and equal rights to all men, allowing the individual to relate to society and God without the constraints of systems or dogmas. Accused of seditious libel for such views, Paine fled to France only to be imprisoned there for his pacifist denigration of the execution of Louis XVI. While in jail, he began his part Deist, part Unitarian tract, *The Age of Reason* (1794), which dissents far further from orthodoxy than even Price would have liked. 'My own mind is my own church', stated Paine, his 'religion' consisting of 'doing justice, loving mercy, and endeavouring to make our fellow-creatures happy'. Organized religion, Paine lamented, was full of corrupt priest-craft, slavish dogmas, and crooked monopolies, the Bible itself a 'cruel and torturous' text full of 'voluptuous debaucheries' and 'unrelenting vindictiveness'.[56]

Wollstonecraft too professed a personal religion, one that Godwin declared was 'almost entirely of her own creation'. Yet even the atheistic Godwin recognized her interest in 'received' religion, a belief founded not on a 'system of forms', but on devotional 'taste' and a passionately committed 'imagination'.[57] Following Godwin, many critics regard Wollstonecraft's faith as a sort of intense feminized sensibility, taking as their blueprint the enthusiastic exclamations of the heroine of her novel, *Mary: a Fiction* (1788). As Barbara Taylor argues, Mary's understanding of God mirrors that of the adolescent Wollstonecraft, moving as it does between a rational, intellectual comprehension of the divine, and a fervent, almost sexualized mysticism.[58] Finally enlightened by a liberally tolerant rational Dissent, Mary comes to recognize a shared oppression between nonconformists and women, both groups struggling to emphasize the importance of private reasoned judgement in religious and social life. Wollstonecraft transcribed Mary's conversion into her political defence of Price in the *Rights of Men*:

my heart is human, beats quick with human sympathies—and I FEAR God ... I fear that sublime power, whose motive for creating me must have been wise and good; and I submit to the moral laws which my reason deduces from this view of my dependence on him.—It is not his power that I fear—it is not to an arbitrary will, but to unerring *reason* I submit.[59]

For Wollstonecraft, God represents a reasoned, enlightened standard to which all must aspire because of its inherent integrity: he functions like an anchor securing the essentially good individual against manipulative or damaging codes of law. Price exemplified such rational faith, 'a man whose habits are fixed by piety and reason', but who also preached a religion of feeling able to accommodate Wollstonecraft's sense that her belief was grounded in her heart, as well as her mind.[60] Like Coleridge, Wollstonecraft claimed that we love and worship God because it makes sense emotionally and rationally: through Christ, God gives the believer a model of being which, when copied, grants self-love and esteem. Taylor suggests that this conviction—that virtue not power elicits God's mercy and respect—underlined Wollstonecraft's feminist argument that successful human relationships necessitated two equal individuals.[61] Human love can only lead to heavenly love once everyone feels equal before each other and God, enabling women to feel passionately without fear of derision. Passion is identified by Wollstonecraft as a component of the rational self in part because it serves to intensify faith, triggering what Taylor calls the 'erotic imagination'.[62] God implants this imagination in individuals to enable them to forge intensely loving relationships with other humans and thus train themselves properly to love God. Wollstonecraft's believer is both psychologically reformed (the individual develops self-esteem) and ethically motivated (being 'good' is the only rational choice), invested primarily in love as that which transforms the individual and therefore society.

This vision of love as a political agent of change looks both forward and back: it prefigures Kierkegaard's proclamation in *Fear and Trembling* (1843) that the whole of reality is made of God's love; and also gestures back to that neo-Platonic religious eroticism Priestley so denigrated. Yet the strategic vagueness of Wollstonecraft's religious position also exempted her from the harsh critiques suffered by more obviously dissenting women, such as Barbauld and Mary Hays. Gilbert Wakefield, for example, who had already attacked Barbauld for promoting public worship over solitary meditation, branded her a '*Platonic visionary*' before going on to more viciously taunt Mary Hays for her radically dissenting opinions.[63] Hays, a close friend of Godwin, is remembered for being the rather ardent author of *Memoirs of Emma Courtney* (1796), its passionate, radical but ultimately compulsive heroine falling obsessively in love with Augustus Harley and worshipping him with an alarming zeal. As Taylor notes, Hays wrote the novel as a warning against, rather than an example of, free thinking and unbridled sexuality, but its boldness mirrored the forthrightness of her sermons, preached by Disney at Essex Street.[64] A similar ambiguity can be perceived in Barbauld's late poem, *Eighteen Hundred and Eleven* (1812), harshly condemned on its publication both for the expression of prophetic strains inappropriate for a woman; and also for its uncompromising, near seditious attack on social and political corruption within Britain.[65] The poem rails bitterly at its readership, the 'loud death drum' of the opening line beating out the demise of a Britain wherein the 'Despot' rules (l. 9) and the 'helpless Peasant but retires to die' (l. 20) even as 'Enfeebling Luxury and ghastly Want' (l. 64) dominates society. As John Wilson Croker despaired, writing in *The Quarterly Review*:

Our old acquaintance Mrs Barbauld turned satirist! The last thing we should have expected, and, now that we have seen her satire, the last thing we could have desired ... We had hoped, indeed, that the empire might have been saved without the intervention of a lady author: ... we must take the liberty of warning her to desist from satire, which indeed is satire on herself alone; and of entreating, with great earnestness, that she will not, for the sake of this ungrateful generation, put herself to the trouble of writing any more party pamphlets in verse.[66]

This we might expect from the conservative Croker, but Godwin too, Henry Crabb Robinson reports, was 'full of his censure of Mrs Barbauld's new poem ... which he called cowardly, time-serving, Presbyterian'.[67] Godwin's dislike of the poem betrays a nervousness around figures like Barbauld, as well as Price, who was succeeded as minister at his chapel in Newington Green by Barbauld's husband, Rochemont, in 1802: all three clung to a sense of divinity Unitarianism promised to stamp out. Barbauld's Presbyterian faith, outlined in the previous chapter, also came to influence her memoir of Estlin, published as the preface to his *Familiar Lectures on Moral Philosophy* (1818). While it is often assumed that Barbauld published nothing after the upset surrounding *Eighteen Hundred and Eleven*, the Estlin memoir reveals that she was still concerned to promote an affective and experiential faith, as well as one rooted in political action. Estlin's belief was ideal, Barbauld wrote, because he claimed to temper his 'zealous regard' for religious questions with his 'comprehensive, elevated, and vigorous' mind: 'goodness of God, and the great practical duties of Christian-ity, were his favourite themes. To those of a different persuasion he always showed the utmost candour: the fervour of his religious feelings never led him to bigotry, nor his liberality to scepticism.'[68] Barbauld herself had been accused of bigotry and scepticism as her fracas with Croker bears out, and as a retaliatory response to the latter's review, her memoir also implies that such readings were rooted in an almost entirely faulty hermeneutics. As Anne Janowitz argues, the poem expresses a sense of ruin and loss that is explicitly related to an emancipatory politics in which defeat is neutralized by a regenerative sense of Romantic liberation.[69] It is perhaps the divine, redemptive, and emotive aspect of Barbauld's note of restored hope that so per-turbed the ever doubting Godwin, the poem clear that 'Religion's light and Freedom's holy flame!' are one and the same, fuelled as they are by 'Science' (a reference to Priestley) and the 'arts' (ll. 70, 74, 78).

'NEW' UNITARIANISM

Barbauld's reading of faith as an organic conviction comprised of freedom, art, and science may have emerged from 'new' Presbyterianism, but it also established the basic ideology of 'new' Unitarianism. Barbauld, like Coleridge, feared that Unitarianism had become too dry and many early nineteenth-century members believed that Priestley's interventions had drained their faith of religious emotion and produced a sense of individualism that prevented denominational feeling.[70] As Barbauld's poem warned society against its increasing infringements on civil and religious liberty, preachers like Belsham began to regret Unitarian support for the French Revolution, the enthusiasm of which had inspired numerous attacks on revealed religion in Europe. Unitarian religion was becoming insipid and languid, a trend the movement's new leaders sought to oppose: William Johnson Fox argued that the movement should be recreated as a society of reform and change; while James Martineau believed that Unitarians should become more sympathetic to some elements of affective and mysterious faith. Both men, however, quickly took advantage of a developing periodical press to disseminate their progressive ideas. Priestley had already led the way with the *Theological Repository* and William Vidler followed with *The Universalist's Miscellany*, renaming it in 1802 as *The Universal Theological Magazine*. In 1805, Robert Aspland reshaped it again as the political and literary *The Monthly Repository*, supplementing it later with the more populist *The Christian Reformer* and passing it to Fox in 1831. John Edward Taylor's *Manchester Guardian* and Edward Baines's *The Leeds Mercury* were also committed to presenting Dissenting concerns and politics favourably. Certainly the Unitarians were freer to circulate their message after 1813, when the Trinitarian Blasphemy Act was overturned, and, in 1825, Aspland and Fox established the British and Foreign Unitarian Association as a way of binding old and new Unitarians together in a shared mission.[71] Yet some old Unitarians did not want to be united with what they perceived as a new radical group that threatened to alienate Anglican sympathizers and disrupt the progress already made. The Lady Hewley Charity was a case in point. Hewley had been a wealthy York Presbyterian who had established a charitable fund in 1704 to educate poor Presbyterian preachers. The Unitarians had inherited the fund, but disputes over its distribution led to a court case in which it was claimed Hewley would never have been sympathetic to 'new' Unitarianism. Further legislation was required beyond the 1813 ruling to ensure the younger generation profited from their predecessors' investments, a need not met until the Dissenters' Chapels Act of 1844.

This struggle nevertheless disconcerted many Unitarians and the situation became more fraught when Fox left his wife to set up house with his female ward, and then tried to justify his actions with reference to his faith. Fox was what Kathryn Gleadle has identified as a 'radical' Unitarian, a figure who was committed to emulating Christ's example and securing religious and civil rights for women as well as men.[72] The radical Unitarians emerged from Fox's Unitarian South Place Chapel in Finsbury, which, like Aspland's chapel in Hackney, attracted a mixed congregation unified by their political and social views, rather than their religious beliefs. As the engraver W. J. Linton proclaimed, Fox was the 'virtual founder of that new school of English radicalism, which looked beyond the established traditions of the French Revolution, and more poetical, escaped the narrowness of Utilitarianism', a view underlined by his involvement with the *Monthly Repository*.[73] Gleadle even argues that Fox's transformation of the journal into a forum for politico-intellectual discussion 'revealed what was to most distinguish the radical Unitarians from their mainstream counterparts: their feminism'.[74] Barbauld's friend, John Estlin, suggested the same, declaring that Unitarianism was 'the religion of females', a movement which promoted female suffrage, rights in marriage, and adult education, and also worked to highlight women's roles in the Chartist programme and the increasingly pressing problem of prostitution.[75] When Fox sermonized on such ideas at South Chapel, many of his congregation walked out, leading to his formal eviction from old Unitarianism and the search for new leadership.

James Martineau succeeded where Fox had failed, ironically because the latter's politics were perceived as too rigid, leaving no space for believers to at least consider ideas of supernatural revelation, miracles, and divinity. Martineau was a member of Tennyson's 'Metaphysical Society', and a co-founder of the Free Christian Union (1868–70) which attempted to unite Dissenters, Anglicans, and those with a personal belief-system in one common Christian body. He certainly attracted many writers to his sermons, preaching to Dickens, Charles Lyell, and Frances Power Cobbe at his Unitarian chapel in Little Portland Street where he was minister from 1859. Martineau was sympathetic to the kind of emotive, intuitive faith of which new Unitarians were wary, and published *Hymns for the Christian Church and Home* (1840) to encourage a return to a religion of poetry and feeling, rather than one of reason. 'Worship', he wrote in the 'Preface', 'is an attitude which our nature assumes, not *for a purpose*, but *from an emotion*':

The plaints of sacred sorrow, the cry of penitence, the vow of duty, the brilliancy of praise, shed forth, like the laughter and tears of infancy ... the churches which begin to justify their outward devotion by appeal to [rationalism] have already lost their inward devoutness; ... it is evident that all natural devotion is but a mode of poetry; while no rationalistic devotion can ever reach it. The spontaneous overflow of the former has only to fall into regular and musical shape, and it becomes a hymn.[76]

Those rationalist, pedantic, or moralizing hymns to which worshippers were used were little more than 'rhymed theology', Martineau argued, including a section on 'Metre-Marks' in the hymn book with a view to teaching his readers how to feel as they read.[77] Including hymns by Barbauld, Cowper, Heber, Hemans, Wordsworth, and William Gaskell, as well as the Wesleys and Watts, Martineau's collection worked to stir the believer into a state of religious emotion.

Martineau's views were fuelled by his reading in two traditions that both offered Unitarianism a way of expressing its agenda: German biblical theory or 'Higher Criticism'; and transcendentalism. German literature in general had been made accessible in Britain by Unitarian writers, notably Coleridge, and the Goethe scholar, William Taylor, whom Barbauld had tutored at her school in Palgrave. The associated biblical theory suggested that the reader approach the Bible sceptically, seeking to recover the 'historical Jesus' from the mythologizing speculation the Gospels produced. Johann Salomo Semler, for example, professor of theology at the University of Halle, suggested that exegesis was culturally relative, so that certain books would seem more significant at particular moments in time, an argument which broke down any unity or authority the Bible had previously claimed.[78] Kant similarly asserted that all religion is no more than a projection of a specific set of moral sensibilities at a given point, contending that the individual must create his or her own meaning from a text like the Bible without the intervention of a ruling body or minister.[79] Such reasoning had a significant impact on many of the Romantic poets, who regarded ancient, authoritative texts, like the Bible, as fragmented memories of irretrievable events. Scripture, no more or less than poetry or prose, then, was one of many reconstructions of what has been lost from the past, a store of references for future writers. Shelley's atheism, for example, did not prevent him from plundering the Bible for literary references, understanding Jesus as a fellow poet and reformer. As he writes in 'Hymn to Intellectual Beauty' (1817), 'the name of God and ghosts and Heaven, | Remain the records' of 'vain endeavour', no more than 'poisonous names with which our youth is fed' (ll. 27–8, 53). Shelley felt guided by a numinous and benevolent power, but it was not Christian in nature:

> The awful shadow of some unseen Power
> Floats though unseen amongst us,—visiting
> This various world with as inconstant wing
> As summer winds that creep from flower to flower.—
> Like moonbeams that behind some piny mountain shower,
> It visits with inconstant glance
> Each human heart and countenance

> (ll. 1–7)

Where Shelley differed from many of his contemporaries was in refusing to connect religious feeling directly to God's truth, one that for thinkers like Coleridge and Martineau grounds the individual's reading of the Bible even where interpretation is fundamentally rational.

The ability to secure an affective experience from a reasoned interpretation of the Bible was the subject of Martineau's first book, *Rationale of Religious Enquiry* (1836), influenced as it was by the German pietist, Friedrich Schleiermacher, who, like Kant, regarded the reading process as a creative act. Schleiermacher, also a professor at Halle and preacher at the Charité in Berlin, held that any interpreter of the Bible necessarily moved between his or her personal and psychological understanding and a linguistic or grammatical sense of the way in which the text reads at different historical moments. His theory was a landmark in biblical hermeneutics. In *On Religion: Speeches to its Cultural Despisers* (1799), he asserted, like Martineau, that religion should be approached both cognitively and experientially: religion's essence is that 'mysterious moment' before 'intuition and feeling have separated' and not the 'mania of system'. Dogma and religious law are constrained to produce a formulaic faith either 'cold or overenthused', whereas turning to the self for religious reflection grants 'sharpened meaning and better-formed judgment'; 'God depends on the direction of the imagination'.[80] For Schleiermacher, this kind of imagination is autonomous in that the believer chooses to enter into an infinite or numinous relationship with God. For his student, the heretical philosopher David Strauss, the imagination instead unintentionally fabricates religious legends and stories to help decode Christ's impact on the world, the apparently

'supernatural' elements of the Gospels a mode of expression for communicating his divine mission. In *Leben Jesu* (1835), promoted by
Martineau and translated into English by George Eliot, Strauss read
Christ's divinity as a kind of fable or 'myth' that was none the less
significant for being so: his book was branded a contemporary example
of 'Iscariotism' as a result. Against a hermeneutics of faith, Strauss
claimed that careful, critical readings of the Gospels should undermine
the position of orthodox Christianity in order that its system might be
rediscovered as a legitimate and progressive philosophy.[81]

The second tradition Martineau folded into his new Unitarianism
also sought to recreate religion as a philosophy, influenced as it was by
Kant's anti-empiricist argument that the individual has access to certain
feelings and experiences that are found within, collectively referred to
as 'the transcendental'. Innate, a priori feelings about ideas like truth,
goodness, and being are privileged above experience of them, guided
by what Emerson called a 'universal soul'.[82] While set against that
rationalist Unitarianism influenced by Locke and Hume, transcendent-
alism shared some traits with Martineau's vision of the faith: utopian,
Idealist, and disdainful of creeds and doctrines. That the divine dwelled
within the human was an idea the transcendentalists partly attributed
to the Unitarian, William Ellery Channing, pastor of the Federal Street
Congregation Church, Boston, from 1803. His sermon on 'Unitarian
Christianity' (1819) was widely circulated, implicitly critiquing New
England Trinitarian Christianity and positing an argument for religious
tolerance that would become the foundation for the 1820 Berry Street
Conference and consequently the American Unitarian Association. A
pacifist, abolitionist, and feminist, Channing was acquainted with many
British Unitarians, and established a long correspondence with Bar-
bauld's niece, Lucy Aikin, after confessing that it was to her aunt that
he owed his religious sensibility and direction.[83]

Where Channing attributed the strength of his faith to Barbauld, the
poet Felicia Hemans claimed that Channing had shaped her particular
approach to belief. She wrote in 1833:

I strive ... to turn, with even deeper and more unswerving love, to the holy
'spirit-land', and guard it with more and more of watchful care, from the
intrusion of all that is heartless and worldly. I find Milton, and Wordsworth,
and Channing, my ministering angels in this resolve.[84]

Much speculation has transpired regarding Hemans's religious position,
which, like that of Wordsworth, wavers close to Unitarianism before

pulling back into a more revelatory and mysterious belief-system. She encountered several kinds of Christianity during her life: a politicized Anglicanism in Liverpool; low church nonconformism at Rhyllon, Wales, where she lived in the 1820s; and Roman Catholicism during her residence in Ireland from 1831.[85] Nanora Sweet even posits a sort of syncretic pagan-Christianity at the heart of poems like 'Superstition and Revelation' and 'Our Lady's Well', Shelleyan in nature but more respectful of establishment orthodoxy.[86] Her friendship with Reginald Heber is key here, an Anglican cleric who would go on to become Bishop of Calcutta, as well as a poet, hymnist, and writer for *The Quarterly Review*. His best known hymns, 'Holy, Holy, Holy', 'Brightest and best of the Sons of the Morning', and 'From Greenland's Icy Mountains', established Heber as an early member of the Oxford Movement, yet he sympathized with Hemans's interest in Druidism, Hellenism, and Zoroastrianism.

Yet one might argue that what really drives Hemans's religious poetry is that dissenting affection discussed in Chapter 1, an emotional faith dependent on the kind of affective experience poetry can produce. A profoundly popular poet at the very moment the Fox–Martineau rift was deepening, Hemans wrote several volumes of religious verse, including *Songs of the Affections* (1830), *Female Characters of Scripture* (1833), *Hymns on the Works of Nature* (1833), and *Scenes and Hymns of Life* (1834), all designed to move the reader and so create a public climate receptive to warm religious feeling. As the *Athenaeum* asserted, the 'fountain and principle of her inspirations' spring from an 'Honour deepened and sanctified by religion', and Hemans claimed in 'The Lyre's Lament' (1828) that only the 'Spirit of God' can enable the 'harp of poesy' to 'regain | That old victorious tone of prophet-years' (ll. 1–2).[87] Hemans sought to re-Christianize religion at a time when Unitarianism threatened to secularize it, describing her 'endeavour' to 'enlarge, in some degree, the sphere of Religious Poetry, by associating with its themes more of the emotions, the affections, and even the purer imaginative enjoyments of daily life' in the 'Preface' to her collection, *Scenes and Hymns*.[88] These poems promote 'daily life' as religion itself, a domesticated faith in which the believer innocently finds God everywhere: in a flower perceived on a walk ('Wood Walk and Hymn'), in a small boy's reverie as he looks over the Scriptures ('The Child Reading the Bible'), in the billow of the waves ('Night Hymn at Sea'), in the love of a mother for her sick child ('Mother's Litany'), and so on. Each of these poems evinces a numinousness which is not simply internal, however, residing outside of the self as an immaterial presence that nevertheless shows itself in the most magical of natural forms. 'Prayer of the Lonely Student', for example, written after Hemans heard William Hamilton's lecture on astronomy at Trinity College, Dublin, in 1832, paints the stars as enchanting little spheres of religious light guiding faith in darkness. In this sense Hemans recalls the eighteenth-century view of astronomy as one of many paths to God, a counter to her contemporaries' understanding of stars as exploding bodies of gaseous energy. Her narrator suggests that perhaps it is only individual doubt, rather than empirical evidence, that casts a shadow over true faith:

> Wherefore is this?—I see the stars returning.
> Fire after fire in Heaven's rich temple burning—
> Fast shine they forth—my spirit friends, my guides,
> Bright rulers of my being's inmost tides;
> They shine—but faintly, through a quivering haze—
> Oh! is the dimness *mine* which clouds those rays?
>
> (ll. 11–16)

On her death in 1835 Hemans fast became a 'Victorian literary monument', St Asaph's Cathedral dedicating a memorial tablet to her and countless poets and reviewers offering devoted eulogies.[89] Mary Carpenter, for example, a Unitarian social reformer and poet, declared that her lyrical voice would continue to Christianize and bond readers in a covenant of emotion: 'Still shalt thou tell | E'en from the tomb, how warm affections swell | In fairest hearts.'[90] Hemans predicted this to be the case in her last poem, 'Sabbath Sonnet' (1835), where she restated her desire to unite the nation in communal religious feeling: 'How many blessed groups this hour are bending, | Through England's primrose meadow-paths, their way | Towards spire and tower' she exclaims (ll. 1–3). This idealized picture of Victorian Sundays and sensitive congregants was one which, for Fox at least, was still to be fought for, however, primarily through a gender- and class-based politics which would grant all worshippers equality in society, as well as before God.

'EARLY FEMINISTS'

Those Unitarians that sided with Fox rather than Martineau mobilized into a significant political and literary movement in the nineteenth century, led by what Mill called the preacher's 'religion of *spirit*, not of *dogma*'.[91] Gleadle argues that the feminist movement itself emerged out of the split Fox initiated, Unitarianism being one of 'the most vital threads binding together the complex radical ideology of the early feminists'.[92] Moreover, the socialist reformer and feminist, Robert Owen, became closely linked with Unitarianism while based in Manchester during the 1790s, working with the Literary and Philosophical Society as well as Manchester College, the new home of the Warrington Academy. Owenism was also committed to the idea of a socialist apocalypse in which all forms of social hierarchy would be banished and women and men from all classes liberated from the psychological and economic chains of capitalism. For some, as Taylor points out, such radicalism was too broad, Engels complaining that Owen's reforming mentality sought 'to emancipate all humanity at once' rather than 'a particular class to begin with'.[93] Yet it was the visionary element of Owen's philosophy that so attracted Unitarians like Fox and the literary coterie he attracted at Craven Hill after his notorious departure from South Place Chapel. The group was certainly mixed, including Mill and Harriet Taylor, Godwin, Sarah Flower Adams, Edward Bulwer Lytton, Leigh Hunt, G. H. Lewes, Robert Browning, and Anna Jameson. A further member was the writer, Mary Leman Grimstone, whose 'Sketches of Domestic Life' (1835), published in the *Monthly Repository*, provided the reader with a series of tales in which women were presented negatively to highlight the consequences of resisting the progressive feminist project. More concerned with beauty than education, romance than reason, Grimstone's women were consequently treated as objects to be controlled, domesticated, and bullied by men. Along with her articles protesting the importance of women's education, Grimstone established a way of using the essay, story, and novel both to forward the feminist cause and put under the microscope its relationship with religious values.

Elizabeth Gaskell was sympathetic to such strategies, having received a Unitarian education in which she studied the Bible, classics, and several languages from an early age. With her husband, William Gaskell, she wrote a Grimstonian poem, 'Sketches of the Poor', for *Blackwood's Edinburgh Magazine* (1837), illuminating an interest in the relationship between religion and social politics developed in her novels. As a congregant at the Unitarian Cross Street Chapel, Manchester, where William was minister, Gaskell used the novel to promote an idea of faith that resided between Fox and Martineau, one that valued reason and progress while recognizing the importance of heartfelt devotion. Yet this seeming compromise between two positions created a tension in Gaskell's work, traceable also in her correspondence, especially those letters she wrote to her close friend, Eliza, Fox's daughter. To Eliza, Gaskell confided that while she found her Unitarian husband progressive in religion, politically he remained in control, managing all their finances and expecting her to assume a domestic and maternal role within the household. Gaskell's dilemma, however, was that she valued her position as a wife and mother as much as that of a novelist and biographer; she confessed to Eliza: 'How am I to reconcile all these warring members? I try to drown myself (my *first* self) by saying it's W[illia]m who is to decide on all these things, and his feeling if right ought to be my rule. And so it is—only that does not quite do.'[94] Such a dilemma is also faced by Margaret Hale in *North and South* (1855), torn as she is between the rational Dissent of her father and the more intuitive faith of the manufacturer, Mr Thornton, with whom she finally falls in love. Gaskell delicately portrays Reverend Hale's religious opinions by using Margaret to represent the assumed astonishment of conformist readers to the conversion of this 'perfect model of a parish priest'.[95] Unable to make 'a fresh declaration of conformity to the Liturgy', Hale sheepishly confesses his doubts regarding the Anglican Church to his daughter:

'Doubts, papa! Doubts as to religion?' asked Margaret, more shocked than ever. 'No! not doubts as to religion; not the slightest injury to that. … Oh! Margaret, how I love the holy Church from which I am to be shut out!' He could not go on for a moment or two. Margaret could not tell what to say; it seemed to her as terribly mysterious as if her father were about to turn Mahometan.[96]

Responding to her bewilderment, Mr Hale cites the testimony of a seventeenth-century Dissenter who crystallizes his own concerns by holding that when 'thou canst no longer continue in thy work without dishonour to God … thou must believe that God will turn thy very silence, suspension, deprivation, and laying aside, to His glory'.[97] Such responsibility to personal will reflects a Foxian Unitarianism, as does Thornton's faith which, free of creeds and anxiety, ultimately affects Margaret more profoundly: 'there was a deeper religion binding [Thornton] to God in his heart, in spite of his strong wilfulness, through all his mistakes, than Mr. Hale had ever dreamed.'[98] Gaskell's own views are betrayed most clearly when she elevates those who express a love of God beyond denominational boundaries, tenderly painting a scene between Margaret, her father, and the impoverished textile worker, Nicholas Higgins, in which doctrinal differences are rendered meaningless: 'Margaret the Churchwoman, her father the Dissenter, Higgins the Infidel, knelt down together. It did them no harm.'[99]

The specific clash between mystical and rational approaches to religion is highlighted further still in *Wives and Daughters* (1866), the two central families—the Gibsons and the Hamleys—both divided in their spiritual allegiances. Mr Gibson's scientific rationalism seems connected in the novel to his infantilization of the more artistic Molly, who is at first spellbound by the initially benevolent poet, Osbourne Hamley, a careful imitator of Hemans. As his adoring mother confesses to Molly:

'Ah! I think I must read you some of Osborne's poetry some day; under seal of secrecy, remember; but I really fancy they are almost as good as Mrs. Hemans'.' To be 'nearly as good as Mrs. Hemans' was saying as much to the young ladies of that day, as saying that poetry is nearly as good as Tennyson's would be in this. Molly looked up with eager interest.[100]

Gaskell maps Osbourne's emotional and physical downfall, however, through the shift that occurs in his poetic style from Hemans to romantic imitations of shallow love poetry. Worse still is that such poetry is addressed to his French Roman Catholic wife, Aimee, whom he has married secretly anticipating Squire Hamley's outrage at his decision:

As for the form of religion in which Mrs. Osborne Hamley had been brought up, it is enough to say that Catholic emancipation had begun to be talked about by some politicians, and that the sullen roar of the majority of Englishmen, at the bare idea of it, was surging in the distance with ominous threatenings; the very mention of such a measure before the squire was, as Osborne well knew, like shaking a red flag before a bull.[101]

Osbourne's sensible brother Roger eventually becomes a softer model of Mr Gibson, a natural scientist who personifies the latter's hope that so 'many new views' are 'opened in science'.[102] Yet Gaskell's narrative reminds us that these 'new views' were enabled by innovative social movements founded on dissenting religions like Unitarianism and Quakerism. The theological impact and effect of such new Dissent, however, is perhaps most apparent in the Oxford Movement's negative response to it as little more than a watering down of religion into a secular politics. The Oxford Movement, as we show in the next chapter, is a clear backlash against Dissent's liberalizing of Christianity, adamantly doctrinaire, uncompromisingly ritualistic, and committed to a patristic religion founded as much in the texts of the Church Fathers as the Bible. For all this, it was as critical of the Established Church as Dissent, seeking both to restore Anglicanism to its original Catholic position, and also to teach the Christian to feel, but always restrain such passionate belief behind a veneer of educated civil courtesy and decorum.

NOTES

1. R Price, *A Sermon, Delivered to a Congregation of Protestant Dissenters, at Hackney, On the 10th of February last*, 2nd edn. (London, 1779), 28.
2. H. Davies, *Worship and Theology in England: From Watts to Wesley to Martineau 1690–1900* (Cambridge: W. B. Erdmans, 1996), 48.
3. A. Fuller, *The Calvinistic and Socinian Systems Examined and Compared, as to their Moral Tendency* (London, 1802), 409, in J. Seed, 'Gentlemen Dissenters: The Social and Political Meanings of Rational Dissent in the 1770s and 1780s', *The Historical Journal*, 28: 2 (1985), 299–325 (314–15).
4. Seed, 'Gentlemen Dissenters', 301.
5. D. Hedley, *Coleridge, Philosophy and Religion:* Aids to Reflection *and the* Mirror of the Spirit (Cambridge: Cambridge University Press, 2000), 36.
6. J. Wesley, 'For the Mahometans', *A Collection of Hymns for the use of the people called Methodists*, ed. F. Hildebrant and O. A. Beckerlegge, in *The Works of John Wesley*, 26 vols. (Nashville, Tenn.: Abingdon Press; Oxford: Clarendon Press, 1983), vii. 608 (ll. 16–18).
7. C. Dickens, letter to W. C. Macready, 17 Aug. 1845, quoted in K. Gleadle, *The Early Feminists: Radical Unitarians and the Emergence of the Women's Rights Movement 1831–51* (Basingstoke: Macmillan, 1995), 11.
8. P. Gibbs, *Letter to the congregation … at Hackney* (1737), in C. G. Bolam et al., *The English Presbyterians: From Elizabethan Puritanism to Modern Unitarianism* (London: Allen and Unwin, 1968), 205.
9. Sabellians, named after the second-century nontrinitarian Sabellius, hold that there is one God comprised of three 'persons', Father, Word (or Son), and Holy Spirit, all part of one personality. Some Sabellians, known as Patripassians, suggested that Christ was God in human form, whereas others view him as a man in intimate union with God, see A. Gordon, *Heads of English Unitarian History* (1895) (Bath: Cedric Chivers, 1970), 23. The first appearance of the word 'Unitarian' was in the anonymously printed *Brief History of the Unitarians, called also Socinians* (1687), written by Stephen Nye at Firmin's request.
10. S. Andrews, *Unitarian Radicalism: Political Rhetoric 1770–1814* (Basingstoke: Palgrave, 2003), 2.

11. See, for example, the first of the Thirty-nine Articles, as it appears in the *Book of Common Prayer*: 'There is but one living and true God, everlasting, without body, parts, or passions; of infinite power, wisdom and goodness; the Maker and Preserver of all things both visible and invisible. And in the unity of this Godhead there be three Persons, of one substance, power and eternity: the Father, the Son, and the Holy Ghost.'

12. Bolam *et al.*, *English Presbyterians*, 228.

13. J. Priestley, *The doctrine of philosophic necessity illustrated an appendix to the Disquisitions relating to matter and spirit. To which is added an answer to the Letters on materialism and on Hartley's Theory of the mind* (1777) (London, 1782), 123.

14. J. Priestley, *Theological and Miscellaneous Works*, ed. John Towill Rutt, 25 vols. (London: George Smallfield, 1817–31), vi. 199 ff.

15. See C. Rowland (ed.), *The Cambridge Companion to Liberation Theology* (Cambridge: Cambridge University Press, 1999).

16. Hedley, *Coleridge, Philosophy and Religion*, 54.

17. S. T. Coleridge, *Table Talk, recorded by Henry Nelson Coleridge and John Taylor Coleridge*, ed. Carl Woodring (London: Routledge, 1990), i. 448.

18. N. Roe, *Wordsworth and Coleridge: The Radical Years* (Oxford: Clarendon Press, 1988), 113.

19. M. D. Paley, 'Apocalypse and Millennium in the Poetry of Coleridge', *The Wordsworth Circle*, 23: 1 (1992), 24–34 (24).

20. J. Mee, *Romanticism, Enthusiasm and Regulation: Poetics and the Policing of Culture in the Romantic Period* (Oxford: Oxford University Press, 2003), 131 ff.

21. S. T. Coleridge, *The Collected Letters of Samuel Taylor Coleridge*, ed. E. L. Griggs, 6 vols. (Oxford: Oxford University Press, 1956–71), i. 86.

22. S. Perry (ed.), *Coleridge's Notebooks: A Selection* (Oxford: Oxford University Press, 2002), 24.

23. S. T. Coleridge, 'Lecture 5: June 5, 1795', *Six Lectures on Revealed Religion its Corruptions and Political Views*, in Lewis Patton and Peter Mann (eds.), *Lectures 1795 On Politics and Religion*, in *The Collected Works of Samuel Taylor Coleridge*, ed. K. Coburn, 16 vols. (Princeton: Princeton University Press, 1971), i. 195–212 (199); Gnosticism was a second-century religious movement which stressed 'gnosis', the revealed knowledge of God which offered the believer redemption and which had been delivered through Christ. Gnostics distinguished between the Demiurge (the creator God) and an unknowable divine power, the latter emanating from the former and assuming a human form (for example, Jesus) or human appearance (divine ghosts).

24. Perry (ed.), *Coleridge's Notebooks*, 26.

25. Ibid. 114.

26. Ibid. 81.

27. Coleridge, *Collected Letters*, i. 578.

28. Coleridge, *Table Talk*, i. 564–5; Barbauld, 'To Mr C[olerid]ge' (1799), l. 34; and see L. Vargo's excellent discussion of their dialogue in 'The Case of Anna Laetitia Barbauld's "To Mr C(olerid)ge"', *Charles Lamb Bulletin*, 102 (1998), 55–63.

29. For a wider discussion of this aspect of Coleridge's faith, see Hedley, *Coleridge, Philosophy and Religion*.

30. S. T. Coleridge, *The Friend*, ed. B. E. Rooke, 2 vols. (London: Routledge, 1969), i. 40–1; and see Hedley, *Coleridge*, 161.

31. S. T. Coleridge, 'An Answer to "A Letter to Edward Long Fox, M.D."' (1795), in L. Patton and P. Mann (eds.), *Lectures 1795 On Politics and Religion*, in *Works*, i. 321–32 (326).

32. M. Mullett, 'Radical Sects and Dissenting Churches 1600–1750', in S. Gilley and W. J. Sheils (eds.), *A History of Religion in Britain: Practice and Belief from Pre-Roman Times to the Present* (Oxford: Blackwell, 1994), 188–210 (201).

33. A. Davies, *The Quakers in English Society 1655–1725* (Oxford: Clarendon Press, 2000), 118–20.

34. J. Punshon, *Portrait in Grey: A Short History of the Quakers* (London: QHS, 1986), 123.

35. A. Mott (ed.), *The Journal and Essays of John Woolman* (London: Macmillan, 1922), 180; on Woolman, see the biography of him written by the Victorian religious poet, Dora Greenwell, *John Woolman* (London: F. B. Kitto, 1871).

36. W. Penn, *More Fruits of Solitude* (1792), in Davies, *Quakers in English Society*, 51.

37. W. Wordsworth, 'Preface' to *Lyrical Ballads, with Pastoral and other Poems* (1802), in *William Wordsworth: Poems*, ed. J. O. Hayden, 2 vols. (London: Penguin, 1977), i. 867–96 (869).

38. C. Lamb, letter to S. T. Coleridge, Feb. 1797, in *The Complete Works of Charles Lamb* (New York: The Modern Library, 1935), 620–1.

39. C. Lamb, 'A Quaker's Meeting', *Essays of Elia* (1823), in *Works*, 44.

40. It is worth noting that pantheism is close in definition to panentheism: however, where the former finds God synonymous with nature, panentheism considers that the universe is part of God, rendering him greater than nature alone.

41. See I. McCalman, *Radical Underworld: Prophets, Revolutionaries, and Pornographers in London 1795–1840* (Oxford: Clarendon Press, 1988), 78–9.

42. See J. Toland, *Socinianism truly stated; an example of fair dealing in all theological controversys; to which is prefixt, indifference in disputes: recommended by a pantheist to an orthodox friend* (London, 1705).

43. Sermon preached to the Nottingham Unitarians, 1796; see J. Cottle, *Early Recollections chiefly relating to … Samuel Taylor Coleridge during his long residence in Bristol*, 2 vols. (London, 1837).

44. Roe, *Wordsworth and Coleridge*, 268–9.

45. Quoted in A. Black, *Political Thought in Europe 1250–1450* (Cambridge: Cambridge University Press, 1992), 32; compare Paul's comment that 'For our comely parts have no need: but God hath tempered the body together, having given more abundant honour to that part which lacked: That there should be no schism in the body; but that the members should have the same care one for another. And whether one member suffer, all the members suffer with it' (1 Corinthians 12: 24–6).

46. P. N. Miller, *Defining the Common Good: Empire, Religion and Philosophy in Eighteenth-Century Britain* (Cambridge: Cambridge University Press, 1994), 17.

47. On the problem of individual 'rights' in the 1790s, see S. Makdisi, *William Blake and the Impossible History of the 1790s* (Chicago: University of Chicago Press, 2003).

48. A. Smith, *The Theory of Moral Sentiments* (1759), ed. Knud Haakonssen (Cambridge: Cambridge University Press, 2002), 199.

49. Ibid. 277.

50. See R. Price, *Observations on the nature of civil liberty, the principles of government, and the justice and policy of the war with America. To which is added an appendix, containing a state of the national debt, an estimate of the money drawn from the public by the taxes, and an account of the national income and expenditure since the last war* (London: T. Cadell, 1776), which sold several thousand copies within days of publication.

51. J. Brewer, 'English Radicalism in the age of George III', in J. G. A. Pocock (ed.), *Three British Revolutions: 1641, 1688, 1776* (Princeton: Princeton University Press, 1980), 342–3.

52. E. Burke, *Reflections on the Revolution in France, and on the proceedings in certain societies in London relative to that event, in a letter intended to have been sent to a gentleman in Paris* (1790), in *Edmund Burke: On Taste, On the Sublime and Beautiful, Reflections on the French Revolution, A Letter to a Noble Lord*, ed. Charles W. Eliot (New York: P. F. Collier, 1909), 177, 213, 159; and see Mee, *Romanticism, Enthusiasm and Regulation*, 86.

53. Burke, *Reflections*, 159.

54. Ibid.

55. See Mee, *Romanticism, Enthusiasm and Regulation*, 90.

56. T. Paine, *The Age of Reason: Being an Investigation of True and of Fabulous Theology: Part I* (1794), in *Political Writings*, ed. B. Kuklick (Cambridge: Cambridge University Press, 2000), 268, 278.

57. W. Godwin, *Memoirs of the Author of* A Vindication of the Rights of Woman (1798) (London: Penguin, 1987), 215.

58. B. Taylor, *Mary Wollstonecraft and the Feminist Imagination* (Cambridge: Cambridge University Press, 2003), 98.
59. M. Wollstonecraft, *A Vindication of the Rights of Men* (1790) in *The Works of Mary Wollstonecraft*, ed. J. Todd and M. Butler, 7 vols. (London: Pickering and Chatto, 1989), v. 18.
60. Ibid. v. 34.
61. Taylor, *Mary Wollstonecraft*, 108.
62. Ibid. 113; and see T. M. Kelley, 'Women, Gender and Literary Criticism', in M. Brown and E. Behler (eds.), *The Cambridge History of Literary Criticism: Romanticism* (Cambridge: Cambridge University Press, 2000), 321–7.
63. G. Wakefield, *A General Reply to the Arguments Against the Enquiry into Public Worship* (London, 1792), 20.
64. Taylor, *Mary Wollstonecraft*, 187–8.
65. On the poem's prophetic element, see *The Monthly Repository of Theology and General Literature*, 74: 7 (1812–13), 108.
66. *The Quarterly Review*, 7 (1812).
67. Quoted in *Henry Crabb Robinson on Books and Their Writers*, ed. E. J. Morley, 3 vols. (London: J. M. Dent, 1938), i. 63–4.
68. J. P. Estlin, *Familiar Lectures on Moral Philosophy*, 2 vols. (London: Longman, Hurst, Rees, Orne, and Brown, 1818), pp. xi–xxxi (pp. xviii, xxix, xxx).
69. A. Janowitz, 'Amiable and radical sociability: Anna Barbauld's "free familiar conversation"', in G. Russell and C. Tuite (eds.), *Romantic Sociability: Social Networks and Literary Culture in Britain 1770–1840*, (Cambridge: Cambridge University Press, 2002), 62–81 (78).
70. Bolam *et al.*, *English Presbyterians*, 235.
71. Ibid. 239–40.
72. Gleadle, *Early Feminists*, 4.
73. W. J. Linton, *James Watson: A Memoir* (1880) (New York: A. M. Kelley, 1971), 58.
74. Gleadle, *Early Feminists*, 34.
75. Quoted in Gleadle, *Early Feminists*, 21.
76. J. Martineau, 'Preface', *Hymns for the Christian Church and Home* (London: John Greenwell, 1840), pp. v–xii (pp. v, vii).
77. See 'Notes on the Metre-Marks in this volume', in Martineau, *Hymns*, pp. xl–xlii.
78. See J. S. Semler, *D. J. S. Semlers Abfertigung der neuen Geister und alten Irtümer in der Lohmannischen Begeisterung ... nebst theologischen Untersicht von dem Ungrunde der gemeinen Meinung von leiblichen Besitzungen des Teufels und Bezauberungen der Christen* (Halle, 1760).

79. See I. Kant, 'An Answer to the question "What is Enlightenment?"'
    (1784), in *Kant's Political Writings*, ed. H. Reiss, trans. H. B. Nisbet
    (Cambridge: Cambridge University Press, 1996), 54–60.
80. F. Schleiermacher, *On Religion: Speeches to its Cultured Despisers* (1799),
    trans. and ed. R. Crouter (Cambridge: Cambridge University Press,
    2003), 28, 31, 32, 53.
81. See D. Jasper, *A Short Introduction to Hermeneutics* (London: Westminster
    John Knox Press, 2004), 92.
82. R. W. Emerson, 'Nature' (1836), in *Ralph Waldo Emerson: Selected Essays*,
    ed. Larzer Ziff (London: Penguin, 1982), 35–82 (49).
83. See A. L. Le Breton, *Memoir of Mrs Barbauld including Letters and Notices
    of her Family and Friends by her great niece* (London: George Bell and Sons,
    1874), 182; and G. A. Ellis, *A Memoir of Mrs Anna Laetitia Barbauld, with
    many of her letters* (Boston: James R. Osgood and Company, 1874), 309.
84. F. Hemans, letter to anon., 17 Mar. 1833, quoted in H. F. Chorley,
    *Memorials of Mrs Hemans: with illustrations of her literary character from
    her private correspondence,* 2 vols. (London: Saunders and Otley, 1836),
    ii. 289.
85. See E. Mason, *Women Poets of the Nineteenth Century*, Writers and their
    Work (Tavistock: Northcote House, 2006).
86. N. Sweet, 'Hemans, Heber, and Superstition and Revelation', in Elizabeth
    Fay (ed.), 'Romantic Passions', Romantic Circles Praxis Series, Apr. 1998,
    http://www.rc.umd.edu/praxis/
87. *The Works of Mrs Hemans with a Memoir by Her Sister*, ed. H. Hughes, 7
    vols. (Edinburgh: William Blackwood and Sons, 1839), i. 28–9.
88. F. Hemans, 'Preface', *Scenes and Hymns of Life, with Other Religious
    Poems* (Edinburgh: William Blackwood; London: T. Cadell, 1834),
    p. vii.
89. The phrase 'Victorian literary monument' is T. Lootens's in *Lost Saints:
    Silence, Gender and Victorian Literary Canonisation* (Charlottesville, Va.,
    and London: University Press of Virginia, 1996), 67; Hemans was buried
    in St Anne's Church, Dawson Street, Dublin, and a memorial tablet to
    her lies in St Asaph's Cathedral, in the Welsh Vale of Clwyd.
90. M. Carpenter, 'On the Death of Mrs Hemans', *Voices of the Spirit and
    Spirit Pictures* (1877), in *Felicia Hemans: Selected Poems, Prose and Letters*,
    ed. G. Kelly (Peterborough, Ontario: Broadview Press, 2002), 80.
91. J. S. Mill, letter to John Pringle Nicol, 17 Jan. 1834, quoted in Gleadle,
    Early Feminists, 46.
92. Gleadle, *Early Feminists*, 8.
93. F. Engels, *Socialism, Utopian and Scientific* (1892), quoted in Barbara
    Taylor, *Eve and the New Jerusalem: Socialism and Feminism in the
    Nineteenth Century* (London: Virago, 1983), p. xiv.

94. E. Gaskell, letter to E. Fox, Feb. 1850, in J. A. V. Chapple and A. Pollard (eds.), *The Letters of Mrs. Gaskell* (Manchester: Manchester University Press, 1966), 108; also see Gleadle, *Early Feminists*, 29–30.

95. E. Gaskell, *North and South* (1854–5), ed. Angus Easson (Oxford: Oxford University Press, 1998), 15.

96. Ibid. 36, 34.

97. Ibid. 35.

98. Ibid. 276.

99. Ibid. 233.

100. E. Gaskell, *Wives and Daughters* (1864–6), ed. Angus Easson (Oxford: Oxford University Press, 2000), 64.

101. Ibid. 271.

102. Ibid. 681.

3

The Oxford Movement: Wordsworth to Hopkins

THE Oxford Movement, also known as Tractarianism, is perhaps the most literary of those nineteenth-century theologies discussed in this book, and emerged in the 1830s from the academic environment of Oxford University.[1] The movement's central figures were poets as well as preachers, and its doctrinal system was grounded in poetics as much as theology. This chapter will discuss both its main leaders, John Keble, John Henry Newman, Edward Bouverie Pusey, and Isaac Williams; and also the poets who were attracted by its theological and aesthetic innovations, notably Wordsworth, Dora Greenwell, Adelaide Anne Procter, Christina Rossetti, and Newman. Grasping Tractarian beliefs can be a slippery task due to internal disagreements regarding key doctrines like reserve, the eucharist, confession, the Incarnation, and analogy. The *Tracts for the Times*, however, a series of treatises published by several of its members, grant us some idea of their collective philosophy. As we will show, the Oxford Movement was rooted in the pre-Reformation liturgical practice of the Church of England, revived primarily by the anti-Calvinist, William Laud, Archbishop of Canterbury from 1633. The ceremonial changes Laud promoted were taken to an extreme within the Movement's late nineteenth-century preference for an intensely medieval 'ritual', a word they used to denote both the words in the liturgy and the ornate ceremonial practised in the church space. This medieval bent of late Tractarianism merged, for some problematically, with a Pre-Raphaelite fascination with Britain's chivalric past and the Movement's theological ideas became both gradually secularized by writers such as Walter Pater, and also Romanized by poets like Gerard Manley Hopkins.

The Movement in turn was not above claiming non-Tractarians for their cause, centrally, Wordsworth, who, by the 1840s, had begun to undertake a series of Christian revisions of his poetry, ostensibly to establish his own beliefs for his critics. Not only had John Wilson charged Wordsworth with obscuring religious truth in his poetry, but the *Eclectic Review* had also accused him of pantheism and crypto-Romanism.[2] For many, he had become the laureate of High Church sensibility, branded so by the Tractarian Frederick William Faber, acting curate of Ambleside and tutor to Wordsworth's cousin, Dorothy Harrison. While Henry Crabb Robinson feared that the prudence of his friend had gone astray under 'this ultra-Puseyite High Churchman', Mary Wordsworth believed the unquestionably charismatic Faber to be 'a perfect *model* of what a deacon of our Church ought to be ... Poetry oozes out of him most gracefully'.[3] Indeed, Crabb Robinson's problem with Faber was that he promoted a sensitive, passionate, and near-sexualized piety packaged in repressed lyrics that addressed both God and his male lovers. 'Ultra-Puseyite' was a criticism that damned him further as a masochist, a phrase that referred to the gloomy Edward Pusey, associated, albeit in an inflated manner, with the more sinister aspects of Tractarianism, to which we return below.

Mary, however, regarded Faber as a graceful poet who directly spoke to the Movement's understanding of religion as a 'poetic' truth: lyrical and yet oblique. The relationship between poetry and Tractarianism was placed centre stage in 1839 during the bestowal of an honorary doctorate on Wordsworth at Oxford. The commemoration speech was delivered by John Keble, the 'founder' of the Oxford Movement and then Oxford Professor of Poetry. Before an immense and strikingly privileged crowd that had flocked to the occasion, Keble venerated Wordsworth as a Christian poet, an implicit Tractarian, and champion of the underprivileged and disenfranchised.[4] The preacher went further in suggesting that Wordsworth's Christian poetry formed the foundation of a radical liberal humanist education that demanded not only university places for the poor, but the direct exclusion of the rich.[5]

Such an education was considered best delivered through poetry, the ideal genre through which to filter High Church religious values. As Stephen Prickett asserts: 'Tractarian poetry was (after Shakespeare's) the most successful ever written in English', Keble's *The Christian Year*, for example, annually selling over 10,000 volumes for at least fifty years after its publication in 1827.[6] No wonder Wordsworth was delighted to be regarded as an associate of the Movement, meeting frequently with Keble and Newman during his Oxford visit and, prompted by Faber, revising a few of his early verses in accordance with Tractarian tenets. Faber in turn wrote extensive footnotes for Wordsworth's *Musings Near*

Aquapendente (1841); and Samuel Wilkinson, editor of the High Church periodical, the *Christian Miscellany*, compiled a selection of the laureate's poetry in a pamphlet called *Contributions of William Wordsworth to the Revival of Catholic Truths* (1842).[7] He even allowed Faber to dedicate his *Sights and Thoughts in Foreign Churches and Among Foreign Peoples* (1842) to him, and yet the very title of this publication hinted at a dangerous interest in Roman Catholicism. Wordsworth's association with Rome via Faber might have fuelled Wilson's attack, but as early as 1812 he had insisted that he would shed his own blood defending the Church of England from the assumed terror of Rome. His vehement opposition to the Catholic Emancipation Act of 1829 also sprang from a fear that this continental religion would enslave the State to the Pope, where Tractarianism promised to reinforce the idea of a nationally shared Christianity.[8] As George Herring points out, the Movement was profoundly revitalizing to nineteenth-century Christianity because of its imaginative and at times Romantic reinvention of a Catholic past in a modern form of Anglicanism.[9] While dogmatic and doctrinal innovation was a key part of this process, a focus on how aesthetic experience might merge with faith in one's relationship to God held a pivotal place for many leading Tractarians, Keble, Newman, and Isaac Williams each an example of a writer who fused his theology with poetic theory.

Keble is necessarily the starting-point of any discussion of the Oxford Movement and literature, forging many of the key poetic and theological theories that fuse so effectively in the work of poets like Hopkins, Faber, and Rossetti. His pastoral benevolence, doctrinal insight, and stunning intellectual grasp of classical tradition granted him an aura of faith and creativity appealing to the Victorians, who read and were affected by *The Christian Year* like no other generation.[10] Keble also recognized that Tractarianism was a dynamic rather than a static phenomenon, and retreated from Oxford into his Littlemore parish in order to enable its progression free from its father figure. As the Movement shifted outside of Oxford, primarily into London, its concerns became channelled into an intensified interest in church ceremony and ritual, rather than doctrinal intricacies, thus appealing to aesthetes such as Pater as well as devout believers in the old medieval Catholic Church. Viewing Tractarianism in this manner explodes common misconceptions of it as nothing more than a group of university clerics trapped within their collegiate squabbles over religious law. On the contrary, its aesthetic and theological preoccupations, eternally married for the Tractarians, were assimilated by public and private nineteenth-century poets alike, who grant us access not only to their own conceptions of God and faith but to the dogmatic imperatives of Tractarianism. Our chapter will turn first, to the emergence of the Oxford Movement as the saviour of the Church of England, under threat, the Tractarians argued, from both Dissent and secularization. We will outline the key beliefs that constitute their meticulously doctrinal religion and explore the Movement's insistence that such law was infused with intense and genuine religious feeling. Our section on the Movement's investment in poetry develops this by addressing Keble's claim that only poetry can provide an adequate outlet for the true believer's religious feelings. If poetry offered relief for overcharged emotion, then church ceremonial was thought to relight it and the chapter closes with a section on the Movement's interest in ritualism. We address both those who seemed to invest in this newly ritualistic Tractarianism, like Hopkins; and also those who implied that the Movement had finally collapsed into nothing more than gothic decadence and pagan sentimentality, like Pater and Wilde.

BEGINNINGS

Newman tells us that the Oxford Movement commenced with Keble's 'Assize' or legislative sermon on the subject of 'National Apostasy', delivered at the University Church in Oxford on 14 July 1833.[11] Here, Keble chiefly attacked the passing of the Catholic Emancipation Act in 1829, and also the government's abolition of ten high-status positions in the Church of Ireland: both undermined the independence and privilege of the Established Church in England and abroad. This was not a new phenomenon. After the repeal of the Test and Corporation Acts in 1828, and the institution of a Whig government in 1830, the top, most elite bishops in the country (the Hackney Phalanx, for example) suddenly lost their influence over the government.[12] Newman, however, did not want to associate the Movement with an outdated and fussy ecclesiastical administration, rendered largely redundant by Dissent. Instead, he positioned the Movement as a new and improved Anglicanism with Keble at its head, a legatee of the Caroline Divines who were a more traditional group of Anglican apologists.[13] The Divines were heavily quoted throughout ninety *Tracts for the Times*, written between 1833 and 1841 by various Oxford men including Keble, Newman, Pusey, and Williams, and which granted the Movement the title, Tractarianism.[14] Arthur West Haddan noted that the Tracts were designed to lift the Church 'into a more substantial orthodoxy' based on a medieval ceremonial introduced by Bishop Laud. Collectively, they defined the Movement as a new and brilliant dynamic able to lead the Church of England out of both the inertia associated with Georgian Anglicanism; and the enthusiasm thought to fuel Dissent.[15] Early historians of the Movement certainly endorse this self-presentation, S. L. Ollard, for example, claiming that: 'No story in the whole history of the English Church, since St Augustine landed in AD 597, is so splendid as the history of the Oxford Movement. It has every sort of interest. It is exciting, romantic, chivalrous, like the story of the Crusade.'[16] Ollard's commentary underlines a strong perception of Tractarianism as the quixotic and gallant saviour of the Church, returning an eroded and unspiritual institution back to the traditions undermined by the Thirty-nine Articles. As Keble declared in the Assize Sermon: 'There was once here a glorious Church, but it was betrayed into the hands of libertines for the real or affected love of a little temporary peace and good order.'[17]

For Keble, Britain was 'fast becoming hostile to the Church', and while he may have overstated his case for effect, these words were echoed by both politicians and poets of the period. William Gladstone claimed that the current state of the Church was as 'bad beyond all parallel known to me in experience or reading', a sentiment echoed by Christina Rossetti in her commentary on Revelation, *The Face of the Deep* (1892):

Already in England (not to glance at other countries) the signs of the times are ominous: Sunday is being diverted by some to business, by others to pleasure; Church congregations are often meagre, and so services are chilled. Our solemn feasts languish, and our fasts where are they?[18]

Like Gladstone, Rossetti called for an infusion of something new and vibrant into the Church, attracted, as the Pre-Raphaelites were for more secular reasons, to the sensuous atmosphere of medieval liturgy. This was accomplished by the Movement's reinstatement of six religious practices: the use of sacraments within the Church; episcopacy, or the governing of the Church by bishops; the notion of the Church as a 'body' in which all believers were linked to Christ; the observance of daily prayers and fasting; visible devotion, that is, church decoration; and the promotion of medieval ritual.[19] Indeed, Oxford had been at the centre of Laud's High Church reforms under Charles I, Cambridge turning the other way towards Evangelicalism. For the Evangelicals, Tractarianism was no less than the devil in disguise, and their *Tracts for the Times* secret Popish documents calculated to lead believers away from God and straight to the 'the land of darkness'.[20]

BELIEFS AND IDEAS

What was it that the Movement's detractors found so offensive? For many critics, the most worrying aspect of this belief-system was its emphasis on Apostolic Succession, that which Newman claimed was the cornerstone of Tractarianism. Apostolic Succession is the sacramental transference of the authority Jesus first gave to his apostles (the power to forgive sins, teach, celebrate the eucharist, and so on) to the present generation of bishops. This chain-like connection linked the Tractarians with the first Christians, granting them not only a cast-iron authority, but also a sort of guarantee that their sacraments were the real and authentic thing. As Geoffrey Rowell points out, Newman declared that Tractarianism was the modern inheritor of early Christianity, and wrote in his Tract, 'The Catholic Church' (1833):

We do not, as much as we ought, consider the force of that article of our Belief, 'The One Catholic and Apostolic Church.' This is a tenet so important as to have been in the Creed from the beginning. It is mentioned there as a *fact*, and a fact *to be believed*, and therefore practical [...] And this surely *is* a most important doctrine; for what can be better news to the bulk of mankind than to be told that Christ when He ascended, did not leave us orphans, but appointed representatives of Himself to the end of time?[21]

The consequences of such a statement were political, as well as theological, in that it implies that no government or sovereign has any authority to create bishops and priests, thus splintering Church from State. While Evangelicals believed that only God could grant individuals entrance into what they called the invisible church (the process of 'election'), many High Churchmen went to the other extreme in seeing a mutually supportive system in which Church and State were one. Moving away from both of these positions, Newman recreated Anglicanism in the image of early Christianity, namely, as an institution that valued the 'super' natural elements of religion, like miracles, as 'fact'. Newman is literally dogmatic here, insisting that Christians need laws both to follow and in which to invest emotionally: 'Many a man will live and die upon a dogma: no man will be a martyr for a conclusion,' Newman claimed, 'man is not a reasoning animal; he is a seeing, feeling, contemplating, acting animal.'[22]

Such an emphasis upon feeling over rationality connected Newman with Romanticism, a poetics many Tractarians wished to Christianize as their own. Although Antiquity was the model of liturgical and spiritual life for the Movement, the process by which this was achieved in sermons and hymns was grounded in an emotional ethos close to that conceived by Wordsworth and Coleridge. As Isaac Williams commented: 'Religious doctrines and articles of faith can only be received according to certain dispositions of the heart', rendering belief an aspect of the emotions. Newman concurred when he wrote to Joseph Blanco White in 1828, insisting that the intellect is 'but the attendant and servant of right and moral feeling in this our weak and dark state of being, defending it when attacked, accounting for it, and explaining it in a poor way to others'.[23] This fusion of feeling and thought is commonly regarded as the foundation of Romanticism and many of the Movement's most important doctrines cannot be understood unless viewed through such a lens. Grounded in a Patristic tradition also regarded as inspired and visionary, Tractarians embraced the Romantic notion of epiphany as a measure of divine guidance and revelation, and the idea of the sublime as a marker of retribution and judgement.[24] Wordsworth's privileging of the 'adult child' was also important to Newman, returning the believer to a state of innocence susceptible to God's messages and promoting a form of 'philosophical meditation' that focuses the believer on 'high principles and feelings'.[25]

Tractarianism, then, was for Newman 'not so much a movement as a "spirit afloat", it was within us, "rising up in hearts"' as a sort of overflow of immanence into transcendence, as Prickett puts it, and thus recalling an aspect of Wordsworth's poetic project.[26] The omnipresence of God in the universe, and therefore in the natural world, elided nature and religion for Wordsworth, offering the believer an otherworldly experience on earth, a kind of silent 'evidence' of God's being. In 'Tintern Abbey' (1798), as we discussed in Chapter 2, this evidence materializes as a 'motion' and 'spirit' that moves through the world like a spiritual energy sparked through the individual's own emotive response to the creation. Nature becomes central to such an experience because it is the stage on which we prepare ourselves to meet God, as Wordsworth attests to countless times throughout his autobiographical poem, *The Prelude*, begun in the 1790s.[27] For the narrator, feeling itself is predicated on encounters with God in the created world: 'I am content', he says, 'With my own modest pleasures, and have lived | With God and Nature communing' (II. 428–30). He is concerned only with the 'God who sees into the heart', a being whose vision is both of the lived world and of humankind, 'in Nature or in Man' (III. 143; IV. 352). The narrator declares:

> More frequently from the same source I drew
> A pleasure quiet and profound, a sense
> Of permanent and universal sway,
> And paramount belief; there, recognised
> A type, for finite natures, of the one
> Supreme Existence, the surpassing life
> Which—to the boundaries of space and time,
> Of melancholy space and doleful time,
> Superior and incapable of change,
> Nor touched by welterings of passion—is,
> And hath the name of, God.
>
> (VI. 129–39)

God then, must be felt through the human capacity for passion, a process which, for Wordsworth and the Tractarians, involved the release of the senses from their intellectual cage, or 'mind forged manacles', as Blake put it.[28] The development of a religious sense-perception is almost entirely necessary truly to see the world, an idea reiterated in Wordsworth's 'Composed Upon an Evening of Extraordinary Beauty and Splendour' (1815):

> No sound is uttered—but a deep
> And solemn harmony pervades
> The hollow vale from steep to steep,
> And penetrates the glades.
> For distant images draw nigh,
> Called forth by wondrous potency
> Of beamy radiance, that imbues
> Whate'er it strikes with gem-like hues.
> In vision exquisitely clear
>
> (ll. 21–9)

Here, the narrator is overcome by the luminosity of the physical world, dazzling and radiant because set alight by God. This coming together of the spiritual and the material mirrors the Incarnation—that Christ is fully divine, fully human, and fully both—a conviction which underlined the supernatural physiology of Christ's body. It was in part too the Incarnation that led to the Tractarian revival of the eucharist, a key belief for the Oxford Movement and which cemented popular readings of it as a mystical and Romantic religion.

Where Romanticism privileged the fusion of the physical, sensual, and emotive within the human, the eucharist exalted the same in Christ's body: an at once intangible and corporeal element that was everlasting and yet transferable into the believer. The Sunday celebration of the taking of bread and wine by Jesus at the Last Supper was derived from Early Church theology by the Movement, which viewed the eucharist as the first Christians had done, the bread and wine materially granting the believer the physical presence of Christ. This differed, as Herring suggests, from three other major interpretations of the eucharist: receptionism, where no connection between Christ and the bread and wine was admitted; virtualism, wherein the consecrated bread and wine alone held Christ's spirit and effect; and memorialism, which regarded the bread and wine as symbolic reminders of Christ. Rendering the eucharist supernatural, however, as the Tractarians did, deemed Christ at once incarnate and present within worship and signified his real presence within the individual believer. The best summary of this position was offered by the clergyman Robert Wilberforce (son of the abolitionist William Wilberforce discussed in Chapter 1) in his *The Doctrine of the Holy Eucharist* (1853), wherein the sacrificial element of the eucharist was stressed. For Wilberforce, Christ's body and blood were both real *and* symbolic, an idea prefigured by Pusey in *The Eucharist a Comfort to the Penitent* (1843) and recalled later by Keble in *On Eucharistical Adoration* (1859), all three figures outraging Evangelicals who believed Christ was received by faith alone.

As we have already suggested, Pusey in particular was vehemently disliked as a suspected agent of Rome, a conjecture intensified by his self-proclaimed interest in spiritual discipline and mortification. Pusey developed this side of his faith after reading the personal writings of the Tractarian, Richard Hurrell Froude, published after his early death by Keble and Newman under the title *Remains* (1838). The book appalled Evangelicals and High Churchmen alike with its stated admiration of medieval saints like Thomas à Becket and advancement of extreme varieties of penance directed by the Roman breviary. Pusey was quick to imitate the Romish stance Froude vacated on his death and self-mortifiers were thereafter labelled 'Puseyites', ridiculed by not only Evangelical critics, but also by the popular press. *Punch*, for example, figured the clergyman as an emaciated moth feverishly drawn to a Roman Catholic candle.[29] Trollope too derided him in *Barchester Towers* (1857), wherein the fragile Mr Slope 'trembles in agony at the iniquities of the Puseyites', with their satanic 'black silk waistcoats' and prayer-books, 'printed with red letters, and ornamented with a cross on the back'.[30] William Conybeare echoed this concern in *The Edinburgh Review* in 1853, warning readers to look out for those dressed in the Puseyite uniform, 'the clipped shirt-collar, the stiff and tie-less neckcloth, the M. B. coat (for "Mark of the Beast") and cassock waistcoat, the cropped hair and unwhiskered cheek'.[31]

Many Tractarian clergy did little to alleviate such criticism, enhancing their cassocks with cotta and biretta to give themselves the appearance of Catholic priests. Pusey regularly endured a hair shirt as well as self-imposed flagellation and fasting routines.[32] His fervid conviction that believers should purge themselves was also evident in his promotion of auricular confession which he practised as early as 1838, forever concerned to enable penitents to become cleansed and regenerated by disclosing their sins.[33] The sacrament of confession had been officially terminated at the establishment of the Anglican Church under Elizabeth I, and Pusey claimed that this outlawing of confession had all but caused the Church of England's current state of spiritual despondency. While commentators such as Bishop Henry Phillpotts suggested that confession should be 'merely recommended to those sinners whose troubled conscience admits not of being quieted by self-examination', Pusey was convinced of its universal imperative.[34] In *The Entire Absolution of the Penitent* (1846), for instance, Pusey maintained that the systematic institution of confession in the Church of England was firmly endorsed by both the Reformers and Caroline Divines.[35] Despite this, confession's closest association was Rome, and its practice was viewed as a kind of secret privilege for Tractarians to indulge in Catholic practices. E. A. Knox described it as 'a rite stigmatized as papistical' and so 'all the more alluring' for being so, the 'thrill of mystery and of persecution for the faith' adding 'to the joy of unburdening the conscience'.[36] Worse still was Walter Walsh's *Secret History of the Oxford Movement* (1898), which inventively painted Tractarianism as a malevolent, monstrous, and deeply flawed cult. Walsh aggressively reviled confession by reciting the story of Miss Cusack ('the Nun of Kenmare'), who, after receiving confession from Pusey, wrote: 'I believe that *the secrecy, and concealment, and devices which had to be used to get an audience with the Doctor, for the purpose of Confessing* had a little, if it had not a good deal, to do with his success.'[37] Despite Pusey's notoriety as an effeminate milksop, he was still 'a *man*', as one Tractarian declared: his critics were intent on hanging him, whether as a hetero-predatory bully or feminized coward.[38]

What Pusey's case suggests is that the re-establishment of confession provoked as much gender trouble as it did anti-Catholic anxiety, an idea voiced by Charles James Blomfield, Bishop of London, in his declaration that confession was 'the source of unspeakable abominations'.[39] These 'abominations' were thought to have the potential to damage two dominant nineteenth-century institutions: first, the Church of England, threatened by the spread of Catholic ideology; and secondly, the Victorian family unit, inexcusably invaded by the questioning priest.[40] Confessing one's sins to God through the medium of a human agent in the space of a confessional box threatened Victorian sensibility because it forced one to broadcast sin outside of the family space to a priest portrayed as perversely eager to listen. The seeping of Rome into Britain's domestic corners was considered more threatening still to women, the narrator of Charles Maurice Davies's Tractarian love story, *Philip Paternoster* (1858), claiming: 'It would be a fatal day for England if ever England's wives and daughters were led to deem the confessional a more sacred place than the home.'[41] The notion of male confessors cajoling female penitents to betray their sins and sexual secrets induced far-fetched anti-Catholic propaganda, verifying the fear that priests might usurp the control husbands and fathers held over the female members of their household. This paranoia was further excited by anecdotes such as that narrated by Sir William Harcourt in a letter to *The Times*, in which he quoted the Catholic confessor of the King of Spain bragging to his penitent: 'I hold your God in my hand, and I have your wife at my feet.'[42] As Miss Cusack attests in recounting her liaisons with Pusey, 'few *men* went to Confession' with the 'Doctor', and Walsh's chapter, 'Ritualistic Sisterhoods', implicates Pusey as an insidious meddler intent on diffusing Catholicism through Britain by way of kidnapping women for his conventual establishments.[43]

Such scandal connected Tractarianism to the gothic, grotesque, and supernatural, and Newman even confessed that one of his early experiences of Roman Catholicism was mediated through the novels of Ann Radcliffe.[44] As Emma Clery writes in her discussion of *The Italian or the Confessional of the Black Penitents* (1797), 'the confessional privileged in Radcliffe's title was intrinsically sinister', alerting her readership that they would have to be 'prepared to encounter the dark influence of the

Catholic priesthood'.[45] The sensational representation of Pusey by the popular press indeed figured him as an English model of Radcliffe's evil priest, Father Schedoni, a macabre advocate of confession and sister-hoods. Yet the establishment of sisterhoods in the Church of England had a decidedly radical impact on some women's lives, directly, for example, on Maria Rossetti, Christina's sister, who joined All Saints sisterhood in 1873. All Saints was established in 1845 and was the Oxford Movement's first Anglican sisterhood, located round the corner from the Rossetti household in Park Village West. Park Village was also close to Christ Church, Albany Street, built as part of Blomfield's scheme to construct fifty new Tractarian churches in London, and funded in part by Pusey.[46] Consecrated in 1837, Christ Church appeared, according to its second incumbent, Henry William Burrows, amidst 'a time of fervour and revival of church principles, and it is not too much to say that Christ Church became the leading church in the movement'.[47] The important status Christ Church occupied is testified to by its not-able congregation, which counted in its numbers the Rossetti women, Christina, Maria, and their mother, Sara Coleridge (daughter of Samuel Taylor), and Margaret Oliphant; as well as distinguished preachers, including Pusey, Manning, Burrows, and William Dodsworth. Pusey is even recorded as being particularly impressed with the 'exceptional zeal of some members of the congregation'.[48]

Pusey took advantage of this zealous feeling by giving it an outlet in confession. Just as Romanticism had enabled the embrace of supernatural phenomenon like the eucharist, so had its new emphasis on the depth of the self paved the way for the reinstitution of the 'talking cure'. Yet this confessing self tended to plunge believers into a discourse that stressed their human frailty and sin before God, reproducing them as profoundly damaged souls. As Pusey himself claimed in his famous confession before Keble:

I am scarred all over and seamed with sin, so that I am a monster to myself; I loathe myself; I can feel of myself only like one covered with leprosy from head to foot; guarded as I have been, there is no one with whom I do not compare myself, and find myself worse than they.[49]

There is a noticeable similarity in tone between Pusey's sorrowful dis-closure and the contents of a letter written by Christina Rossetti to a dying Dante Gabriel, concerned with the past actions of his life:

I want to assure you that, however harassed by memory or anxiety you may be, I have (more or less) heretofore gone through the same ordeal. I have borne myself till I became unbearable to myself, and then I have found help in confession and absolution and spiritual counsel, and relief inexpressible.[50]

Rossetti's continual mission to achieve heavenly comfort certainly left her vulnerable as both a poet and believer. While Wordsworth found solace in nature, Rossetti considered the material world, natural and technological alike, a barrier to the religious fulfilment granted only in death. This perhaps dark-seeming proclivity might be read as pathological; then again, it is also rooted in a firm Christian faith that arguably stabilizes much of Rossetti's work, constituted as it is of almost entirely scriptural quotation and allusion. She is no mere plagiarist of the Bible, however, the typological basis of her writing understanding Old Testament figures and events as forerunners (types) of New Testament figures and events (anti-types); and eloquently mapping out the individual spiritual life with reference to biblical motifs.[51] Her sonnet 'Seven vials hold thy wrath' (1893) exemplifies this technique:

> Seven vials hold thy wrath: but what can hold
> Thy mercy save Thine own Infinitude
> Boundlessly overflowing with all good,
> All loving kindness, all delights untold?
> Thy love, of each created love the mould;
> Thyself, of all the empty plenitude;
> Heard of at Ephrata, found in the Wood,
> For ever One, the Same, and Manifold.
> Lord, give us grace to tremble with that dove
> Which Ark-bound winged its solitary way
> And overpast the Deluge in a day,
> Whom Noah's hand pulled in and comforted:
> For we who much more hang upon Thy Love
> Behold its shadow in the deed he did.

Rossetti shifts here between New and Old Testament references as Catherine Musello Cantalupo argues in her useful reading of the poem's types. She notes how Rossetti begins with Revelation ('seven vials'), shifts to Paul's notion of God as overflowing love ('of all the empty plenitude'), and moves back to David as a model poet in his establishment of God's presence in an ark. The reader is then directed to Noah as a 'type' of God's loving being amidst the disorder—the 'deluge'—of divine anger.

Biblical events, like material things or natural objects, are simply types of God, then, what Newman called 'the Sacramental system', or 'real things unseen'.[52] Certainly this recalls St Paul's declaration that 'the invisible things' of God 'are clearly seen, being understood by the things that are made, *even* his eternal power and Godhead' (Romans 1: 20). Yet for Rossetti, these tangible things are to be discarded as quickly as possible in order to embrace fully the spiritual life. 'A Better Resurrection' (1857), for example, fiercely endeavours to annihilate all mortal attachments and distractions in order to reach Christ:

> I have no wit, no words, no tears;
> My heart within me like a stone
> Is numbed too much for hopes or fears;
> Look right, look left, I dwell alone;
> I lift my eyes, but dimmed with grief
> No everlasting hills I see;
> My life is in the falling leaf:
> O Jesus, quicken me.

The better Resurrection searched for here looks past the conventional rebirth associated with spring and looks instead to the autumn's fading leaves as that which will herald in winter, representative of death and so heaven.[53] As Jerome McGann notes, Rossetti wants something that goes beyond the human into paradise, 'a life in falling leaves', that removes her from the material frame of the poem as it roots her in a kind of spiritual energy. Where Wordsworth locates God in this 'motion' as an external observer, Rossetti immerses herself within it to privilege only faith. A middle way between these two positions is arguably struck upon by Hopkins's inscape and instress to which we return shortly, but before doing so it is worth contemplating why so many Tractarian writers chose poetry as a way to explore belief and doctrine alike.

POETRY

Rossetti's choice of poetry to convey her Christian belief is not accidental in light of her Tractarian associations. For the Oxford Movement, poetry was synonymous with religious truth and offered believers the best, and most appropriate, way of communicating and understanding their faith. Romantic poetic theory had already indicated the abstract and supernatural, even sacramental, aspect of the genre, and Keble in particular extended this work by Christianizing the spontaneous overflow of feeling as a spiritual process. Poetic feeling did not simply explode for Keble, however, being rather the product of a build up of pressure or tension albeit contained within a religious frame. Writing to J. T. Coleridge in 1832, he stated:

My notion is to consider poetry as a vent for overcharged feelings, or a full imagination, and so account for the various classes into which poets naturally fall, by reference to the various objects which are apt to fill and overpower the mind, so as to require a sort of relief.[54]

These various classes were outlined in his *Lectures on Poetry* (1832–41) as 'primary' poets 'who, spontaneously moved by impulse, resort to composition for relief and solace of a burdened or over-wrought mind'; and 'secondary' poets, who 'imitate the ideas, the expression, and the measures of the former'.[55] Into the first group fall classical poets like Virgil, Horace, and Dante, while the second comprises of the more modern Byron and Shelley, all linked together by a poetic that carries with it a healing power. Poetry does not simply offer relief, but is actually defined *as* relief, soothing the harried individual by producing tender feelings within the heart and guiding and composing the mind to worship and prayer.[56] The Prayer Book and Gospels are also essentially poetic in this sense, full of balmy truth and, like poets, prophets, and apostles, suggestive of the potentially sacramental nature of human experience. If primary poets settle the reader, secondary poets create the space in which to feel such composure, writing of ecclesiastical tradition and the Church itself. The latter is a metaphor for poetry in Keble's work, offering a location in which the believer might forge emotion and then articulate it both within prayer and also by participating in the liturgy. Isaac Williams, Felicia Hemans, and Wordsworth were among many who fashioned poetical sequences on the Church following George Herbert's *The Temple* (1633), reshaping the scaffold of poetry as essentially religious.[57]

While the *Lectures* remained untranslated until 1912, Keble had already spelled out his theory in English within his widely disseminated 1838 review of J. G. Lockhart's *Life of Sir Walter Scott*.[58] Here, he argued that: 'Poetry is the indirect expression in words, most appropriately in metrical words, of some overpowering emotion, or ruling taste, or feeling, the direct indulgence whereof is somehow repressed.'[59] One word we might focus on here is 'indirect', the final spillage of emotion in poetry veiled to indicate the sacred status 'poetic,' and consequently 'religious', truth occupies. The idea of encoding religious knowledge in poetry was called 'reserve' by the Tractarians, a central aspect of their doctrine and indicating that God's scriptural laws should remain hidden to all but the faithful. Devotional writing and biblical exegesis alike were thus meant to present religious truth using metaphor, figure, and allegory in a manner only the initiated believer could understand. Reserve also prevented an increasingly literate secular audience from accessing scriptural law, while underlining the fact that some of God's tenets were simply beyond human comprehension and would only be revealed to the faithful in heaven. Poetry ideally conveyed messages in a reserved manner as an oblique and subtle genre able to pave a gentle route to God opposed to the forthright and sometimes aggressive directness of Evangelical writing, condemned by Tractarians for crudely spilling religious mysteries. Advocating a submissive, restrained, and therefore feminized approach to religion, reserve's male adherents were even labelled effeminate and delicate by their critics.[60] Such reproach was fuelled by the tendency of many Tractarian men to address each other as 'darling'; Newman and his friend Ambrose St John regularly held hands while walking together in Oxford and their tearful farewell on the former's departure to Littlemore became a mythical scene of heartfelt devotion within the Movement.[61]

This feminized aesthetic also justified poetical careers for women, able to adopt reticently the role of theological observer, but at the same time freed from accusations of vainly flaunting religious learning suitable only for men. Employing reserve also enabled women to stress their contemplative nature as believers and poets and thus claim a clerical role almost equivalent to that of a priest or theologian. Dora Greenwell, for instance, proved herself to be a far greater theological thinker than her Tractarian brother, Alan, who held a living at Golbourne Rectory in Lancashire. Indeed, her religious essays and poetry disclose a concern, not that theology is inappropriate for a woman to study, but that the individual cannot be both poet and believer at the same time. In 'The Spirit of Poetry' (1875) Greenwell writes that 'poetry would seem the natural ally of Christianity', both giving 'wings to the fettered soul', while speaking 'to man of something that is far beyond'.[62] She worried, however, that poetry might intoxicate the soul, urging 'onward the passions which nature herself would seek to hold in leash' and finding 'food for a "darker ecstasy" '.[63] Christianity, she suggested in line with Rossetti, depresses nature, Christ 'at war' with it in his role as 'the pruner, the purifier', purging the 'vine' of its opiate fruit where poetry rather dangerously encourages the untamed budding of 'many clustered' 'wild grapes'.[64] Moreover, religion 'lives to order and to law; its object is to repress nature, to suppress passion', while poetry 'can only exist in an atmosphere of emotion, which, if it fails to find, it will go out of its way to create'.[65]

Greenwell, then, was extremely anxious regarding the prospect of being a poet herself, alarmed that poetry might amount to little more than 'a morbid mental condition', albeit 'a *brilliant disease*'.[66] Like Keble, she recognized that poetry itself is defined through the writer's emotions seeking relief through veiled articulation as her simply titled 'Reserve' (1861) conveys:

> Now would I learn thee like some noble task
> That payeth well for labour; I would find
> Thy soul's true Dominant, and thus unwind
> Its deeper, rarer harmonies, that ask
> Interpreting; for like a gracious mask
> Is thy calm, quiet bearing; far behind
> Thy spirit sits and smiles in sunshine kind,
> And fain within that fulness mine would bask.
> Set if thou wilt this bar betwixt thy tide
> Of feeling and the world that might misknow
> Its strength; use ever with the crowd this pride,
> 'Thus fare, and yet no farther shall ye go;'
> But not *with me*, dear friend, whose heart stands wide
> To drink in all thy Being's overflow.

Addressing God, the narrator longs to understand and decode the fathomless mysteries of the divine—'Its deeper, rarer harmonies'—yet acknowledges that what she seeks lies behind a veil of benevolence: a 'gracious mask'. Like Rossetti's narrators, Greenwell's speaker believes there is a truth to be reached, a 'fulness' or 'tide | Of feeling' in which to bathe and 'drink in' when fully prepared. Making ready for such an experience, however, is blocked not only because reserve prohibits its pronunciation—you cannot have what you cannot ask for—but also, due to the essential nature of the human, unfinished until realized in heaven. 'The crowd' may not comprehend this as such, denied access at the pearly gates and, for the Tractarians, confined to purgatory until they have made ready, a process enabled further by the reintroduction of prayers for the dead.[67] Yet once fully prepared, like the narrator here, the believer becomes part of God's vast divine body, a kind of Wordsworthian 'heart' which joins the faithful in a shared religious feeling.

The impossibility of articulating one's desire or acceptance of God was addressed in Christian poetry by the fact that, as a genre, it is defined by its endless repetition and recollection of phrases from Scripture and liturgy. As Dolores Rosenblum suggests, lyric prayers and devotional utterances 'are inexhaustible in that the suppliant cannot say the same thing often enough, nor can she say too much': reserve checks dangerous expression while the recital of prayer allows the believer's faithful feelings to run over.[68] Adelaide Anne Procter, the best-selling favourite of Queen Victoria, also explored restrained narration, sometimes even obscuring the religious messages behind her lyrics. 'Murmurs' (1856), for example, characterizes the prospect of annunciation as a whispered undertone unable to become fully vocalized, the speaker, as one who fears remaining unheard, begging the reader to 'Listen, and I will tell thee | The song Creation sings' (ll. 13–14). Yet clarity becomes not only unobtainable but also a veritable torment:

> Why wilt thou make bright music
> Give forth a sound of pain?
> Why wilt thou weave fair flowers
> Into a weary chain?
>
> (ll. 1–4)

Softly intimating the poem's religious nature by calling it a 'holy song', the narrator cloaks her meanings in shadowy metaphors: they echo, ripple, and glitter in an attempt to be amplified through the 'little voice' of the believer, one that turns down its own volume in accordance with reserve. 'Unexpressed' (1858) too bares the silent soul the believer owns until seated in heaven, the poem a catalogue of varying attempts, all failed, to express what 'Dwells within the soul of every Artist' (l. 1). Like Blake, Procter uses the word 'Artist' to embrace all who profess faith, the very process of doing so an aesthetic creation.[69] The innate beauty of such a creation, however, always remains veiled 'to mortal eyes', and only God has access to the full resonance of what the artist endeavours to fix in form:

> No real Poet ever wove in numbers
> All his dreams; but the diviner part,
> Hidden from all the world, spake to him only
> In the voiceless silence of his heart.
>
> (ll. 21–4)

The poet's most divine harmonies are thus too bright for the mortal world; they are whispered inside the confines of the human heart that contains and restricts powerful feeling until it is ready to burst forth in more sacred realms. The poet's 'numbers'—the stanzaic units that contain and regulate the feeling put forth—cannot entirely effuse his or her dreams or feelings; but their diviner part—their poetical nature—is so obviously prayer-like that God hears the poet's faith even when he or she is silent. As Keble wrote in his *Lectures*, 'the variety of the poet's numbers are of great import in guiding us to his personal feeling and disposition: just as a man's walk is an index to the movements of his mind.'[70]

The model of Keble's poetic theory for many nineteenth-century readers was Newman's celebrated 'Lead Kindly Light' (1833), a poem which portrays religious life as a journey moving from darkness to light:

> Lead, kindly Light, amid the encircling gloom,
> Lead thou me on;
> The night is dark, and I am far from home,
> Lead thou me on.
> Keep thou my feet; I do not ask to see
> The distant scene; one step enough for me
>
> (ll. 1–6)

This is no crude 'enlightenment' poem of progress, betraying instead the challenge of a faith that requires both steady trust and an absolute dependence on a God who cannot be known. Such conviction in what is essentially recondite, however, may have been Newman's downfall, as it was Procter's: caught for so long in religious obscurity both turned to Roman Catholicism as the headstrong 'true' Church, offering as it did concrete answers to all mysteries. In contrast, Tractarianism operated in an almost Keatsian realm of uncertainty, offering what Newman called a *via media* to believers that even he ultimately found deficient. As he declares in the *Apologia Pro Vita Sua* (1864), from the time of his conversion, he was

in perfect peace and contentment. I never have had one doubt. I was not conscious, on my conversion, of any inward difference of thought or of temper from what I had before. I was not conscious of firmer faith in the fundamental truths of revelation, or of more self-command; I had not more fervour; but it was like coming into port after a rough sea; and my happiness on that score remains to this day without interruption.[71]

For Newman, conversion solidified his religious beliefs in the eucharistic transubstantiation, the immaculate conception, and God's infallibility, as well as underlining the need for physical discipline (the body was to be 'extricated, purified, and restored') and the necessity of open faith. Tractarianism suddenly seemed like a club in which the rules were kept secret, marked by 'half-measures' and 'economical reserve'. By contrast, Newman thought, Roman Catholicism had produced a more 'definite circle of thought', freeing him from uncertainty and restraint. He felt liberated but also guilty, leaving behind a religion in which his role had been formative; as he wrote in 'The Dream of Gerontius' (1865), later set to music by Elgar:

> (Jesu, have mercy! Mary, pray for me!)
> 'Tis this new feeling, never felt before,
> (Be with me, Lord, in my extremity!)
> That I am going, that I am no more.
> 'Tis this strange innermost abandonment
>
> (ll. 5–9)

The power of such verse was troubling to say the least for Tractarianism, damaged by the conversion not only of Newman, but also of Henry Manning and Faber. Worse still had been the ensuing 'Gorham Judgement' (1850), an event which led over fifty Tractarians straight to the Roman Catholic Church. The Gorham Judgement was named after the High Church Bishop of Exeter, Henry Phillpotts, who prosecuted an Evangelical clergyman, G. C. Gorham, for refusing to teach the doctrine of baptismal regeneration. This doctrine ruled that baptism marked the believer's point of entry into the Church, and was supported by many Tractarians who were shocked when the Judicial Committee of the Privy Council overturned Phillpotts's accusation. Heresy upheld by a secular court drove numerous Tractarians over to Rome, devastating staunch Anglicans like Keble and Williams who saw this passage as a profound betrayal of the Church of England and God. On the other hand, the overall number of Tractarian incumbents working in Britain actually increased in the aftermath of the events of 1845 and 1850, and many in the faith began to be more concerned about the practice of religious ceremony than doctrinal wrangling.[72] While theological debate had dominated the movement from Keble's Assize Sermon to the Gorham Judgement, the 1860s saw a renewed focus on liturgy and ritual. The particulars of dogma could be discussed and outlined in pulpit and print, but for a still largely illiterate society, the symbolic and visual representation of these ideas—'ritualism'—was fundamental.

RITUALISM

While the debate around ritualist ceremony came to dominate religious concerns by the 1860s, its presence was also increasingly felt in newly built Tractarian churches, ornamental and colourfully decorated. A florid medieval ritual ceremony was present in Rossetti's Christ Church as early as the 1830s, but became slowly commonplace within most Tractarian churches from the mid-nineteenth century, both in and outside of Oxford. Benjamin Jowett, for example, expressed his surprise at the extent of ritualism in London in a letter to a friend of 1865, declaring:

If you walked abroad you would be greatly astonished at the change which has come over the churches of London; there is a sort of aesthetico-Catholic revival going on.[73]

Most Tractarians understood ritualism as the practice of a baroque, Laudian ceremonial, but it also registered a gothic liturgy evinced by the use of altar lights, candles and veils, the kneeling of the congregation at the consecration, prayers for the dead, the burning of incense, the mixing of water and wine in the chalice, and the elevation of the eucharist. Some clergy would wear a chasuble to deliver the eucharist, the old traditional vestment worn by Roman aristocracy in late antiquity and deriving from the paenula, or outdoor cloak.[74] Other markers of ritualism included a sung service, the regal procession of the clergy and choir from the vestry, the assumption of the eastward position when celebrating the eucharist, and the adoption of seasonal coloured coverings for an altar often adorned by a back-lit cross.[75] A few priests even attempted to introduce the Three Hours devotion on Good Fridays, a clear sign of Roman Catholic ritual: when Alexander Mackonochie, rector of St Albans, Holborn, decided to implement the practice, he was indicted by the Church Association for 'Popery'.

The Association's fears regarding the Popish implications of ritual were echoed by many critics of Tractarianism in the period, the seventh Earl of Shaftesbury a striking example. After attending St Albans in 1866, he recorded in his diary: 'Such a scene of theatrical gymnastics, of singing, screaming, genuflections, such a series of strange movements of the priests, their backs almost always to the people, as I never saw before even in a Romish Temple.' The church, Shaftesbury complained, was littered with iconic pictures and crosses, the atmosphere choked with 'Clouds upon clouds of incense, the censer frequently refreshed by the High Priest, who kissed the spoon, as he dug out the sacred powder, and swung it about at the end of a silver chain'. What he called the 'melodrama' of ritual was heightened further by the peals of 'soft music' and intimidating presence of a 'tall iron grille' hiding the high altar, a chancel or 'rood' screen designed to reserve and make secret the most sacred part of the church interior.[76] Yet such ceremony also had its vehement defenders, Rossetti's confessor, Richard Frederick Littledale, arguing that ritual had never been legally outlawed and was, in fact, a direct fulfilment of the proclamations of Anglican Divines. Burrows also defended the use of ritualism in his book *The Half-Century of Christ Church* (1887), even though he is unable to refrain from mentioning that 'a section of the religious world' was 'alarmed by the first tokens of the approach which had not then taken the name of Ritualism, but was voted downright Romanism'.[77] Careful to distinguish Christ Church as Tractarian after the desertion of its previous intendent, William Dodsworth, to Rome in 1851, Burrows nevertheless fixates on the amount of money spent on decorating the church with ornate artwork, a decorated font, jewelled communion plate, oak pews, marble floors, and stained glass windows.[78]

Meditating and praying while surrounded by such decor seems to have had an impact on Rossetti, whose poetry evokes Sara Coleridge's description of the religious atmosphere at Christ Church as one that produced 'a flavour of combined learning and piety, and of literary and artistic refinement'.[79] Many of Rossetti's poems invite the reader into the spiritual space of the poem, what Pater would call a 'cloistral refuge'.[80] 'Advent Sunday', for example, invokes the 'lighted lamps and garlands' that illuminated the church; where 'Light in all eyes' describes the 'mitred priests' who lead the service. 'Christmas Carols' refers to the prayer bells, while 'Lift up thine eyes to seek the invisible' describes the 'golden harps' and joyous saints. Incense near smothers the worshippers in 'Thy lovely saints do bring Thee love'; and precious stones—rubies, diamonds, pearls—are set into the structure of poems like 'His Banner over me was Love', 'Whence death has vanished like a shifting sand', and 'Beautiful for situation'. Such imagery creates a kind of luminous atmosphere within these devotional poems, enhanced further by persistent references to seraphs and cherubs who float gently around a grandly crowned and robed Christ.

Ritualist poetry like Rossetti's, then, offered an incandescent portal into God's mysteries, just as the sombre and shadowed ritualist church space was illuminated by endless candles catching the light from priests' vestments, crystalline chalices, and stained glass. The depiction of glittering light amidst overwhelming darkness is a common religious metaphor representing the defeat of iniquity by good, and ritualism vividly animated this idea. In doing so, it shifted Tractarian poetic trends away from the gothic writing of Williams and Faber, fixated as it was with a bloody continental piety conveyed through gory and torturous dramatizations of Christ's death.[81] Williams's 'The Cross Dripping Blood', for example, pours over the 'Blood from His Hands', 'falling drop by drop, | And from His Temples', hanging 'on His pale Body'.[82] This eerie dwelling on the butchery of the crucifixion is replaced in subsequent ritualist poetry by a more ethereal focus on the divine spirit, removing God from empirical and materialist attacks and into the celestial moments of kindled embers or radiant angels.

We might compare the early Tractarian poetry of Williams with the later ritualist verse of Hopkins to gauge this shift, the latter's electrically charged poetry catching God within the flashing of foil or hum of the dragonfly, rather than drowning the reader in his blood. For Williams, like Keble, a notion called 'analogy' structured this latter way of accessing God, an idea inherited from Bishop Joseph Butler's *Analogy of Religion* (1736), required reading for ordinands in the early nineteenth century. Analogy connotes a belief in the correspondence between the natural and the supernatural, or moral world, so that religion and God are 'revealed' within what is observable around us. Newman described it as the 'doctrine that material phenomena are both the types and the instruments of real things unseen', the 'Mysteries of the faith' that are reserved within physical objects.[83] Hopkins, however, considered Butlerian analogy slightly myopic, unable to capture the intrinsic vision within the natural world: material phenomena are not so much types as tiny jigsaws made up of molecular sense data. Hopkins called this 'inscape', a word that denoted the energy of natural objects which for him, almost buzz with vitality only to be kept going by 'instress', that which stops the buzz from fizzling out.

This near scientized poetics wherein the world vibrates beneath an invisible film suggests that religion is not hidden behind natural objects, but is found within them. Hopkins intimates this in a journal entry written in 1870 wherein he describes the process of almost losing oneself in the at once hypnotic and devotional aura produced by a bluebell:

I do not think I have ever seen anything more beautiful than the bluebell I have been looking at. I know the beauty of our Lord by it. Its inscape is mixed of strength and grace like an ash tree. The head is strongly drawn over backwards and arched down like a cutwater drawing itself back from the line of the keel. The lines of the bells strike and overlie this, rayed but not symmetrically, some lie parallel. They look steeling against the paper, the shades lying between the bells and behind the cocked petal-ends and nursing up the precision of their distinctness, the petal-ends themselves being delicately lit.[84]

J. R. Watson reminds us of how 'delicate, detailed', and 'loving' this passage is, revealing the import of careful aesthetic perception whilst signalling a process of looking into the world's effervescence, rather than past it to a divine afterlife.[85] Penetrating *in* to the scape of a thing, the representation of its view, and *in* to the stress, or emphasis, of individual reading, Hopkins created a renewed form of analogy which was unable to render Christ drenched in blood due to the generalized form of cognition such a reading entailed. 'Without stress,' he wrote in his notebook, 'we might not and could say | Blood is read | but only | This blood is red | or | The last blood I saw was red | nor even that, for in later language not only universals would not be true but the copula would break down even in particular judgements.'[86]

What this kind of stress shared with its predecessor, analogy, was a reserve or retreat from the universal and an affection for the mystery of nature. Yet Hopkins believed such mystery was decoded, not through the learning of Latinate ceremony or complex doctrine, but through the more tricky process of seeing through faith. As he mourned in his journal: 'I thought how sadly beauty of inscape was unknown and buried away from simple people and yet how near at hand it was if they had eyes to see it and it could be called out everywhere again.'[87] Hopkins's aesthetic merged Tractarian liturgy and reserve with a powerful insight into nature as art, reflecting both his friendships with Pater and Swinburne, each magnetized by the pattern and design of nature, and his undergraduate experience at Oxford. Here, he became a member of the Balliol ritualists, spellbound by Pusey, and then Newman, and working always to recreate the magical realm of the ritualistic High Church in the supernatural world he accessed through his senses. Yet as a convert to Rome, and finally to the Society of Jesus in 1868, the poet was also profoundly invested in asceticism, obsessively noting down his 'sins' for confessional purposes in as detailed a manner as he would render the bluebell. Hopkins's extreme discipline provoked him to burn his early poetry, and on becoming a Jesuit he 'resolved to write no more, as not belonging to my profession, unless it were by the wish of my superiors'.[88]

Famously, however, his superiors did encourage him to write, his rector at St Beuno's, North Wales, motivating Hopkins to respond to a piece he had read in *The Times* regarding the wreck of the *Deutschland*, which had been carrying a group of nuns expelled from Prussia.[89] The factual detail he garnered from the newspaper article interlocked with the doctrinal implications he recognized in the event enabled him to realize a poetics able to balance perfectly meaning, expression, rhythm, and emotion.[90] As Hopkins conveys in the first verse of 'The Windhover: To Christ our Lord' (1877):

> I caught this morning morning's minion, king-
> dom of daylight's dauphin, dapple-dawn-drawn Falcon, in his
> riding
> Of the rolling level underneath him steady air, and striding
> High there, how he rung upon the rein of a wimpling wing
> In his ecstasy! then off, off forth on swing,
> As a skate's heel sweeps smooth on a bow-bend: the hurl and
> gliding
> Rebuffed the big wind. My heart in hiding
> Stirred for a bird,—the achieve of, the mastery of the thing!
>
> (ll. 1–10)

The 'mastery of the thing' communicates the instress of God within nature, represented here by the bird, who transmits religious feeling to the narrator by 'instressing' God into him. The narrator's tucked away heart thus waits in reserve until reawakened by the sacramental flutter of the falcon, a eucharistic figure who physically imbues God. While Hopkins rarely invoked the liturgical calendar in his poetry, relying instead on a doctrinal sense of mystery, he remained invested, like many Tractarians, in the eucharist, considering it an exemplary model of instress. 'The Bugler's First Communion', 'Morning, Midday and Evening Sacrifice', 'Easter Communion', and 'Communion' each portray a eucharistic transference of God into material things, solidifying an ethereal-seeming faith. Indeed, like his direct predecessor, Rossetti, by whom he was much influenced, the emphasis falls always on divine love, transcendent of ceremonial specificity, and animating his concepts of instress and inscape. As he suggests in an early undergraduate verse, 'I have found the dominant of my range and state—| Love, O my God, to call Thee Love and Love.'[91]

How to differentiate such divine feeling from the sensuality of human desire remains troublesome in reading Tractarian poetry throughout the nineteenth century, Hopkins's nerve-tingling verse perhaps evocative of more than prayer-like emotion. The same issue plagued ritualists, accused as they were of what Edward Monro called 'hollow aestheticism'. In his 1850 sermons on ministerial office, Monro warned his fellow clergy that ritualistic ornamentation was 'but a chrysalis, in which the immortal soul is preparing to spread its wings into eternal day. We must not spend our time there', but focus instead on 'the hearts' of 'people'.[92] The 'fruit of experience', then, was to be elevated above the experience itself, a ranking that Hopkins's tutor, Walter Pater, audaciously reversed in his art for art's sake manifesto, *The Renaissance* (1873). Consisting of a series of impressionistic essays on Italian art, the study won Pater the tarnish of hedonist, provoked by his suggestion that existence was ideally the sustained forbearance of 'intellectual excitement' and 'exquisite passion': 'To burn always with this hard, gem-like flame, to maintain this ecstasy, is success in life.'[93] Such a proposal was regarded by critics as scandalously dangerous, leading to a confusion between art and religion, truth and beauty. Pater had already insisted in his first published essay on Coleridge that 'modern thought' should be 'relative' rather than 'absolute', a shocking premiss for believers invested in a pure conception of the divine.[94] At the same time, Oscar Wilde was flamboyantly writing of the 'careless habits of accuracy', mocking the entanglements in which theologians and scientists alike were mired and turning instead to Hellenic ideals of harmony, sensuality, and passion.

Pater's own conflation of pagan sentiment with the formation of religious systems in *The Renaissance* implied that all faith was feeling, an offensive idea to some, but for others a liberating one in which God could be accessed through emotion, rather than esoteric Latin texts. This was no nonconformist brand of religious feeling, however, precisely because Pater was so grounded in a High Church ritualism which allowed him to render religion aesthetic.[95] Certainly Pater, like Hopkins, had been an Oxford ritualist in his youth, rebelling temporarily against his faith, and, as Mrs Humphrey Ward remarked almost fifty years after reading *The Renaissance*, striving to vocalize an 'entire aloofness' from 'the Christian tradition of Oxford'. In its place, she suggested, Pater glorified 'the higher and intenser forms of esthetic [*sic*] pleasure' to counter the 'Christian doctrine of self-denial and renunciation'.[96] Neutralizing Tractarianism's disciplining rigour, Pater retained a hunger for its liturgical mysteries. Like Keble, his essays on poetics blur into discussions of religion, poetry elevated as sublime, spectral, and paradisial in an at once religious and decadent sense.[97] As John Shelton Reed argues, there 'was a good deal of overlap and more or less continuous exchange between the circles of advanced Anglo-Catholicism and the secular avant-garde' in the nineteenth century, both associated with luxury, languor, and the excesses of capricious youth.[98]

Again, the concern that such vices, whether religious or secular, would spill over into a preoccupation with Roman Catholicism fostered Evangelical critiques of Tractarianism, to which we will turn in the next chapter. We might conclude this discussion, however, by stating that, while many Evangelicals challenged Tractarians for being unworldly and unaware of social issues, ritualism motivated a succession of charitable missions into the poorest areas of Britain's main cities. While Hopkins may have emotionally crumbled during his preaching experience at his parish in Liverpool, many ritualist 'slum priests', as they became known, were devoted to the physical and spiritual welfare of the poor. Accommodating the homeless, educating the underprivileged, and offering welfare to the impoverished was granted a ritualist tone within flower missions, in which volunteers would shower inner-city streets with floral reminders of God's vitality and presence in the world. Moreover, the discipline ritualism demanded of the believer produced individuals committed to hard work and self-sacrifice, and the form of worship it encouraged appealed to the unlettered where previous models of missionary work had failed.[99] As Rossetti's friend, Littledale, argued: 'Ritualism is a sort of excursion train on the Sunday, to bring the poor man out of his dull, squalid, every-day life into a land of beauty, colour, light and song.' Its critics, he suggested, were blind to its uses, 'having pictures, musical wives, spacious rooms, curtains and gilding in profusion'.[100] Dickens would have had some sympathy with such a point, but fretted that ritualism's emphasis on the sensual and visual feminized believers or led them to Rome. We will look more at this anxiety in Chapter 6, exploring the resurgence of public interest in spiritualism, the occult, and mysticism. The Oxford Movement's legacy, however, remained social, doctrinal, and aesthetic, coming to ground modern Anglo-Catholicism both in Britain and abroad.[101]

NOTES

1. The academic and slightly fusty bent of the Oxford Movement earned it the nickname, 'British Museum religion', see N. Yates, *Buildings, Faith and Worship: The Liturgical Arrangement of Anglican Churches 1600–1900* (Oxford: Clarendon Press, 1991), 144–5.

2. J. Wilson (Christopher North), 'Was Margaret a Christian?', *The Eclectic Review*, 12 (1842), 568–79; see S. Gill, *William Wordsworth: A Life* (Oxford: Oxford University Press, 1989), 416–17.

3. J. Barker, *Wordsworth: A Life* (London: Viking, 2000), 726.

4. See J. T. Coleridge's extract from the Oration, in *Memoir of the Rev. John Keble* (Oxford and London: James Parker, 1869), 249.

5. See S. Prickett, 'Keble's Crewian Oration', in K. Blair (ed.), *John Keble and his Contexts* (London: AMS, 2004).

6. S. Prickett, 'Tractarian Poetry', in R. Cronin, A. Chapman, and A. H. Harrison (eds.), *A Companion to Victorian Poetry* (Oxford: Blackwell, 2002), 279–90 (279).

7. Compiled for the series, *The Christian's Miscellany; Conducted by Members of the Church of England*, see S. Gill, *Wordsworth and the Victorians* (Oxford: Clarendon Press, 1998), 63.

8. Barker, *Wordsworth*, 545, 611.

9. G. Herring, *What was the Oxford Movement?* (London: Continuum, 2002), 1 ff.

10. See M. Wheeler, 'Keble and Rome', in Blair (ed.), *John Keble and his Contexts*.

11. Newman wrote: 'I have ever considered and kept the day, as the start of the religious movement of 1833', in *Apologia pro Vita Sua* (1864), ed. I. Ker (London: Penguin, 1994), 50.

12. See Herring, *Oxford Movement*, 8.

13. Ibid. 9.

14. Ninety Tracts were written between 1833 and 1841, twenty-nine by Newman, eight by Keble, seven by Pusey, and many others by various Oxford men including Froude and Williams. Some of the Tracts were reprinted from the works of past writers (mostly from the seventeenth century), from Catenas and from biblical commentaries by the Anglican divines. Only Newman's Tract 90 of 1841, 'Remarks on Certain Passages in the Thirty-nine Articles', pushed both ecclesiastical and public opinion too far by declaring that the Thirty-nine Articles did not contradict the doctrines of Roman Catholicism, an argument interpreted as a sly attempt to Romanize the Church of England.

15. A. W. Haddan, 'On Party Spirit in the English Church' (1861), in P. B. Nockles, *The Oxford Movement in Context: Anglican High Churchmanship 1760–1857* (Cambridge: Cambridge University Press, 1994), 322.

16. S. L. Ollard, *A Short History of the Oxford Movement* (1915), in Herring, *Oxford Movement*, 98.

17. J. Keble, *The Assize Sermon on 'National Apostasy', Oxford Movement Centenary preached by the Rev. J. Keble in St Mary's Church at Oxford on 14 July 1833; reprinted with report of the service and historical introduction by the Rev. R. J. E. Boggis BD, Vicar of St John's, Torquay* (Torquay: Devonshire Press, n.d.), in *Bodleian Pamphlets on Church Finance, 23* (1850–1935), 7, 18, 14–15.

18. W. Gladstone, 'The Church of England and Ritualism', *Contemporary Review*, 24 (1874), in M. H. Bright, 'English Literary Romanticism and the Oxford Movement', *Journal of the History of Ideas*, 40: 3 (1979), 385–404 (398–9); C. Rossetti, *The Face of the Deep* (London: S.P.C.K., 1892), 243.

19. O. Chadwick, *The Mind of the Oxford Movement* (London: Adam and Charles Black, 1960), 51; much of this was popular with High Churchmen who welcomed any rejuvenation of the Christian Church: the *Christian Remembrancer* stated in 1841: 'with the earlier numbers of [the Tracts] the great mass of the clergy fully agreed. They were glad to find men bold enough to advance opinions which they themselves had always implicitly received ... In the very moment when they were calling upon the church to abandon her established principles, at this very moment arose a company of men, strong in knowledge, faith and self-denial, who proved, in a manner which could not be questioned, that those truths instead of being abandoned, needed only to be acted upon', in *Christian Remembrancer*, New Series, 1 (Apr. 1841), in Nockles, *Oxford Movement*, 275.

20. Herring, *Oxford Movement*, 27; the comment is Edward Bickersteth's, a prominent Evangelical divine who helped promote the Evangelical Alliance, founded in 1846 to oppose Tractarianism; the Methodist Conference also countered the Movement by publishing its own *Wesleyan Tracts for the Times* that directly targeted the six Tractarian ideas noted above.

21. J. H. Newman, 'The Catholic Church', *Tracts for the Times*, 2 (1833); Herring, *Oxford Movement*, 105.

22. J. H. Newman, 'Tamworth Reading Room', in *Discussions and Arguments on Various Subjects* (London: Longmans and Green, 1911), 293–5.

23. J. H. Newman, letter to J. B. White, 1 Mar. 1828, in D. Newsome, *The Parting of Friends: A Study of the Wilberforces and Henry Manning* (London: John Murray, 1966), 89.

24. See D. Goslee, *Romanticism and the Anglican Newman* (Athens, Oh.: Ohio University Press, 1996).

25. Newman, *Apologia*, 100.

26. S. Prickett, *Romanticism and Religion: The Tradition of Coleridge and Wordsworth in the Victorian Church* (Cambridge: Cambridge University Press, 1976), 87.

27. All references are to the 1805 version of *The Prelude*.

28. W. Blake, 'London', in *Songs of Experience* (1791).

29. 'The Puseyite Moth and Roman Candle', *Punch* (1850), in J. S. Reed, *The Cultural Politics of Victorian Anglo-Catholicism* (Nashville, Tenn., and London: Vanderbilt University Press, 1996), p. xiii.

30. A. Trollope, *Barchester Towers* (1857), ed. John Sutherland (Oxford: Oxford University Press, 1998), 28.

31. W. J. Conybeare, 'Church Parties', *The Edinburgh Review*, 98 (1853), 273–342, in J. S. Reed, *Glorious Battle: The Cultural Politics of Victorian Anglo-Catholicism* (Nashville, Tenn.: Vanderbilt University Press, 1996), 80.

32. See G. Rowell, *The Vision Glorious: Themes and Personalities of the Catholic Revival in Anglicanism* (Oxford: Oxford University Press, 1983), 86.

33. Reed, *Glorious Battle*, 47.

34. Bishop H. Phillpotts, *Letters to Charles Butler* (London, 1825), in Nockles, *Oxford Movement*, 249.

35. See E. B. Pusey's sermon, *The Entire Absolution of the Penitent*, delivered to the University of Oxford in 1846, see Nockles, *Oxford Movement*, 250.

36. E. A. Knox, *The Tractarian Movement: 1833–1845* (London: Putnam, 1934), in Reed, *Glorious Battle*, 49.

37. N. F. Cusack, *The Story of my Life* (1891), in W. Walsh, *The Secret History of the Oxford Movement*, 3rd edn. (London: Swan Sonnenschein and Co., 1898), 87.

38. Or what Goslee calls Newman's 'spiritual androgyny', *Anglican Newman*, 126.

39. C. J. Blomfield, *A Charge to the Clergy of London* (1842), in J. Bentley, *Ritualism and Politics in Victorian Britain: The Attempt to Legislate for Belief* (Oxford: Oxford University Press, 1978), 30.

40. Bentley, *Ritualism*, 30–1.

41. C. M. Davies, *Philip Paternoster: A Tractarian Love Story by an Ex-Puseyite*, 2 vols. (London: Richard Bentley, 1858), ii. 65.

42. W. Harcourt, letter to *The Times*, 30 July 1874, in Bentley, *Ritualism*, 34; an excessive measure of 'No Popery' literature was issued in the nineteenth century and certain volumes republished from the eighteenth, to warn women of the lascivious ways of priests, see S. D. Bernstein, *Confessional Subjects: Revelations of Gender and Power in Victorian Literature and Culture* (Chapel Hill, NC, and London: University of North Carolina Press, 1997), 50 ff.

43. Walsh, *Secret History* (1898), 87, 164.

44. Newman, *Apologia*, 24.

45. E. Clery, 'Introduction', in Ann Radcliffe, *The Italian or the Confessional of the Black Penitents: A Romance*, ed. F. Garber (Oxford: Oxford University Press, 1998), pp. vii–xxxi (p. xiii); see also Clery's *The Rise of Supernatural Fiction 1762–1800* (Cambridge: Cambridge University Press, 1995).

46. Pusey contributed £1,000 in cash; see H. W. Burrows, *The Half-Century of Christ Church, Albany Street, St. Pancras* (London: Skeffington and Son, 1887), 9.

47. Ibid. 14.

48. Ibid. 16.

49. See H. P. Liddon, *Life of Edward Bouverie Pusey*, ed. Rev. J. O. Johnston and the Rev. R. J. Wilson, 4 vols. (London: Longmans and Co., 1893–97).

50. C. Rossetti, letter to D. G. Rossetti, 2 Dec. 1881, in J. Marsh, *Christina Rossetti: A Literary Biography* (London: Pimlico, 1995), 60.

51. C. M. Cantalupo, 'Christina Rossetti: The Devotional Poet and the Rejection of Romantic Nature', in D. A. Kent, *The Achievement of Christina Rossetti* (Ithaca, NY, and London: Cornell University Press, 1987), 274–300 (275–6).

52. Newman, *Apologia*, 37.

53. See E. Mason, 'Christina Rossetti and the Doctrine of Reserve', *The Journal of Victorian Culture*, 7: 2 (2002), 196–219.

54. Prickett, 'Tractarian Poetry', 281.

55. J. Keble, *Lectures on Poetry 1832–41*, trans. E. K. Francis, 2 vols. (Oxford: Clarendon Press, 1912), i. 53–4.

56. Ibid. ii. 482–3.

57. For example, I. Williams, *The Cathedral, or the Catholic and Apostolic Church in England* (Oxford, 1838); Wordsworth, *The Excursion* (1814); and Hemans's unfinished *The Christian Temple*.

58. See J. Keble, 'Life of Sir Walter Scott', *British Critic* (1838), in Keble, *Occasional Papers and Reviews* (Oxford and London: James Parker and Co., 1877), 1–80; the review text was J. G. Lockhart, *Memoirs of the Life of Sir Walter Scott, Bart*, 7 vols. (London: Murray and Whittaker, 1838).

59. Keble, 'Life of Sir Walter Scott', 6.

60. See, for example, D. Hilliard, 'UnEnglish and UnManly: Anglo-Catholicism and Homosexuality', *Victorian Studies*, 25: 2 (1982), 181–210; and J. S. Reed, ' "Giddy Young Men": A Counter-Cultural Aspect of Victorian Anglo-Catholicism', *Comparative Social Research*, 11 (1989), 209–26.

61. Prickett, 'Tractarian Poetry', 280.

62. D. Greenwell, 'The Spirit of Poetry', *Liber Humanitatis: A Series of Essays on Various Aspects of Spiritual and Social Life* (London: Daldy, Isbister and Co., 1875), 119.

63. Ibid. 123, 125.

64. Ibid. 124.

65. Ibid. 127.
66. D. Greenwell, 'Stray Leaves', in W. Dorling, *Memoirs of Dora Green-well* (London: James Clarke and Co., 1885), 20–1; 'Stray Leaves' is not in print, the only existing copy, the original, is held in the Janet Camp Troxell Collection of Rossetti Manuscripts in the Firestone Library, Princeton University; for more on the manuscript, see J. Gray, 'Dora Greenwell's Commonplace Book', *Princeton University Library Chronicle*, 57: 1 (1995), 47–74.
67. On this subject, see 'Archbishop Ussher on Prayers for the Dead: Against Romanism No. II', *Tracts for the Times*, 72 (1835), a reprint of Archbishop James Ussher's seventeenth-century pamphlet on prayers for the dead.
68. D. Rosenblum, 'Christina Rossetti and Poetic Sequence', in Kent, *Achievement of Christina Rossetti*, 132–56 (152).
69. See the discussion of Blake's *Läocoon* in Chapter 1.
70. Keble, *Lectures*, 106.
71. Newman, *Apologia*, 214.
72. Herring, *Oxford Movement*, 71.
73. In P. Thureau-Dangin, *The English Catholic Revival in the Nineteenth-Century*, 2 vols. (New York: E. P Dutton and Co., n.d.), in Reed, *Glorious Battle*, 60–1.
74. Herring, *Oxford Movement*, 90.
75. Rowell, *Vision Glorious*, 128.
76. In E. Hodder, *The Life and Work of the Seventh Earl of Shaftesbury, K.G.*, 3 vols. (London: Cassell, 1886), iii. 213.
77. Burrows, *Half-Century*, 10–11.
78. Ibid. 21, 31, 47, 50, 66.
79. See ibid. 67 ff.; and Sara Coleridge, *Memoir and Letters of Sara Coleridge*, 2 vols. (London: Henry S. King and Co., 1873).
80. W. Pater, 'Style', in *Appreciations: With an Essay on Style* (London: Macmillan, 1889), 1–36 (14).
81. G. B. Tennyson, *Victorian Devotional Poetry: The Tractarian Mode* (Cambridge, Mass.: Harvard University Press, 1981), 168.
82. I. Williams, *The Altar: Or, Meditations in Verse on the Great Christian Sacrifice* (London: James Burns, 1847), XXII. 1–4.
83. Tennyson, *Victorian Devotional Poetry*, 52, 143.
84. 18 May 1870, *The Journals and Papers of Gerard Manley Hopkins*, ed. H. House and G. Storey (Oxford and London: Oxford University Press, 1959), 199.
85. J. R. Watson, *The Poetry of Gerard Manley Hopkins* (London: Penguin, 1987), 18.
86. Ibid. 127.
87. In *Poems and Prose of Gerard Manley Hopkins*, ed. W. H. Gardner (London: Penguin, 1953), p.xxi.

88. See Hopkins's letters to R. W. Dixon of 12–17 Oct., 23–5 Oct., 29 Oct.–2 Nov., and 1–16 Dec., in *The Correspondence of Gerard Manley Hopkins and Richard Watson Dixon*, ed. C. C. Abbott (Oxford and London: Oxford University Press, 1935).

89. N. White, *Hopkins: A Literary Biography* (Oxford: Clarendon Press, 1992), 250.

90. Ibid. 283.

91. See *Poems and Prose*, ed. Gardner, p. xxi.

92. E. Monro, *Sermons Principally on the Responsibilities of the Ministerial Office* (London: J. H. Parker, 1850), 105–7, quoted in Herring, *Oxford Movement*, 90.

93. W. Pater, *The Renaissance* (1873), ed. Adam Phillips (Oxford: Oxford University Press, 1986), 152.

94. Pater, 'Coleridge' (1866), in *Appreciations*, 64–106 (65).

95. Pater, *Renaissance*, 129–30.

96. M. A. Ward, *A Writer's Recollections 1856–1900* (London: W. Collins Sons and Co. Ltd., 1918), 120–1.

97. Pater, 'Aesthetic Poetry' (1868), in *Appreciations* (1889), 213–27 (213); the essay was omitted from the 1890 and subsequent editions.

98. Reed, *Glorious Battle*, 218.

99. Ibid. 149.

100. R. F. Littledale, 'The First Report of the Ritual Commission', in O. Shipley (ed.), *The Church and the World: Essays on Questions of the Day in 1868* (London: Longmans, Green, Reader and Dyer, 1868), 24.

101. Tractarianism was welcomed in the United States and British North America and encouraged several missionary projects to Africa, New Zealand, Australia, and Asia. Its hold on the modernist imagination is also apparent, see J. Pearce, *Literary Converts: Spiritual Inspiration in an Age of Unbelief* (London : Harper Collins, 1999).

4

Evangelicalism: Brontë to Eliot

In October 1855 George Eliot published an essay in the *Westminster Review* entitled 'Evangelical Teaching: Dr Cumming', which, among other things, made it clear how far away she had moved from her Evangelical roots.[1] Eliot used the essay to critique the inconsistent and rhetorical arguments advanced by Dr John Cumming, an Evangelical writer and preacher whom she had taken issue with. The critique centred on his use of a crude, popular apologetic for the Christian faith, and his tendency to construct a false caricature of his opponent's intellectual position in order to make his own counter-arguments sound more persuasive. Though Eliot's argument is characteristically sharp and insightful, it mimics the behaviour that she is complaining about: the syntactical arrangement of the title of the essay implies that Cumming is illustrative of Evangelical teaching per se, thus creating an Evangelical type that is no more a reflection of historical reality than the figures constructed by Cumming. Eliot's desire to cast Cumming as the embodiment of Evangelical teaching is made explicit towards the end of the essay:

One more characteristic of Dr. Cumming's writings, and we have done. This is the *perverted moral judgement* that everywhere reigns in them. Not that this perversion is peculiar to Dr. Cumming: it belongs to the dogmatic system which he shares with all Evangelical believers. But the abstract tendencies of systems are represented in very different degrees, according to the different characters of those who embrace them; just as the same food tells differently on different constitutions: and there are certain qualities in Dr. Cumming that cause the perversion of which we speak to exhibit itself with peculiar prominence in his teaching.[2]

The claim that Cumming is a particularly perverse type of Evangelical is accompanied by the insistence that he is not altogether unusual: the complaint of a fault with the 'dogmatic system' of Evangelicalism suggests something intrinsic and substantive rather than accidental.

In *Everywhere Spoken Against: Dissent in the Victorian Novel,* one of the most important accounts of the engagement between literature and religious Dissent (including Evangelical Dissent) in the nineteenth century, Valentine Cunningham argues persuasively that Eliot was more sympathetic towards dissenting life and practice than fellows novelists such as Charles Dickens and Anthony Trollope. Yet while novels such as *Adam Bede* (1859) and *Middlemarch* (1871–2) capture the intellectual and emotional struggles of Evangelical life with imaginative sympathy, Eliot's simultaneous dismissal of figures such as Cumming has contributed, like the unhelpful caricatures deployed by Dickens and Trollope, to a general misreading of the Evangelical presence in literature and culture during the mid-nineteenth century. At the heart of this misreading is a view that the cultural force of Evangelicalism was narrow, limited, and in recession by the middle of the nineteenth century. Even the helpful chapter on religion provided by Philip Davis in *The Oxford English Literary History,* viii. *1830–1880,* tells us that 'by the mid-1830s Evangelicalism was becoming a victim of its own initial success, a rigidified force'.[3] This depiction of Evangelicalism as a spent force by the mid-1830s is one that owes a great deal to the testimony of several Victorian writers, from John Henry Newman to John Ruskin, who ultimately rejected their Evangelical upbringing on the grounds of its intellectual and cultural inadequacy.[4] Like the products of nineteenth-century writers who wrote of their unconversion (including Anthony Trollope, Samuel Butler, and George Eliot), these accounts of Evangelical decline contain a strong polemical intent that is often hidden and/or ignored. Having noted that '[l]ooking back from the vantage point of the 1850s, George Eliot was inclined to share Newman's conviction that the mid-1830 had witnessed the Evangelical Movement's watershed', Elisabeth Jay goes on to observe that the 'diagnoses offered by Newman, Eliot, Trollope and Butler in conjunction with one another should encourage a healthy scepticism about the apparent objectivity of such assessments'.[5] By treating more sceptically the history of Evangelicalism that these writers provide, and by turning to the vast body of religious material that circulated throughout the mid-nineteenth century, one becomes more alert to the variety and impact of Evangelicalism. Evangelicals were a major cultural force well beyond the 1830s, and this chapter will explore some of their points of influence, struggle, and interaction with literature and society. The chapter begins by thinking about Evangelical identity, and then goes on to consider some of the ways in which Evangelicalism engaged with the surrounding culture. Material from a variety of mid-nineteenth-century authors is used throughout the chapter, with detailed close readings of novels by Charles Dickens and Wilkie Collins being central to the line of argument pursued. Both Dickens and Collins explore the way in which Evangelicals perceived themselves to be people of the Word, but the two writers also expose some of the problems that this perception gave rise to. General challenges to the cultural authority of the Bible in the period, along with specific questions about interpretation and the relation of the divine Word to other literature, highlighted unresolved issues in the Evangelical reliance on Scripture. In an attempt to affirm the authoritative qualities of their message, Evangelicals became increasingly reliant on rhetorical preaching, revivalism, and conversion, and these are considered in detail. The chapter concludes by turning to ideas of temptation and judgement, with particular reference to two issues that occupied the thinking of Evangelicals: gender and hell.

IDENTITY

The term Evangelical was coined in the mid-eighteenth century to describe a revival of interest in the personal experience and promulgation of the Christian 'evangel' (gospel). As several historians have noted, Evangelicals saw themselves in a line of continuity stretching back to the Reformation, and, before that, the Early Church. In many respects, Evangelicals saw themselves as the authentic expression of Christianity. Margaret Oliphant captures the potential arrogance of this self-perception in her biography of Edward Irving (1792–1834), a controversial Evangelical figure whose increasing interest in millenarian speculation and charismatic experiences eventually marginalized him from the Evangelical mainstream. Describing a sermon delivered to the London Missionary Society in 1826, in which Irving caused considerable offence, Oliphant writes: '[T]his is the first point upon which Irving fairly parted company with his Evangelical brethren, and exasperated that large, active, and influential community which, as he somewhere says, not without a little bitterness, "calls itself the religious world".'[6] Although the Evangelical perception of themselves as 'the religious world' may arrogantly exclude certain denominations and groups not considered authentically Christian, it simultaneously points to the breadth and diversity of Evangelicalism. Evangelicalism was a movement rather than a denomination. Its adherents differed in both theology and politics—the former exemplified in the divide between Calvinists (who emphasized divine sovereignty and believed that an elect had been chosen by God for salvation) and Arminians (who emphasized human free will and believed that salvation could be freely chosen by anyone), and the latter in the vociferous differences of opinion between Anglicans and Dissenters. Internal debates concerning theology and politics were defining controversies of the nineteenth century and have rightly attracted much scholarly attention; however, examination of them runs the risk of failing to acknowledge an Evangelical identity that transcended such divisions.

Evangelical diversity and the lack of a clear membership structure leave us with the question of how the movement can be identified and understood. The problem is epitomized by the propensity of scholars to turn to extreme literary depictions, such as Miss Clack in Wilkie Collins *The Moonstone* (1868), for examples of Evangelicalism: such characters are far easier to recognize and categorize than the majority of the movement's adherents. It is understandable, even inevitable, that critics should seek common recognizable points of reference when discussing nineteenth-century Evangelicalism; yet relying on extreme incarnations in an attempt to circumvent the challenge of identity is problematic. Unfortunately, there is no easy solution to the predicament. Recognizing historical Evangelical figures rather than fictional Evangelical characters is no easier: once we move beyond well-known persons such as William Wilberforce, Hannah More, and Lord Shaftsbury, it is virtually impossible to determine exactly who is and who is not an Evangelical, particularly when much of the historiography is written by those unfamiliar with, or even antagonistic to, Evangelicalism. Some help is at hand in Donald Lewis's two-volume *The Blackwell Dictionary of Evangelical Biography, 1730–1860* but even this valuable reference work necessarily ignores the large number of Evangelical figures who helped shape the thought and life of the period. When, at the start of the book, Lewis outlines his criteria for selection, one is struck by the methodological difficulties raised, particularly the confession that, after 1860, it becomes increasingly difficult to distinguish the boundaries of the Evangelical and non-Evangelical clearly.

In an attempt to delineate the boundaries, albeit provisionally, most scholarship on Evangelicalism, including Lewis's work, turns to belief for criteria. Of course, identifying certain beliefs as fundamental to Evangelicalism runs the risk of excessive interpretive subjectivity. In addition, the pragmatic nature of Evangelicalism—evident, for example, in the title of William Wilberforce's influential *A Practical View of the*

Prevailing Religious System of Professed Christians (1797)—makes it impossible to separate belief from practice, and resists the idea of an explicitly dogmatic framework to which one can go in order to determine core Evangelical beliefs. That said, belief does offer a constructive point of reference. Although one might reasonably question Jay's assertion that 'the essentials of Evangelical doctrine remained unchanged', a number of beliefs have been widely acknowledged as integral to Evangelical identity.[7] Recent work on Evangelicalism frequently cites the summary of belief provided by David Bebbington in *Evangelicals in Modern Britain*, which identifies four main characteristics: *conversionism*, the belief that lives need to be changed by the Gospel; *biblicism*, a high opinion of and deference to the Bible as the primary source of God's revelation; *activism*, the expression of the Gospel in effort; and *crucicentrism*, a stress on the atoning sacrifice of Christ on the Cross.[8]

Given the 'quadrilateral of priorities' that Bebbington identifies, it is hardly surprising that Evangelicals came together in the first part of the nineteenth century for a number of projects and initiatives that sought to transform their culture. Most famously, the Clapham Sect, a group of influential and socially concerned Anglicans, was instrumental in bringing about the abolition of slavery. Elsewhere, Evangelical activism and concern for the salvation of others found expression in the work of the London City Mission (founded 1835) and the Religious Tract Society (founded 1799).[9] The Evangelical predilection for inaugurating societies devoted to the promotion of the Gospel is satirized mercilessly by Charles Dickens in *Bleak House* (1852–3). On the surface of this text, the condemnation of Mrs Jellyby's interest in foreign mission at the expense of her own family implies that the work of such societies was misguided, implicating Evangelicalism as complicit in a society that failed to address the real socio-economic need all around. However, it may well be the case that Evangelicalism provided Dickens with a convenient scapegoat with which to mask the underlying conservative message of his narrative. Despite its ostensibly neutral and innocent perspective, Esther's narrative clearly privileges domestic over foreign interests. It also views the frenetic pace of the city negatively, hence Esther's claim that '[i]t was delightful to see the green landscape before us, and the immense metropolis behind'.[10] Given this preference for rural domestic order over an urban environment that insists on change and life outside one's own immediate sphere, Esther's negative description of Mrs Jellyby's activity needs to be reinterpreted. The claim that 'Mrs Jellyby, sitting in quite a nest of waste paper, drank coffee all the evening, and dictated at intervals to her eldest daughter'[11] notably insists on reading Mrs Jellyby's activity in terms of a domestic framework ('sitting in quite a nest') and reveals, through its concern with time ('all the evening' and 'dictated at intervals'), a desire for activity to be clearly ordered and regulated. Thus Esther's account of Evangelical activity may be motivated more by the threat Evangelicals pose to the status quo than their conservative refusal to address pressing social problems in London.

Many of the Evangelical societies and organizations formed to bring about social transformation were centred round Exeter Hall. Opened on 29 March 1831 and located on the Strand in London, Exeter Hall was built to provide a large meeting place for Evangelicals. Its subsequent notoriety as the centre for Evangelical gatherings makes it a significant marker of Evangelical identity. In his account of the history of the building, F. Morell Holmes uses the same descriptor of Evangelicalism that Irving had complained of ('the religious world'), and writes:

The opening of Exeter Hall marked a new era in the history of the religious world—if indeed before that date the religious world may be said to have borne that name, or existed as an organized body.

It is true that many godly persons lived and did their work, but that work was confined mostly to the sphere of the various churches to which they belonged ... There were also various religious societies in existence, but they did not come so boldly before the world as they now do; and it was not until the Hall was opened and religious effort and philanthropic zeal had a 'local habitation and a name', apart from any sectarian building, that we find the phrase 'religious world' used. We might speak of Exeter Hall, then, as the outward sign and symbol, the emblem and monument of religious and philanthropic organisation and work.[12]

One of the effects of Exeter Hall was to increase the self-consciousness of Evangelicals regarding their own identity. Ironically, the same period (the 1830s and 1840s) that some scholars see as marking the eclipse of Evangelicalism is the period in which Evangelicals became increasingly aware of their collective identity. Following an important meeting at Exeter Hall in June 1843 for the promotion of Christian Union among 'Christians and Ministers of all Evangelical Protestant communions', the impetus for an umbrella organization that would foster Evangelical unity and sit at a tangent to pre-existing denominations gathered pace, leading to the creation of the Evangelical Alliance in 1846.[13] A series of disagreements, especially transatlantic differences over attitudes towards slavery and Evangelical slave owners, meant that the original plan for a global alliance of Evangelicals was abandoned in favour of national organizations. In their account of the history of the British Evangelical Alliance, David Hilborn and Ian Randall insist that a desire for Evangelical unity was the primary motivation behind the creation of the organization, citing *Essays on Christian Union* (1845), among other texts, in support of their claim. However, while the outward expression of a desire for Evangelical unity in the cause of the Gospel permeates this collection of essays, lending credence to the claim of a positive rationale behind the creation of the Alliance, other, more negative, factors are also present, particularly concern about the rise of Roman Catholicism.[14] The struggle between the Tractarians and Evangelicals during and after the 1830s for control of the Church of England, and the Maynooth controversy of 1844, in which the British government gave additional money to a Catholic seminary in Ireland, encouraged anti-Catholic prejudice. Many of the contributions to *Essays on Christian Union* suggest that anti-Catholicism was more important to the emergence of the Alliance than Randall and Hilborn are willing to admit. Like the identity of any other group, Evangelical identity was constructed partly in terms of what they were not, and opposition to Catholicism was integral to their growing self-consciousness. In response to the perceived threat of Catholicism, a threat that one of the contributors to *Essays on Christian Union*, Ralph Wardlaw, equates with the antichrist, another contributor, Reverend J. A. James, urged:

Our appeal, therefore, is made to all Evangelical Protestants—Is it not time to unite? Does not your situation require it? Strike hands, then, in a covenant of love and friendship, and form a holy league, aggressive and defensive, against a system which is aiming to destroy you utterly, that it may be left at liberty to pursue its unobstructed course through the world, the consummation of which would be reached in overthrowing Evangelical religion, and planting everywhere a baleful superstition in its place.[15]

The position articulated by James is not unusual: similar sentiments are evident throughout the early issues of *Evangelical Christendum*, a periodical launched by the Evangelical Alliance in 1847 and conspicuous in its choice of a title that seems to propose an Evangelical alternative to the Christendom of the Roman Catholic Church.

As the nineteenth century progressed, Evangelicals became increasingly alarmed by the growth of the Broad Church, a term used to describe Christians who were more theologically liberal in their beliefs, less rigid in their insistence on the fundamentals of the faith, and generally more receptive to the latest developments in critical thought. Whereas the Broad Church saw their receptivity to new ideas as a good thing, Evangelicals thought that it conceded too much to 'Rationalism'. Much of the Evangelical hostility to 'Romanism' and 'Rationalism' was predicated on the perceived threat of ritual and the intellect to the universal appeal of the Gospel. As Jay notes in *The Evangelical and Oxford Movements*: 'Evangelicalism prided itself on making a simple creed intelligible to any one who would listen and this populist approach contrasts strongly with the arduous searching after truth engaged in by some of the Tractarians.'[16] For some writers, including John Ruskin and George Eliot, the anti-intellectualism of the Evangelical faith was a major factor in their decision to move away from a set of beliefs they found deficient and inadequate. In the case of Eliot's essay on Dr Cumming though, it is difficult to distinguish the charge of anti-intellectualism from a broader snobbery towards writing aimed at a popular audience.

It would be wrong to dismiss all Evangelicals as anti-intellectual, despite definite tendencies in this direction. In an attempt to explain some of the disparaging comments about the intellect expressed by Evangelicals, Bebbington helpfully notes the movement's debt to the common-sense epistemology of figures such as the Scottish philosopher Thomas Reid: eschewing the scepticism of David Hume, common-sense philosophy insisted that certain beliefs were to be viewed as axiomatic and basic.[17] In the hands of thinkers such as Thomas Chalmers and James McCosh, common-sense philosophy found thoughtful expression in a form that engaged intelligently with a variety of challenges posed by contemporary culture; in the hands of other, less articulate, Evangelicals, however, the simplicity espoused by common-sense philosophy legitimized views that were naïve and unequivocally anti-intellectual.

CULTURAL (DIS)ENGAGEMENT

Evangelical attitudes to culture varied considerably and were influenced by different political, geographic, and theological factors. Perhaps the most important theological determinant was the well-known Evangelical belief in human sinfulness. In the fictional autobiographies *David Copperfield* and *Jane Eyre* Charles Dickens and Charlotte Brontë draw upon their own childhood experiences of Evangelical discourse, with its emphasis on human depravity, to create caricatures in the form of the Murdstones and Mr Brocklehurst. Describing an 'austere and wrathful' religion, David Copperfield recalls sitting in church and listening to Miss Murdstone speak of 'miserable sinners' and other 'dread words with a cruel relish'.[18] The fictional Murdstones are at the extreme end of a theological spectrum but while the influence on Evangelical thought of hyper-Calvinism had lessened considerably by 1850, the Calvinist emphasis on total depravity continued to affect broader Evangelical theology throughout the century. Total depravity was even embedded in the minimal statement of faith adopted by the Salvation Army, a theologically Arminian denomination founded in 1878 as an offshoot of Methodism: their fifth doctrine declared a consequence of the fall to be that 'all men have become sinners, totally depraved, and as such are justly exposed to the wrath of God'. The individualistic tendency of Evangelicalism meant that total depravity was seen primarily in terms of personal human sinfulness, yet it extended to the belief that all of society was fallen. As a result, many Evangelicals sought to separate themselves from the evil of their society and its corrupt 'worldly' influences. The resulting cultural disengagement is evident in Charlotte Brontë's *Jane Eyre* when Mr Brocklehurst identifies Jane as an agent of the Devil and advises the other pupils to shun her evil influence: 'You must be on your guard against her; you must shun her example: if necessary, avoid her company, exclude her from your sports, and shut her out from your converse.'[19]

The picture Jane paints of the Evangelical Brocklehurst is notably biased and incomplete, however. Intrinsically linked to the Evangelical preoccupation with sin was a belief in the possibility of salvation through faith in Christ. The absence of any reference to this redemptive hope in Brocklehurst's talk may well be intended as a critique of the perverted version of the Gospel preached by some Evangelicals: *Jane Eyre* often seems to attack localized expressions of religion rather than religion per se. Alternatively, the account of Brocklehurst may be read in terms of Jane's strong desire for independence and her rejection of the need for assistance from any external agent. After all, *Jane Eyre* is Jane's story, and her exaggerated depiction of Brocklehurst could be seen as masking her own refusal either to submit to any sort of external authority or recognize fundamental limits on her individual autonomy. Further evidence for this reading can be found later in the novel when, in a scene echoing her earlier rejection of Brocklehurst's beliefs, Jane describes her objection to the theology preached by St John Rivers. She explains that the 'Calvinistic doctrines' she hears in St John's sermon 'sounded like a sentence pronounced for doom'.[20] It is not easy to reconcile this interpretation of St John's sermon with the 'evangel' (or good news) that presumably motivates his missionary vocation, and Jane's negative interpretation of the message that St John preaches may well be linked closely to her unwillingness to entertain the Evangelical belief that salvation is a gift of grace rather than something that individuals merit. Certainly Jane's account of her own life is notable for the way it boasts of her ability to survive and succeed. Given this underlying confidence in her own limitless ability and potential, it is perhaps unsurprising that Jane refuses to contemplate the idea that anyone else has access to a religious experience that she does not possess herself: 'I was sure St John Rivers—pure-lived, conscientious, zealous as he was—had not yet found that peace of God which passeth all understanding: he had no more found it, I thought, than had I.'[21]

Paradoxically, the Evangelical desire to separate themselves from the heathen was accompanied by a belief in the possibility of salvation and a commitment to converting contemporaries and transforming the world in which they found themselves. Indeed, part of the difficulty of locating the Evangelical presence in the middle of the nineteenth century results from this diffusion of influence. Evangelicals committed to incarnating their beliefs in the context of daily life sought involvement in a range of cultural, social, and political activities. The more successful their involvement, the harder it becomes to view their Evangelical distinctiveness in a discrete manner. Those willing to look for the marks of Evangelicalism find them in almost every aspect of Victorian society—for example, Boyd Hilton has argued that the contribution of Evangelical theology to the British economic expansion in the nineteenth century is evident in the language of atonement used in economic discourse—yet it remains easier for commentators to observe failed attempts by Evangelicals to reach out to their culture.[22] Confrontation is always more visible than synthesis. Wilkie Collins pens a striking example of a disastrous Evangelical attempt at cultural engagement in *The Moonstone* through Miss Clack's description of the persuasive prowess of the publication *The Serpent at Home*: 'The design of the book—with which the worldly reader may not be acquainted—is to show how the Evil One lies in wait for us in all the most apparently innocent actions of our daily lives. The chapters best adapted to female perusal are "Satan in the Hair Brush"; "Satan behind the Looking Glass"; "Satan under the Tea-Table"; "Satan out of the Window"—and many others.'[23] The reason the description seems comical is not because there is no attempt to engage its 'heathen' audience but because the book's 'design' and 'adapted' language fail so spectacularly.

It is no coincidence that Miss Clack's attempts at evangelizing those around her takes place in a novel that has been read by many critics in terms of its treatment of imperialism. The problem that Evangelicals struggled to address in their mission work at home—i.e. distinguishing between the Christian Gospel and their own cultural prejudice—was reflected in their mission work abroad. In some quarters, the yoking together of the light of the Gospel and the light of British civilization was deliberate, as Anna Johnston reminds us: 'Throughout the history of imperial expansion, missionary proselytising offered the British public a model of "civilised" expansions and colonial community management, transforming imperial projects into moral allegories.'[24] Elsewhere, the Evangelical conflation of the Christian Gospel and their own cultural practices had more to do with the (typically unacknowledged) inevitability of interpreting religious belief within the framework of one's cultural experience. Either way, Miss Clack's narrative epitomizes the problematic nature of Evangelical attempts to interact with other cultures. Despite the convincing case that Lillian Nayder makes in *Unequal Partnerships: Charles Dickens, Wilkie Collins, and Victorian Authorship* for reading *The Moonstone* as a novel written, in contrast to Dickens's work, to highlight the crimes of the Empire, Miss Clack displays considerable cultural prejudice when she describes the Brahmins who kidnap her 'Christian hero', Godfrey Ablewhite: 'At the end of it some words were exchanged, among the invisible wretches, in a language which he [Godfrey] did not understand, but in tones which were plainly expressive (to his cultivated ear) of disappointment and rage.'[25] Miss Clack's vocabulary recasts cultural difference in terms of a dichotomy between animalistic ignorance and refined cultivation, and demonstrates a fundamental failure to engage respectfully with the heathen she wishes to reach, a failure underlined by Godfrey's inability to understand what is going on.

PEOPLE OF THE WORD

One of the points that Nayder draws attention to in her discussion of *The Moonstone* is the effectiveness with which the Brahmins read the mysterious events that take place. In contrast, Gabriel Betteredge lacks critical sophistication in his interpretation of texts, a quality exemplified in his frequent and random turning to *Robinson Crusoe* 'the one infallible remedy'.[26] Betteredge's obsession with seeking divine inspiration in a work of fiction rather than the Bible, combined with his inability to read this new sacred text intelligently, serves to focus attention on the cultural challenges to the status and interpretation of Scripture during the mid-nineteenth century. The questions raised about the Bible were particularly troubling for Evangelicals, who saw themselves as people of the Word. In a pamphlet published in 1867, entitled 'Evangelical Religion: What it is and What it is not', the Reverend J. C. Ryle insisted: 'The first leading feature in Evangelical Religion is the *absolute supremacy it assigns to Holy Scripture*, as the alone rule of faith and practice, the alone test of truth, the alone judge of controversy.'[27] This dogmatic claim is questioned in *The Moonstone* through the conduct of Miss Clack, who, in spite of the Evangelical belief in the Bible as the sufficient and authoritative Word of God, relies on other textual forms for her evangelistic endeavours. When tracts fail to engage an audience, Miss Clack uses short letters to help introduce 'all my precious passages'.[28] Not only does Miss Clack's willingness to substitute new texts in place of the Bible call into question the sufficiency of the divine Word; her attempts to capture her aunt's interest by hiding the texts in unusual places reflect an Evangelical message that is explicitly performative.

To appreciate the anxieties about the status and interpretation of the Bible that surface in *The Moonstone*, we need to consider the impact of the publication of *Essays and Reviews* in 1860.[29] Containing contributions from seven prominent theologians, *Essays and Reviews* disseminated the insights of German Higher Criticism for a British audience. Although higher critical readings of the Bible were in the public domain before 1860—George Eliot, for instance, had translated Strauss's *Life of Jesus* in 1846—the publication of *Essays and Reviews* had a significant effect on Evangelicals' consciousness and elicited a far stronger reaction from them than the publication of Charles Darwin's *The Origin of Species* in 1859. German Higher Criticism insisted on a more sceptical and critical read-ing of the biblical text, declaring that the 'Word of God is in the Bible' as opposed to the Evangelical belief that the Word of God is the Bible.[30] One of the many Evangelical publications to insist upon the dramatic consequences of this shift in perspective was *The Christian Observer*, which declared: 'If the Bible is plainly declared to have a great falsehood intertwined with its every page, how is it possible to build anything upon it?'[31] The repercussions of *Essays and Reviews*, which, among other things, suggested that the Bible should be placed on a level with and interpreted '*like any other book*', were felt throughout the decade.[32] An article in *Evangelical Christendom*, written in 1865 as a response to the Broad Church theology of Dean Stanley, complained of a substantive shift in the status of Scripture: '[A]lthough the new theologians are always ready to eulogise the Bible as a literary monument, and to extol its character-istics as compared with those of other books, they habitually evade the essential and vital question of the whole controversy—namely, whether the Bible has, or has not a just claim to speak with divine authority.'[33]

Miss Clack's anxiety about the Bible can also be seen in her attempts to make its message clear. Upon giving Lady Verinder some tracts, Miss Clack adds the instruction: 'You will read, if I bring you my own precious books? Turned down at all the right places, aunt.'[34] The suggestion that Miss Clack's interpretive efforts are a necessary mediation of the biblical message stands in contradistinction to the claim by leading Evangelicals that: 'The truth that the Bible is self-interpreting is as precious and all-important as the corresponding truth that it is the inspired Word of God. The message from heaven would, indeed, be of no use to men if it required any interpreter besides itself.'[35] In the same way that Miss Clack's compulsive mediation of the biblical message undermines the claim for a self-interpreting text, the narrative structure of *The Moonstone*, in which several narrators interpret the evidence rather than allowing it to speak for itself, makes textual indeterminacy seem inescapable.[36]

Questions over the authority of the Bible were compounded by the growing popularity of fiction in general and the novel in particular. Evangelicals had a long history of suspicion towards literature, and although this had lessened significantly by the middle of the nineteenth century—several households possessed copies of Christian classics such as Bunyan's *Pilgrim's Progress* and John Milton's *Paradise Lost*, older Evangelical writers such as Hannah More and Mrs Sherwood were widely read, and many Evangelical periodicals printed a large amount of religious fiction—a sizeable level of distrust persisted. In 1860 *The Christian Observer* published the following review of Thomas Bowdler's *The Family Shakespeare: in which nothing is added to the original text, but those words and expressions are omitted which cannot with propriety be read in a family*: 'Is it desirable that Shakespeare should be read in Christian families? Is it becoming that the *Christian Observer* should write a line to promote acquaintance with the great tragic poet? We must confess that we are not prepared with a precise answer. But if Shakespeare must be read, this is the edition, and the only edition, that ought to lie upon the table of a Christian family.'[37] Evangelical concerns about the propriety of what people read were accentuated by the rise of the novel and its growing respectability. Although the circulation of novels had expanded dramatically earlier in the century, the form increasingly came to dominate reading habits when Dickens, among others, utilized serialized instalments and periodical publication to make fiction cheaply available for a growing middle-class market. Popular demand for novels challenged the pre-eminence of the Bible at the same time as new intellectual trends began to undermine the aura surrounding the Sacred Text.[38] As a consequence, Evangelicals became increasingly anxious about contemporary reading habits. An article in *The Evangelical Magazine* in December 1864 asked its readers: 'What sort of books do you read? How much of the literature of the day is there, of which we may read whole columns, without there being suggested a single thought to quicken the life of our souls ... ?' The article continued: 'If we read little else ... especially neglecting God's own word, the flower and crown of all books, it can scarcely be otherwise than that we should have to complain of spiritual lethargy and decay.'[39]

Internal debate among Evangelicals about how they should view fiction and respond to the shift in reading habits came to a head in 1863 with the clash between two Evangelical periodicals: *Good Words*, edited by the moderate Scottish Evangelical, Norman Macleod, and *The Record*, arguably the most extreme mainstream Evangelical periodical of the period. *Good Words* had been launched by the publisher Alexander Strahan in 1860. Seeking to develop the broadly religious middle-class family magazine format of *The Leisure Hour* and appeal to both the religious and secular markets, *Good Words* positioned itself as a competitor to Thackeray's *Cornhill*.[40] For Norman Macleod, the resulting combination of material, ranging from travel writing to sermons and sensation novels, was part of a deliberate missionary strategy: 'Now I have a purpose—a serious, solemn purpose—in *Good Words*. I wish in this peculiar department of my ministerial work to which I have been "called", and in which I think I have been blessed, "to become all things to all men, that I might by all means gain some".'[41] However, Macleod's willingness to include fiction from writers such as Margaret Oliphant, Mrs Henry Wood, and Anthony Trollope, as well as his use of contributions from non-Evangelical theologians such as Dean Stanley, caused considerable consternation. The alleged 'mingle-mangle' of forms, texts, and persons in Macleod's periodical drew the following complaint from *The Record* in April 1863: 'it is no easy matter to disentangle the finespun web of sophistry, and to lay one's hand on the precise point where deviation from the truth begins.'[42]

The increasing number of novels sold each year in the Victorian period was part of a much wider increase in textual production. Faced with so many words, all of which were transitory and continually recycled, it was difficult to isolate the permanent and unchanging quality of the divine Word that Evangelicals viewed as so essential. Even the large-scale production of Bibles—'the B.F.B.S [British and Foreign Bible Society] would claim full or partial responsibility for the distribution of more than 250 million Bibles, in whole or in part, around the world'—paled into insignificance when compared with the seemingly infinite number of tracts, periodicals, and other religious material produced during the nineteenth century.[43] The increasingly difficult question of what it meant to be a people of the Word posed a challenge for all Evangelicals, some of whom responded by seeking refuge in a more dogmatic insistence on the fundamentals of their faith. By the 1880s, a perceived decline in conservative Evangelical theology meant that the Evangelical Alliance felt the need to organize rallies across the country to defend the truth of the Gospel. The choice of Charles Spurgeon to lead the London rallies of 1888 was significant because of his association with the 'Downgrade Controversy' the previous year. In 1887 a series of articles in *The Sword and the Trowel*, the magazine of Spurgeon's large and influential church in London, argued that ' "rationalism" was threatening evangelical truth, and that as a result, evangelicals as well as liberals were in danger of "going downhill at breakneck speed" '.[44] Other Evangelicals, however, were more willing to adapt their beliefs to a world in which textual meaning seemed increasingly open-ended, and the themes of sin, repentance, and conversion were regularly recycled in novels, albeit with a more qualified and less overt Evangelical tone.

It would be a mistake to presume that the challenge posed by novels simply threatened to replace the biblical narrative with a different story and/or submit the divine Word to market forces in a way previously unparalleled; the way in which Scripture was interpreted was also challenged. In recent times critics have typically emphasized the Bible's plurality and multivocality, but mid-nineteenth-century Evangelicals were far more likely to insist on the essential unity of Scripture. Thus the growth in popularity of the novel, a textual form marked by interpretive indeterminacy, called the dominant Evangelical hermeneutic into question. Evangelicals who regularly read novels were bound to start thinking about the biblical narrative differently. In theory, multiple readings were in keeping with the Evangelical emphasis on individual rather than ecclesial interpretation, but in practice they challenged Evangelical reliance on the alleged univocality, transparency, and simplicity of the Gospel message.

J. Hillis Miller reminds us that *Bleak House* offers a prime example of a novel that actively presents the reader with an indeterminate text:

Bleak House presents the reader with a sick, decaying, moribund society. It locates with profound insight the cause of that sickness in the sign-making power, in the ineradicable human tendency to take the sign for the substance, and in the instinctive habit of interpretation, assimilating others into a private or collective system of meaning. At the same time the novel itself performs a large-scale act of interpretation. If there were no interpretation there would be no novel. It frees itself from the guilt of this only by giving the reader, not least in its inconsistencies, the evidence necessary to see that it *is* an interpretation.[45]

While Miller's theoretical orientation means that his reading does not look for, nor depend upon, the historical setting of *Bleak House*, his claim that Dickens's novel is 'a document about the interpretation of documents', providing infinite interpretive possibilities, points to important cultural parallels with Evangelical attitudes to the divine Word.[46]

In a recent essay that revisits his earlier reading of *Bleak House*, Miller notes the heavy reliance on bodily metaphor in Dickens's novel and details multiple references to the materiality of words, both written and spoken: 'Law documents, for example, are, the reader is often reminded, written on sheepskin (the name of one of Miss Flite's birds). Lady Dedlock's letters are written on paper, the "little bundle" that Bucket at a crucial moment "produces from a mysterious part of his coat".'[47] As Miller goes on to point out, the description of the second Jarndyce will, passed from Grandfather Smallweed to John Jarndyce, is equally revealing: 'a stained discoloured paper, which was much singed upon the outside, and a little burnt at the edges'.[48] Such references lead Miller to shift his focus from how words might be interpreted to the effect that they have: if the writing in *Bleak House* is accompanied by references to material decomposition, the message that *Bleak House* would seem to communicate is that public speech acts, or, as Miller calls them in the title of his essay, 'moments of decision', register little or no positive impact on the world, a claim at odds with Dickens's alleged attempt to bring about social change through writing the novel. The dilemma that Dickens appears to struggle with—whether words register a positive impact on the world—is similar to the one faced by Evangelicals. Inevitably, questions hung over the efficacy of Evangelical preaching, which, when added to a growing realization, conscious or otherwise, that the self-interpreting Word would be misinterpreted without ecclesial guidance, left Evangelicals needing to find every possible way of protesting the authoritative qualities of their message.

PREACHING, REVIVALISM, AND CONVERSION

Some of the question marks that hung over Evangelical preaching surface in *Bleak House* via the overly rhetorical sermonizing of Mr Chadband. His oratory is not only condemned directly—at one point the narrative refers to the 'length of time [he spends] uttering such abominable nonsense'—but also indirectly through the industrial vocabulary used to describe him.[49] References to Chadband's 'general appearance of having a good deal of train oil in his system' and the way in which he 'makes his accustomed signal, and rises with a smoking head', place considerable emphasis on the mechanical process of his preaching.[50] Given the difficulty that Jo, other characters, and the reader have in identifying precisely what it is that Chadband is talking about, this emphasis on process rather than content is significant. Later on in the novel the narrative tells us that:

It happens that Mr. Chadband has a pulpit habit of fixing some member of his congregation with his eye, and fatly arguing his points with that particular person; who is understood to be expected to be moved to an occasional grunt, groan, gasp, or other audible expression of inward working; which expression of inward working, being echoed by some elderly lady in the next pew, and so communicated, like a game of forfeits, through a circle of the more fermentable sinners present, serves the purpose of parliamentary cheering, and gets Mr. Chadband's steam up.[51]

In this case the text's emphasis of process over content implies that Chadband's preaching has nothing to say: his refusal to stop speaking can be read as an attempt to defer endlessly the moment of decision, when his listeners will have the opportunity to stop and evaluate what has been said to them.

Dickens was not the only writer to equate Evangelicalism with empty rhetoric. One of the most dramatic moments in Eliot's *Middlemarch* occurs when Bulstrode proves unable to live up to the belief he forcefully professes, while the insincerity of the Evangelical characters in Trollope's *Rachel Ray* (1863) caused *Good Words* to renege on its original agreement to publish this novel.[52] Collins levels further charges of insincerity in two of his novels from the 1860s, *Armadale* (1864–6) and *The Moonstone*. At the conclusion of the former, Mother Oldershaw's eloquence is the subject of Mustapha's cynical invitation to Pedgrift Senior: 'They stop acting on the stage, I grant you, on Sunday evening—but they don't stop acting in the pulpit. Come and see the last new Sunday performer of our time.'[53] Mustapha's juxtaposition of the 'last' and the 'new' locates Evangelicalism as both anachronistic and culpable amid the development of a culture that is increasingly reliant on performance. The make-up worn by the ladies in attendance symbolizes the lack of authenticity in the message, as does the sceptical Pedgrift Senior's admiration of Mother Oldershaw's ability to hold forth: 'You never listened to anything more eloquent in your life.'[54] By focusing on the impressiveness of the thing that has been said rather than the reality behind it, Pedgrift Senior's remark shows how the Evangelical reliance on preaching inadvertently shifts the focus to performance rather than the message's essential content.

Despite insisting that they held to an unmediated Bible that spoke clearly, Evangelicals were renowned for their mediation and performance of the Gospel message. This is a major theme of *The Moonstone*, where Godfrey Ablewhite, a man whose true nature is rather different from the one that impresses Miss Clack with 'all the fascination of his Evangelical voice and manner', is seen to embody the emptiness and potential hypocrisy of Evangelical rhetoric.[55] Godfrey's claim to godliness is intrinsically linked to his ability to perform, and his reputation is built upon the success of his speaking performances at Exeter Hall. The first time the reader is introduced to Godfrey, Betteredge writes: 'He was quite a public character. The last time I was in London, my mistress gave me two treats. She sent me to the theatre to see a dancing woman who was all the rage; and she sent me to Exeter Hall to hear Mr Godfrey. The lady did it, with a band of music. The gentleman did it, with a handkerchief and a glass of water. Crowds at the performance with the legs. Ditto at the performance with the tongue.'[56] Elsewhere in *The*

Moonstone, Evangelicalism is shown to be caught up in the emptiness of its own rhetoric, a point underlined by the susceptibility of Miss Clack to Godfrey's performances: 'The heavenly gentleness of his smile made his apologies irresistible. The richness of his deep voice added its own indescribable charm.'[57]

The reference to Exeter Hall in *The Moonstone* indicates the importance of this establishment as a marker of Evangelical identity. Beyond being a convenient gathering point for Evangelicals in the mid-nineteenth century, Exeter Hall offered, in the words of one critic, 'the great theatre for the concentration of Protestant Christianity'.[58] Like actors, preachers on the stage of Exeter Hall were praised for their dynamism and reputations were built on their ability to impress the audiences who flocked to hear them.[59] Commenting on the so-called May Meetings, in which religious and philanthropic societies gathered at Exeter Hall for their annual public meetings, W. M. McDonnell described the 'anticipation' with which the 'religious world' attended, and how 'each particular church or society makes a strong endeavour to win pious fame on the great platform'.[60] While Exeter Hall was not the only forum in which the reputation of preachers was built, it highlighted the Evangelical dependence on large events and dramatic accounts of religious experience. These qualities also lay behind the Evangelical association with Revivalism, which emphasized powerful experiences of conversion and a renewal of faith through meetings at which the presence of God was felt to be especially present. The experience of a revival of faith had been central to John Wesley, George Whitefield, and others throughout the rise of Evangelicalism in the eighteenth and nineteenth centuries, and although Revivals were invariably short lived, they successfully renewed and invigorated Evangelicalism, albeit at the cost of sharp criticism about the conditions they allegedly manipulated. Valentine Cunningham explains: 'The 1859 Revival in Ireland signalled, according to J. Edwin Orr, a Second Evangelical Revival to match the eighteenth-century awakening: an era of Spurgeon and the Salvation Army, of Moody and Sankey, of Missions and Lord Shaftsbury. Atheists, like John Chapman, were expectably antagonistic. Prominent among the conditions for revival, Chapman claimed, were ignorance, and illiteracy, and emotionalism triumphing over intellect.'[61]

A subconscious recognition of the force of Chapman's critique may help to explain Evangelical participation in the widespread condemnation of the sensation novel during the 1860s. Although sensation novels existed before 1860 and continued well beyond 1870, the genre gained notoriety in the 1860s as the result of several vehement attacks on the propriety of these tales by critics, several of whom were Evangelicals. It makes sense to read the complaints within Evangelical periodicals such as *The Christian Observer*, which warned of 'real evils connected with a sensational literature', in the light of criticisms about the emotional manipulation of Revivalism and the Evangelical reaction to these criticisms.[62] Ostensibly, Evangelicals attributed the 'real evils' of sensation fiction to its alleged immorality, but given the conservative narrative of the genre (villains are usually killed, disfigured, or incarcerated) and the fact that Evangelicals were not averse to using sensational techniques themselves, the real reason is less straightforward.[63] Upon turning to the article on 'Sensational Literature' in *The Christian Observer*, we find that its attack is prefaced by an insistence that '*sensationalism*' is not 'a necessary evil'.[64] After noting the possible American origin of the word—a reference to the transatlantic source of Revivalism—the article admits: 'we cannot help thinking that, were sensationalism altogether ostracised [from pulpits], many a strong and telling method of impressing men and moving the conscience would have to give place to tame platitudes and intolerable iteration.'[65] This suggests that the Evangelical reaction against sensation fiction is best explained in terms of an anxiety arising out of the recognition that sensation fiction and the conversion narratives favoured by Evangelicalism in general and Revivalism in particular, shared much in common.

In an attempt to accentuate their account of God's work in people's lives, Evangelical testimonies frequently described in lurid detail the pre-conversion experience of sin. One of the few distinctions between sensation fiction and Evangelical testimony lay in the teleology of the narrative, but even this distinction was often blurred: on the one hand, by the assertion of a conservative moral code at the conclusion to many sensation novels, and on the other, by the depiction of Evangelical converts (such as Bulstrode in *Middlemarch*) falling back into sin after their initial conversion. Moreover, the difference between descriptions of falling into sin and converting from sin were minimal. In both cases, personal responsibility was offset by a series of other factors (e.g. persuasive comments, social pressures, individual distress) and the decision to change was typically located in contexts that were emotionally charged and open to the possibility of manipulation. In *East Lynne* (1860–1) Isabel's 'sinful' decision to leave her husband takes place amid 'bitter distress and wrath', and 'a storm of sobs'; her subsequent conviction of sin is concurrent with a 'recent and depressing illness, the conviction of Sir Francis Levison's complete worthlessness, [and] the terrible position in which she found herself'; and her final deathbed request for forgiveness is motivated by guilt and anxiety: ' "The longing for you was killing me", she reiterated wildly, as one talking in a fever. "I never knew a moment's peace after the mad act I was guilty of, in leaving you ... Oh, forgive me, forgive me! My sin was great, but my punishment has been greater. It has been as one long scene of mortal agony".'[66] What troubled Evangelicals was not that sensational characters such as Lady Audley (in *Lady Audley's Secret*) and Lydia Gwilt (in *Armadale*) committed sinful acts, but that these acts appeared to be motivated by emotional and environmental reasons similar to the conversions on which they laid so much store.

The problem for Evangelicals was exacerbated by the contiguous manifestation of the Ulster Revival of 1859 and the 1860s controversy over sensation fiction. Many critics expressed alarm at the way in which sensation novels sought to bypass the mind and stimulate the nerves. The Evangelical emphasis on the need for individuals to repent of their sin meant that they were keen to resist any attempt at undermining human volition, yet the prominence of bodily manifestations during the Ulster Revival was open to the same charge of emotional manipulation. Ironically, the contradiction in the Evangelical position towards preaching to the nerves was mirrored by sensation writers such as Dickens, whose literary manipulation of the nerves of his readers (through the use, for instance, of cliffhangers in the serial instalments of his novels) coincided with a critique of the bodily manifestations of Revival (such as Mrs Cruncher's 'flopping' in *A Tale of Two Cities*). In response to criticisms of the Ulster Revival, the Evangelical Alliance commissioned the Reverend Dr James McCosh, Professor of Mental Philosophy at Queen's College Belfast, to write a defence for the October 1859 issue of *Evangelical Christendom*. Responding to 'the physician of wide and diversified experience [who] tells me, "Oh, I have, in my visits, seen precisely similar bodily effects, and these having no connexion with religion" ',[67] McCosh could only respond by shifting emphasis away from bodily manifestations and insisting that the authenticity of the Revival was contingent on spiritual rather than physical signs. While his claim that a genuine revival of faith could be seen in a 'newness of life and conduct' was perfectly reasonable, McCosh's inability to escape the possibility that, at least in some instances, physical manifestations might be the consequence of emotional manipulation, conscious or otherwise, helps explain why Evangelicals were so anxious to insist, at times hysterically and unreasonably, that there were clear differences between conversion narratives and sensation fiction.[68]

TEMPTATION, FALLEN WOMEN, AND JUDGEMENT

Several novels sought to question Evangelical claims about the power of conversion by depicting pious men who continued to struggle with sin. In *Barchester Towers* (1857) Mr Slope is powerless to stop himself falling for the married Siagnora Neroni: 'Mr Slope could not help himself. He knew that he was wrong ... He knew that he was acting against the recognised principles of his life ... But as we have said, he could not help himself. Passion, for the first time in his life, passion was too strong for him.'[69] The repetitive textual insistence on Slope's helplessness is evident again a few pages later, when he is said to be incapable of walking away from temptation: 'he could not do it'.[70] This narrative challenge to Evangelical claims about the power of the Cross is mirrored in *Middlemarch*, where Eliot offers a deeper and more thoughtful portrayal of an Evangelical, Bulstrode, unable to live consistently with his beliefs. The narrator explains: 'He was simply a man whose desires had been stronger than his theoretic beliefs, and who had gradually explained the gratification of his desires into satisfactory agreement with those beliefs.'[71] Although the narrator is sympathetic and willing to defend Bulstrode's hypocrisy on the grounds that 'it is a process which shows itself occasionally in us all', the defence is offered at the cost of a belief in the power of conversion to transform an individual's life and conduct.[72] Given the force of this critique, it is significant that one of the major forces within Evangelicalism during the late nineteenth and early twentieth centuries was the Keswick Movement, a movement dedicated to the pursuit of individual holiness and the ongoing work of sanctification in the life of the believer.

Gloomy assessments of the Evangelical struggle with temptation were even more marked when applied to women who ventured outside of the home. In the influential *Family Fortunes* Leonore Davidoff and Catherine Hall devote considerable space to assessing the cultural impact of Evangelical theology, and its contribution to 'the emergence of a series of beliefs and practices as to the distinct and separate spheres of male and female'.[73] Central to this ideology was a belief that the home was the most appropriate sphere for women. If, as Davidoff and Hall go on to argue, '[d]ependence was at the core of the Evangelical Christian view of womanhood', it followed that women who ventured outside the secure environment of the home were at particular risk of falling into sin.[74] The Evangelical preoccupation with certain New Testament letters that, when read 'literally', seemed to promote female subjection, allied with the general importance of the home for Evangelicalism, encouraged the view that women needed the spiritual guidance of a husband to resist temptation.[75] This perspective was hardly new—Milton's *Paradise Lost* offers a similar perspective in its revision of the Genesis myth, depicting Eve as the weaker party who succumbs to Satan's flattery when she is isolated from her husband—but it was promoted actively by a stream of influential Evangelical writers going back to Hannah More.[76]

At the same time, one has to be careful about interpreting the concurrence of Evangelical theology and patriarchal ideas of female domesticity within a simplistic framework of religious cause and cultural effect. Even if one accepts the view that Evangelical theology was causal to some degree, a nuanced reading is required, such as that offered by Kathryn Gleadle in her introduction to *Radical Writing on Women, 1800–1850: An Anthology*:

By essentializing the supposedly female characteristics of loving, caring and morality, Evangelical literature not only provided a route whereby women could claim a duty to intervene in community and philanthropic endeavours, it also paradoxically refocused attention upon women's domestic and maternal roles. This was a complex ideological configuration; but undoubtedly, the Evangelical insistence on recognizing women's worth and significance played an important part in shifting cultural attitudes towards positive roles for women.[77]

Support for Gleadle's claim that the Evangelical focus on domesticity implicitly undermined the separate-sphere ideology it sought to promote can be found in the figure of Catherine Booth and the work of the Salvation Army. In contrast to many other denominations, the Salvation Army followed the example of their female co-founder and encouraged women to preach the Gospel, a role traditionally seen by Evangelicals as a male preserve. Pamela Walker tells us that Catherine 'exemplified a new model of Christian womanhood, articulating a new approach to female ministry and creating an influential career as an evangelist. As well as formulating the Salvation Army's egalitarian policies, she served as an inspiration to thousands of young women who preached under the aegis of the organization.'[78] While the example of Catherine

Booth might be seen as an exception that proves the rule (the Booths suffered considerable criticism from fellow Evangelicals for encouraging female ministry), it reminds us that Evangelicalism was capable of accommodating and even encouraging female emancipation.

In 1885 the Salvation Army joined forces with W. T. Stead to expose the danger of children and young women falling into prostitution. With the aid of members of the Salvation Army, who helped him procure a child from a brothel, Stead wrote up his sensational investigative journalism in a series of pieces for the *Pall Mall Gazette*.[79] One consequence of the subsequent outcry was to lend support to the campaign of Josephine Butler, another prominent Evangelical, for the age of consent for women to be raised to 16. Although this episode shows Evangelical women exerting significant influence in the public sphere, it also illustrates the complicity of Evangelicalism in perpetuating a view of women as being at greater risk of sin than men and thus in need of additional legal protection. Commenting on the previous generation, Sally Mitchell helpfully traces the Evangelical vocabulary embedded in popular attitudes towards women and temptation during the 1860s: 'A woman who falls from her purity can never return to ordinary society, and a woman's soul is so refined that it has, ironically, grown too thin and fragile to protect her: a woman is in greater danger than a man.'[80]

The enduring trope of the fallen women and its debt to Evangelicalism are visible beyond the mid-nineteenth century, in Thomas Hardy's *Tess of the D'Urbervilles* (1891). Hardy depicts Tess as a tragic heroine, prone to sin and incapable of resisting the dark hand of providence that seemingly conspires to bring about her demise. Although the main Evangelical character in the novel, Reverend Clare, an 'Evangelical of the Evangelicals' described with great sympathy and respect by the narrative, is seen to belong to an era whose time has passed, his legacy inadvertently contributes to Tess's suffering in two ways.[81] First, the inability of Reverend Clare's Evangelical faith to answer the critical questions posed by his son forms an important part of Angel Clare's subsequent failure to forgive Tess the 'sin' she confesses. The inherited vocabulary of sin and shame is no longer accompanied by the possibility of grace, and Angel is left trying 'desperately to advance among the new conditions in which he stood. Some consequent action was necessary; yet what?'[82] Second, when Reverend Clare's preaching leads to the conversion of Alex d'Urberville, it inadvertently provides a vocabulary that Alex uses to justify his selfish ongoing desire for Tess. Alex complains:

I ask myself, am I, indeed, one of those 'servants of corruption' who, 'after they have escaped the pollutions of the world, are again entangled therein and overcome'—whose latter end is worse than their beginning? ... I was firm as a man could be till I saw those eyes and that mouth again—surely there never was such a maddening mouth since Eve's! ... You temptress, Tess; you dear damned witch of Babylon—I could not resist you as soon as I met you again![83]

In the case of both Angel and Alex, the legacy of Evangelical theology is judgement. Although the novel strips this doctrine of the support needed to make it intellectually coherent, it signals helpfully the way in which judgement was a significant corollary of nineteenth-century Evangelical thought.

One of the ways in which Evangelicals sought to accentuate the power of and need for salvation, was to describe the danger of hell in graphic detail. Particularly in popular Evangelical tracts and preaching, sinners were frequently urged to repent in order to avoid the terrors of hell. However, not everyone found this emphasis on hell satisfactory, and the influence of other viewpoints, such as the universalism of the Unitarians, made substantial inroads by the middle of the century into the way many Victorians thought about the afterlife. In 1853 growing doubts over hell were made public when F. D. Maurice, professor of theology at King's College, London, published *Theological Essays*. Maurice was highly equivocal in the position he took over the reality of hell, but his willingness to question the nature and duration of separation from God caused considerable outcry, as did his willingness to entertain universal views on the matter of salvation. Although the Evangelicals at King's College were able to force Maurice's resignation, the matter refused to go away. Reverend H. B. Wilson questioned everlasting punishment in his contribution to *Essays and Reviews*, and Bishop Colenso followed suit in his *Commentary on Romans* (1861). If, at first, the debate over hell seemed to be located outside of strict Evangelical confines, this was not to last: when Thomas Rawson Birks, secretary of the Evangelical Alliance and one of its co-founders, published a reinterpretation of hell in *Victory of Divine Goodness* (1867), he came under criticism from certain members of the Alliance and ended up resigning his office. As Randall and Hilborn explain in their history of the Evangelical Alliance, Birks 'took a broadly restitutionist line, going so far as to suggest that "the lost" might develop in the afterlife to a point where they could eventually share some of the joy of God's re-made cosmos, if not its full blessings'. In some ways, Birks's position was compatible with the Evangelical Alliance's formal statement of belief: 'His scheme *did* maintain unbelievers in an eternal realm rather than annihilating them, and this eternal realm *was* divided off from heaven. It was, however, palliative (if not exactly remedial), and this hardly reflected the intent of those Americans who had first inserted the "hell" clause into the Basis of Faith.'[84]

As the century developed, Evangelicals became less confident in asserting that those who had died were going to endure everlasting conscious torment, and fewer writers, Evangelical or otherwise, ended their stories by condemning individuals to severe providential judgement. Nevertheless, the language of hell and judgement did not disappear: 'While the theologians wrangled over key words and doctrines, the leading novelists and poets, most of whom held liberal or radically revisionary views on the subject, continued to find in the language traditionally associated with hell a repertoire of resonances and associations through which to describe spiritual experience in the here-and-now.'[85] The ability of writers to reinterpret the language of hell raises interesting questions about the extent and nature of secularization towards the end of the nineteenth century, which are examined further in the next chapter. For now, the capacity of the doctrine of hell to be reinterpreted rather than forgotten leads us back to the question of what it meant for Evangelicals to define themselves in terms of faithful adherence to the Word of God. Commenting on the controversy over Birks, Geoffrey Rowell explains how, 'in 1846, the confession of faith of the Evangelical Alliance had been expanded, [and] a clause affirming eternal punishment had been added, chiefly at the request of American delegates, alarmed by the spread of universalist and annihilationist ideas'; but the example of Birks highlights the difficulty of relying on doctrinal statements as a means of securing theological orthodoxy among Evangelicals.[86] As the diversity of its adherents attests, a capacity for interpretive freedom and slippage was integral to Evangelicalism, rather than an isolated phenomenon, even if Evangelicals were slow to acknowledge that this was so. Eliot highlights the problem within Evangelical hermeneutics when attacking Dr Cumming for the inconsistency with which he insists on the 'rigorous literality' of words.[87] She complains how, when talking about the doctrine of Eternal Punishment, 'the text becomes elastic for him when he wants freer play for his prejudices'.[88] Although Eliot's assessment of the Evangelical propensity for reading the script in different, even contradictory, ways is fair, it inadvertently undermines the one-dimensional caricature of Evangelicalism that her essay on Cumming seeks to construct. Evangelicals may have sometimes been oblivious to their capacity for interpreting the Word in different ways, but it is this variation in reading the Word that helps explain how an apparently narrow movement was able to exert such a substantial and diverse influence upon the whole gamut of nineteenth-century culture.

NOTES

1. Eliot was a fervent Evangelical in her early years. Useful discussions of her changing beliefs can be found in V. Cunningham, *Everywhere Spoken Against: Dissent in the Victorian Novel* (Oxford: Clarendon Press, 1975), and G. Levine (ed.), *The Cambridge Companion to George Eliot* (Cambridge: Cambridge University Press, 2001).

2. G. Eliot, 'Evangelical Teaching: Dr Cumming', *Westminster Review*, 16 (Oct. 1855), 436–62 (457).

3. P. Davis, *The Oxford English Literary History*, viii. *1830–1880: The Victorians* (Oxford: Oxford University Press, 2002), 105.

4. For a helpful account of Ruskin's Evangelical upbringing and his subsequent turn from it, see M. Wheeler, *Ruskin's God* (Cambridge: Cambridge University Press, 1999).

5. E. Jay, *Faith and Doubt in Victorian Britain* (Basingstoke: Macmillan, 1986), 8.

6. M. Oliphant, *The Life of Edward Irving*, 2nd edn. (London: Hurst and Blackett, 1862), i. 202.

7. Jay, *Faith and Doubt*, 1.

8. D. W. Bebbington, *Evangelicalism in Modern Britain: A History from the 1730s to the 1980s* (London: Unwin Hyman, 1989), 2–3.

9. Thoughtful discussions concerning the London Missionary Society and Religious Tract Society in the nineteenth century can be found in A. Johnston, *Missionary Writing and Empire, 1800–1860* (Cambridge: Cambridge University Press, 2003), and A. Fyfe, *Science and Salvation: Evangelical Popular Science Publishing in Victorian Britain* (Chicago: University of Chicago Press, 2004). For a broader overview of Evangelical activism in the nineteenth century, see Bebbington, *Evangelicalism in Modern Britain*, and I. Bradley, *The Call to Seriousness: The Evangelical Impact on the Victorians* (London: Cape, 1976).

10. C. Dickens, *Bleak House* (1852–3), ed. O. Sitwell (Oxford: Oxford Illustrated Dickens, 1991), 60.

11. Ibid. 41.

12. F. Morell Holmes, *Exeter Hall and its Associations* (London: Hodder & Stoughton, 1881), 29–30.

13. Christian Union, *A Full Report of the Proceedings of the Great Meeting Held at Exeter Hall, 1st June 1843 to promote and extend Christian Union* (London: D. Stroud, 1843), 10.

14. Anti-Catholicism might be seen as endemic to Protestantism rather than just Evangelicalism. This is the implied position of V. Sage, *Horror Fiction in the Protestant Tradition* (Basingstoke: Macmillan, 1988), which locates the anti-Catholic subtext of the Gothic novel as a Protestant rather than an Evangelical phenomenon. For a helpful account of the relationship between Protestant and Evangelical identity, see J. Wolffe, *The Protestant Crusade in Great Britain, 1829–1860* (Oxford: Clarendon Press, 1991).

15. T. Chalmers *et al.*, *Essays on Christian Union* (London: Hamilton, Adams and Co., 1845), 163.

16. E. Jay (ed.), *The Evangelical and Oxford Movements* (Cambridge: Cambridge University Press, 1983), 16.

17. For helpful introductions to the work of Thomas Reid (1710–96), see N. Wolterstorff, *Thomas Reid and the Story of Epistemology* (Cambridge: Cambridge University Press, 2001), and T. Cuneo and R. van Woudenberg (eds.), *The Cambridge Companion to Thomas Reid* (Cambridge: Cambridge University Press, 2004).

18. C. Dickens, *David Copperfield* (1849–50), ed. R. H. Malden (Oxford: Oxford Illustrated Dickens, 1996), 52.

19. C. Brontë, *Jane Eyre* (1847), ed. M. Smith (Oxford: Oxford World's Classics, 2000), 66.

20. Ibid. 352.

21. Ibid.

22. Famously, Max Weber offers an extended argument regarding the link between capitalism and Protestantism. See M. Weber, *The Protestant Ethic and the Spirit of Capitalism*, trans. T. Parsons (London: Allen and Unwin, 1930).

23. W. Collins, *The Moonstone* (1868), ed. J. Stewart (Harmondsworth: Penguin Classics, 1986), 268.

24. Johnston, *Missionary Writing and Empire*, 13. Further discussion of the crossover between missionary activity and imperialism can be found in A. Porter, *Religion versus Empire: British Protestant Missionaries and Overseas Expansion, 1700–1914* (Manchester: Manchester University Press, 2004), and J. Cox, *Imperial Fault Lines: Christianity and Colonial Power in India, 1818–1940* (Stanford, Calif.: Stanford University Press, 2002).

25. Collins, *The Moonstone*, 240.

26. Ibid. 518.

27. J. C. Ryle, 'Evangelical Religion: What it is, and What it is not', in *Truths for the Times* (London: William Hunt and Company, 1867), 138.

28. Collins, *The Moonstone*, 273.

29. For more detailed accounts of the reception of *Essays and Reviews* in Victorian culture, see J. L. Altholz, *Anatomy of a Controversy: The Debate over Essays and Reviews 1860–1864* (Aldershot: Scholar Press, 1994), I. Ellis, *Seven Against Christ: A Study of 'Essays and Reviews'* (Leiden: Brill, 1980), and V. Shea and W. Whitla (eds.), *Essays and Reviews: The 1860 Text and its Reading* (Charlottesville, Va.: University Press of Virginia, 2000).

30. Adelphos, 'Modern Spurious Revivals', in *The Revival: An Advocate of Evangelical Truth,* 14 (6 Feb. 1866), 71–3 (72).

31. Anon., 'Theodore Parker and the Oxford Essayists', *The Christian Observer,* 60 (July 1860), 467–87 (485).

32. B. Jowett, 'On the Interpretation of Scripture', in Shea and Whitla (eds.), *Essays and Reviews: The 1860 Text and its Reading*, 504.

33. Anon., 'The Defects of Broad Church Theology', *Evangelical Christendom,* 6 (1 May 1865), 211–16 (216).

34. Collins, *The Moonstone*, 258–9.

35. Anon., 'Unity of Creed: The Union of the Christian Church', *The Revival: An Advocate of Evangelical Truth,* 15 (1866), 71–3 (71).

36. For a good account of the changing legal and theological views of evidence in the nineteenth century, see J. Melissa Schramm, *Testimony and Advocacy in Victorian Law, Literature and Theology* (Cambridge: Cambridge University Press, 2000).

37. Anon., 'Review of Thomas Bowdler's *The Family Shakespeare; in which nothing is added to the original text, but those words and expressions are omitted which cannot with propriety be read in a family*', *The Christian Observer*, 60 (May 1860), 360–1 (360).

38. The term 'aura' is used by Walter Benjamin in his famous essay 'The Work of Art in the Mechanical Age of Reproduction' (1936). See W. Benjamin, *Illuminations*, ed. H. Arendt (London: Pimlico, 1999).

39. Anon., 'Cleaving to the Dust', *The Evangelical Magazine*, 6 (Dec. 1864), 791–4 (792).

40. See P. Srebrnik, *Alexander Strahan: Victorian Publisher* (Ann Arbor: University of Michigan Press, 1986). Srebrnik points out that the sales figures of the two periodicals were comparable in the early 1860s.

41. D. Macleod, *Memoir of Norman Macleod,* 2 vols. (London: Daldy, Isbister and Co., 1876), ii. 110.

42. Anon., *Good Words: The Theology of its Editor and of Some of its Contributors,* 2nd edn. (London: The Record Offices, 1863), 2.

43. S. Zemka, *Victorian Testaments: The Bible, Christology, and Literary Authority in Early-Nineteenth-Century British Culture* (Stanford, Calif.: Stanford University Press, 1997), 191.

44. I. Randall and D. Hilborn, *One Body in Christ: The History and Significance of the Evangelical Alliance* (Carlisle: Paternoster Press, 2001), 114.

45. J. Hillis Miller, 'Introduction', in C. Dickens, *Bleak House* (Harmondsworth: Penguin Classics, 1971), 33–4.

46. Ibid. 11.

47. J. Hillis Miller, 'Moments of Decision in *Bleak House*', in J. Jordan (ed.), *The Cambridge Companion to Charles Dickens* (Cambridge: Cambridge University Press, 2001), 54–5.

48. Dickens, *Bleak House* (1991 edn.), 841.

49. Ibid. 270.

50. Ibid. 262, 269.

51. Ibid. 358.

52. For a more detailed discussion of the events leading up to Norman Macleod's decision to change his mind about publishing Trollope's novel, see the chapter on *Good Words* and *Rachel Ray* in M. Turner, *Trollope and the Magazines: Gendered Issues in Mid-Victorian Britain* (Basingstoke: Palgrave, 2000).

53. W. Collins, *Armadale* (1864–6), ed. J. Sutherland (Harmondsworth: Penguin Books, 1995), 674.

54. Ibid.

55. Collins, *The Moonstone*, 280.

56. Ibid. 89.

57. Ibid. 246.

58. W. M. McDonnell, *Exeter Hall: A Theological Romance,* 10th edn. (Boston: Colby & Rich Publishers, 1885), 3. First published in 1869, McDonnell's text was an explicit attack on Evangelical Christianity. The first chapter of his story offered some introductory remarks on the history and significance of Exeter Hall.

59. In this regard, Exeter Hall was firmly rooted in the Evangelical tradition. In his biography of the great Evangelical preacher George Whitefield, Harry Stout details the continuity between Whitefield's acting experience and his skill as a preacher. See H. Stout, *The Divine Dramatist: George Whitefield and the Rise of Modern Evangelicalism* (Grand Rapids, Mich.: Eerdmans, 1991).

60. McDonnell, *Exeter Hall: A Theological Romance,* 3.

61. Cunningham, *Everywhere Spoken Against,* 34.

62. Anon., 'Sensational Literature', *The Christian Observer,* 65 (Nov. 1865), 809–13 (810).

63. Commenting on Evangelical publications earlier in the century, Samuel Pickering writes: 'Although the *Methodist Magazine* was particularly given to printing sensation tales, such stories appeared in all popular religious journals. Not only did they undermine the periodicals' jeremiads against the novel but they also whetted appetites for novels.' See S. Pickering, *The Moral Tradition in English Fiction, 1785–1850* (Hanover, NH: The University Press of New England, 1976), 69.

64. Anon., 'Sensational Literature', 810.

65. Ibid.

66. E. Wood, *East Lynne* (1860–1), ed. A. Maunder (Peterborough, Ontario: Broadview, 2002), 322, 350, 680.

67. J. McCosh, 'The Ulster Revival and its Physiological Accidents', *Evangelical Christendom,* 13 (1 Oct. 1859), 368–75 (371).

68. Ibid. 371.

69. A. Trollope, *Barchester Towers* (1857), ed. J. Sutherland (Oxford: Oxford University Press, 1998), 270.

70. Ibid. 279.

71. G. Eliot, *Middlemarch* (1871–2), ed. D. Carroll (Oxford: Oxford World's Classics, 1998), 581.

72. Ibid.

73. L. Davidoff and C. Hall, *Family Fortunes: Men and Women of the English Middle Class, 1780–1850*, 2nd edn. (London: Routledge, 2002), 74.

74. Ibid. 114.

75. A number of Evangelicals eschewed Paul's comments in Galatians in favour of the advice given in 1 Corinthians, Ephesians, and 1 Timothy regarding the relative positions of men and women. For a useful account of the importance of the home for Evangelicalism, see E. Jay, *Religion of the Heart: Anglican Evangelicalism and the Nineteenth-Century Novel* (Oxford: Clarendon Press, 1979), 131–48.

76. Although Hannah More died in 1833, her writings remained popular throughout the mid-nineteenth century and were frequently reprinted. In a useful corrective to the commonplace idea that Hannah More's domestic focus was at the expense of any public political engagement, Anne Stott reminds us: 'Whether it was sending money to an election campaign, petitioning parliament, dashing off an election ballad, or painstakingly distilling the fruits of her wide reading into an advice book for a princess, she used the ways available to women to enter the great public debates. Indeed, More believed that it was her *duty* to intervene in such issues.' A. Stott, 'Patriotism and Providence: The Politics of Hannah More', in K. Gleadle and S. Richardson (eds.), *Women in British Politics 1760–1860: The Power of the Petticoat* (Basingstoke: Macmillan Press, 2000), 39–55.

77. K. Gleadle (ed.), *Radical Writing on Women, 1800–1850: An Anthology* (Basingstoke: Palgrave, 2002), 13.

78. P. J. Walker, *Pulling the Devil's Kingdom Down: The Salvation Army in Victorian Britain* (Berkeley: University of California Press, 2001), 8–9.

79. Further discussion of Stead's association with the Salvation Army can be found in the next chapter of this book.

80. S. Mitchell, *The Fallen Angel: Chastity, Class and Women's Reading, 1835–1880* (Bowling Green, Oh.: Bowling Green University Popular Press, 1981), p. x.

81. T. Hardy, *Tess of the D'Urbervilles* (1891), ed. D. Skilton (Harmondsworth: Penguin Classics, 1985), 217.

82. Ibid. 300

83. Ibid. 402.

84. Randall and Hilborn, *One Body in Christ*, 122.

85. M. Wheeler, *Heaven, Hell and the Victorians* (Cambridge: Cambridge University Press, 1994), 196.

86. G. Rowell, *Hell and the Victorians: A Study of the Nineteenth-Century Theological Controversies Concerning Eternal Punishment and the Future Life* (Oxford: Clarendon Press, 1974), 127.

87. Eliot, 'Dr Cumming', 456.

88. Ibid.

5

Secularization: Dickens to Hardy

ACCORDING to the sociologist of religion Steve Bruce, writing in *God is Dead: Secularization in the West*, 'modernization creates problems for religion'.[1] By evoking Nietzsche's infamous pronouncement in the book's title, Bruce signals from the outset his belief that the problems had proved too much for Christianity by the beginning of the twentieth century, and the rest of his book details the ways in which the forces of modernity brought this to pass. Despite Bruce's confident and articulate defence of the secularization thesis, his writing is notably defensive at several points, inadvertently revealing the extent to which secularization theory has been the subject of vociferous criticism over the past twenty years. Following Rodney Stark and William Bainbridge's rejection of the secularization paradigm in *The Future of Religion: Secularization, Revival and Cult Formation*, which claimed that religion has shown a capacity to renew itself amid modernity through cults and sects, scholars from a multitude of disciplines have become increasingly sceptical about the notion that a linear and inescapable erosion of faith was at an advanced stage by the second half of the nineteenth century. Historians have questioned the assumption that late Victorians were significantly less religious than their predecessors; sociologists have expressed doubts about the quantitative data used to chart a decline; and literary and cultural critics have shown a renewed interest in the multitude of writings from the second half of the nineteenth century pertaining to the supernatural.[2]

Nevertheless, the disruption of the secularization paradigm has its limits; as Alex Owen reminds us in her magisterial *The Place of Enchantment: British Occultism and the Culture of the Modern*: 'however much the theory of secularization has been critiqued—and the notion of the secular itself differently defined—the concept of a rational secularized culture as a key signifier of modernity has remained a constant.'[3] Through her examination of the occult, Owen seeks to reconfigure our understanding of the relationship between spirituality and modernity, and contest the assumption that religion simply disappeared as modernity advanced. Such work is a helpful corrective to the implicit and explicit accounts of decline provided by famous Victorian chroniclers of religion such as George Eliot, Matthew Arnold, and Samuel Butler. While there can be little doubt that modernity revolutionized society and posed major challenges for religion, it does not follow that modernity disrupted a profoundly Christian era and necessitated its decline. Modernity disrupted a pre-modern era, and Christianity was forced to try to adapt accordingly, as it had been forced to respond to other dramatic cultural changes throughout history. Rather than applying secularization theory in an indiscriminate and dogmatic fashion to insist upon the historic inevitability of religious decline, it is more constructive, and more accurate, to think about the ways in which Christianity adapted its form and message to engage with widespread cultural change. Not only does this help uncover a strong religious presence beyond the period when it was supposed to have fallen into dramatic decline; it resists the monolithic assumption of secularization theory that religion cannot have a place in the modern world.

Like many other well-known writers of the Victorian period, Charles Dickens translated and reinterpreted the religious beliefs he inherited. The tendency among certain critics to treat his work as secular rather than religious erects a false dichotomy. To describe Dickens as a religious writer does not stop us thinking about the secular in his writing any more than it requires a typological or decontextualized 'Christian' reading of his texts; instead, it calls for an openness to the breadth of religious discourse that one might expect to find in the writings of a mid-nineteenth-century writer. Only then can one appreciate how Dickens's writing embodies the religious and the secular simultaneously. Janet Larson frames the blurred distinctions astutely in *Dickens and the Broken Scripture* when she argues that Dickens sought to invoke and revise the Bible in his work.[4] Although the most explicit example of this rewriting is evident in a text that Dickens intended solely for private circulation — *The Life of our Lord* (1846) — one finds it throughout his writing. Recognizing the prevalence of biblical references elsewhere in Dickens's work leads to greater interpretive weight being placed on the absences in the religious narrative of *A Christmas Carol* (1843). In the story the supernatural intervention of Marley's ghost prompts an investigation into the real meaning of Christmas. The investigation concludes by replacing the explicit theological detail of the Christmas story with a new carol, one that translates the Gospel in terms of human charity and love for one's neighbour. Dickens deliberately recalls the Gospels' accounts of Jesus as the light of the world—for example, Scrooge attempts, unsuccessfully, to smother 'the light, which streamed from under [the extinguisher-cap], in an unbroken flood'—only to empty the symbol of any direct reference to Deity.[5] The 'Wise Men' are only mentioned in passing, the (Holy) Ghost proceeds from Marley rather than the Father, and the narrative displays no interest in exploring the 'sacred name and origin' of the Incarnation.[6]

The narrow parameters of secularization theory insist that texts like *A Christmas Carol* be read as unambiguous evidence for the decline of religion by the mid-nineteenth century. To move with such ease, however, from a local text to a grand narrative is problematic. Leaving aside the difficulties involved in any historical generalization, it is hard for twenty-first-century critics to reconstruct how readers in the 1840s, living in an age where religious discourse was integral to daily life, would have interpreted the absence of explicit theological references. Whatever the answer to this, the text requires some theological awareness for its effect: the sentimentalized moral injunction for Scrooge to cease his commercial exploitation depends upon the underlying assumption that Christmas is a special time of year, an assumption inseparable from its religious roots. Even if the text is to be read as a deliberate attempt to empty the Christmas narrative of its theological content rather than translating the Gospel in a way consistent with the confessional community of the Church, its secularity remains contingent on religion.[7] Yet the religious remnant that the secular feeds upon is something that traditional secularization theory struggles to acknowledge or comprehend. Dickens's text may appear to remove certain theological references from the Christmas story but these references continue to haunt the narrative: from the very start the narrator's excessive insistence that Marley is 'dead' infers the possibility of an afterlife and this thought is continued in the second paragraph via multiple references to 'sole', a word with obvious double meaning.

The theological remnant in *A Christmas Carol* refuses to go away, despite the text's efforts to quantify and objectify the supernatural content of religion. But there can be no doubt that the cultural drive towards materialism evident in Dickens's text had consequences for religion. This chapter will begin by analysing the impact of materialist philosophy on religious thought in the mid- to late nineteenth century. Materialist philosophy had been increasingly influential since the Enlightenment, but the growing cultural status of science and the energetic polemics

by advocates such as T. H. Huxley did much to familiarize the public
with a materialist vocabulary. Ultimately, it was materialism rather than
science per se that posed problems for religion. As we shall explain, the
difficulties were caused largely by the limited theological understanding
of a previous generation, exemplified in the natural theology of William
Paley. The failure of theology to deal adequately with the mediated
nature of reality meant that it was threatened by the ambition of materialism to account for all unexplained phenomenon. One of the places
where the reaches of materialism are particularly apparent is in ghost
stories, a genre that Dickens's Christmas numbers did much to promote
and popularize. Although the genre initially seems predicated on the
disruption of received scientific knowledge by supernatural phenomena,
many ghost stories proceed to frame these disruptions within a scientific
and evidential context that seeks to explain the unknown and fill in the
gaps traditionally accounted for by belief in God. Among other things,
materialism questions the possibility of transcendence in the modern
world: when George Eliot, for example, tries to return to transcendent
motifs in *Daniel Deronda*, she does so in a manner that makes them
subservient to materialist methodology and concerns. The turn away
from transcendence has been observed by a number of commentators
writing about nineteenth-century religion, and explains the next section
of the chapter, on immanent theology and the rise of the social Gospel.
A key figure in this respect is F. D. Maurice, whose dispute with Henry
L. Mansel in the late 1850s helped ensure that 'Mansel's was the last
great nineteenth-century effort at a theology of transcendence'.[8] Instead
of reading Maurice's Christian socialism as contiguous to the secular,
humanistic religion advocated by Ludwig Feuerbach, the chapter argues
that the social Gospel, for all its weaknesses, was grounded in a clear theological vision. After exploring the philosophy of the Christian Socialists
further, the chapter moves on to examine the impact of the Gospel in
the new urban environment of the nineteenth century. In many respects
the city provides an ideal focus for the strands elucidated in the chapter,
particularly in the way that it complicates our understanding of religious
and secular space. While both atheists and believers were inclined to read
the city as a symbol of secularization, accounts of urban life often feature
the surprising re-emergence of the prophet, a role subsequently contested by the orthodox, heterodox, and irreligious alike. This jostling for
the right to interpret and construct the essence of true religion will be the
subject of the concluding part of the chapter, focusing on blasphemers,
atheists, and freethinkers at the end of the nineteenth century.

MATERIALISM

Virtually all accounts of nineteenth-century religion and/or secularization draw attention to the importance of Charles Darwin's *The Origin of Species* (1859). While it is difficult to overstate the long-term cultural impact of Darwin's work, it is easy to exaggerate its immediate effect on Christian belief and/or simplify the divergent responses that met its publication.[9] Many leading religious figures responded positively to the text, while others expressed relative indifference. A perusal of a selection of Evangelical periodicals from the early 1860s, for example, reveals that the main threat to the status and authority of the Bible was perceived to come from *Essays and Reviews* not *The Origin of Species*. Moreover, those Christians who did criticize Darwin's account of evolution often did so on diverse and even contradictory grounds. One should not, therefore, conclude that *The Origins of Species* initiated or exposed an essential divide between science and religion. Many of the leading scientists of the eighteenth and nineteenth centuries were believers, and, as Aileen Fyfe explains in *Science and Salvation: Evangelical Popular Science Publishing in Victorian Britain*, groups such as the Religious Tract Society played a major role in the promotion of science during the mid-nineteenth century.[10] So what contribution did Darwin's text make to secularization? A useful starting-point is Darwin's fascination with the work of William Paley. Published in 1802, Paley's *Natural Theology* is best remembered for its use of a watch as an analogy by which one might infer that the world was created by God: in the same way, argued Paley, that the complex mechanism of a watch presupposed design by a maker, the complexity of the natural world inferred a divine author behind it. But, as Stephen Prickett helpfully reminds us in *Narrative, Religion and Science: Fundamentalism versus Irony, 1700–1999*, Paley's 'analogy of a watch [was] first used by the British scientist, Robert Boyle, popularized by the French philosopher, Leibniz, and developed with minute precision by Paley's contemporary, Pierre Laplace'.[11] Paley's argument from design continued a tradition of natural theology that had been popular in English theology since the time of John Locke. Central to the enterprise of natural theology was an attempt to reason from the natural world to an understanding of God. Instead of breaking with this tradition, Darwin continued it: his personal writings reveal the influence of Paley on his early thought, and the attention devoted to the eye in

The Origin of Species (another example used by Paley), along with the telescope (a modern equivalent, as Prickett reminds us, of the watch), shows how Darwin inherited the methodology of natural theology. In the words of Prickett: 'By the time Darwin came to write *The Origin* he had clearly appropriated Paley to the point where the structure and contents of *Natural Theology* were a part of his own mental furniture.'[12] Where Darwin differed from Paley, however, was in the conclusion he reached about where this methodology might lead. The failure of much of the Church to deal with Immanuel Kant's critique of natural theology, along with the failure of those (typically Calvinists) who rejected natural theology to articulate an alternate theology that took adequate account of the mediated nature of reality, meant that popular Christian belief often relied upon a god-of-the-gaps theology, in which God was used to account for the mysteries of the universe. In the wake of the scientific revolution that took effect in the second half of the nineteenth century, the gaps that God was needed to fill diminished rapidly, and some were left wondering what place belief in God had in the modern world.

In terms of positioning scientific materialism as a methodological alternative to a religion predicated on either natural theology or special providence, Huxley was a far more important figure than Darwin. The common description of Huxley as 'Darwin's bulldog' belies the contribution of Huxley to the professionalization of science and its growing cultural status.[13] In one of his most important essays, 'On the Physical Basis of Life' (1868), Huxley set out his philosophical objection to seeking an explanation for strange and unusual phenomena in religion and the supernatural. He argued that the only reasonable explanation was one that was materially based: 'the materialistic terminology is in every way to be preferred. For it connects thought with the other phenomena of the universe, and suggests inquiry into the nature of those physical conditions, or concomitants of thought, which are more or less accessible to us ... whereas, the alternative, or spiritualistic, terminology is utterly barren, and leads to nothing but obscurity and confusion of ideas.'[14] In an attempt to avoid the charge that his reliance upon physical explanations constituted an a priori materialist philosophy, Huxley invoked the scepticism of Hume and claimed that his position was predicated on a provisional hypothesis rather than necessary truth. However, his unwillingness to countenance anything other than a physical basis for life suggests that Huxley's position was a materialist one, if not in theory then at least in practice.

The position Huxley articulates in 'On the Physical Basis of Life' is anticipated by the narrator in 'The Haunted and the Haunters' (1859), a ghost story by Edward Bulwer Lytton. In a statement that accords with Bulwer Lytton's own position on the supernatural, the narrator declares:

I had witnessed many very extraordinary phenomena in various parts of the world—phenomena that would be either totally disbelieved if I stated them, or ascribed to supernatural agencies. Now, my theory is that the Supernatural is the Impossible, and that what is called supernatural is only a something in the laws of nature of which we have been hitherto ignorant. Therefore, if a ghost rise before me, I have not the right to say, 'So, then, the supernatural is possible', but rather, 'So, then, the apparition of a ghost is contrary to received opinion, within the laws of nature—i.e. not supernatural'.[15]

This attempt to respond to the supernatural within the parameters of materialism shows the extent to which supernatural accounts of religion were forced on to the back foot. Whereas the popularity of ghost stories in the nineteenth century has often been read as a disruption to the explanatory potential of science, a closer examination of the way in which they frame this disruption suggests otherwise. In Sheridan Le Fanu's 'The Green Tea', first published in *All the Year Round* in 1869 and then reprinted as the opening story of *In a Glass Darkly* (1872), the interruption of the supernatural is described as follows: 'It [the phantom monkey] amounted at last to a dreadful interruption. You will ask, how could a silent immaterial phantom effect that? It was thus, whenever I meditated praying; it was always before me, and nearer and nearer'.[16] The language used here is revealing: not only is the supernatural transformed from that which is truly other to an objectified 'it' capable of being quantified ('amounted'); the inexplicable phenomena is read in terms of basic scientific categories of time ('whenever') and space ('before me, and nearer and nearer').

One of the most striking fictional attempts to relocate the supernatural within a scientific framework can be found in George Eliot's *The Lifted Veil* (1859). Latimer, the narrator of this tale, is troubled by inexplicable powers of foresight and an ability to read the minds of others, but his unusual powers prove incapable of penetrating the mystery of Bertha, a woman he describes as 'my oasis of mystery in the dreary desert of knowledge'.[17] After marrying her, Latimer claims to see Bertha for who she really is, and yet the mystery continues when she appears to enter into a conspiracy with her new maid, Mrs Archer. The nature of this conspiracy is revealed in the final moments of the tale when Latimer's friend, the scientist Charles Meunier, helps him extract from the lifeless body of Mrs Archer hidden information regarding an attempt to poison Latimer. Just before Mrs Archer's death, Meunier proposes 'an experiment on this woman' that involves transfusing his blood into her after her heart has stopped beating.[18] Meunier and Latimer's desire to dominate the mystery of femininity leads them to transform Mrs Archer's death chamber into a scientific laboratory, and the text clearly marks this refurbished space as male. Just before the experiment is carried out, Bertha is led out of the room, and her attempt to send two female attendants to keep watch in her place is subverted by Latimer:

When they entered, Meunier had already opened the artery in the long thin neck that lay rigid on the pillow, and I dismissed them, ordering them to remain at a distance till we rang: the doctor, I said, had an operation to perform—he was not sure about the death. For the next twenty minutes I forgot everything but Meunier and the experiment in which he was so absorbed ... It was my task at first to keep up the artificial respiration in the body after the transfusion had been effected, but presently Meunier relieved me, and I could see the wondrous slow return of life; the breast began to heave, the inspirations became stronger, the eyelids quivered, and the soul seemed to have returned beneath them.[19]

In many respects, this final, climactic scene is more disturbing than the secret it uncovers: not only is female space violated, but the attempt to master the unknown and position the mystery of the female 'soul' beneath the two men results in the subject of human death becoming subservient to an absorbing experimental operation.

Consistent with the materialist framing provided by tales of the supernatural is the repeated emphasis on mediation. Throughout the mid-nineteenth century ghost stories freely use haunted houses and other material objects to mediate the supernatural. Despite the fact that some narrators, such as the one in Sheridan Le Fanu's 'An Account of Some Strange Disturbances in an Old House in Aungier Street' (1853), draw attention to the limitations of '[p]en, ink, and paper' as 'vehicles for the marvellous', they continue to rely on text to communicate their tales.[20] The centrality of mediation to manifestations of the supernatural extends also to the implied critical reader referred to at the start of many stories, whose anticipated scepticism helps to shape the form of the ghost story and without whom there would be no ghost story. By maintaining an ambivalence regarding the supernatural origin of the events they narrate, many ghost stories highlight this mediatory role of the reader. In this respect they accord with the central insight offered by Sludge in Browning's dramatic monologue 'Mr Sludge, the Medium' (1864). Sludge insists that those attending séances collude in the production of a plausibility structure for the supernatural: attendees expect the supernatural and see what they want to see. At one point Sludge even suggests that this desire to see the supernatural is equivalent to those who interpret historical circumstances providentially:

> When you and good men gape at Providence,
> Go into history and bid us mark
> Not merely power-plots prevented, crowns
> Kept on kings' heads by miracle enough,
> But private mercies—oh, you've told me, sir,
> Of such interpositions! …
>
> (927–32)

Although he draws attention to the mediated nature of all belief in the supernatural, whether in the form of séances or religion, Sludge never dismisses the possibility that those beings refer to some aspect of reality. His cynicism and self-interest may prevent us from accepting his arguments uncritically but the focus of the poem is on reminding us how supernatural belief is mediated, not on dispelling the supernatural altogether.

Mediation is also central to the complex treatment of materialism in George Eliot's last novel, *Daniel Deronda* (1876). On one level this novel appears to leave behind the interest in science found in earlier novels such as *Middlemarch*, but, on another level, Daniel's preference for the realm of the prophetic over 'that dead anatomy of culture which turns the universe into a mere ceaseless answer to queries' continues to ground itself in Eliot's sophisticated understanding of materialism.[21] Through Mordecai, Eliot reminds her readers that the prophetic vocation is to be understood as thoroughly material and organic, not as a synonym for the immaterial and unmediated. In response to his question—'what is it to feel the light of the divine reason growing stronger within and without?'—Mordecai declares: 'It is to see more and more of the hidden bonds that bind and consecrate change as a dependant growth—yea, consecrate it with kinship: the past becomes my parent, and the future stretches towards me the appealing arms of children.'[22] Given Mordecai's concern to root his understanding of the prophetic within a materialist framework, it may be significant that Eliot chooses Jewish prophecy over its Christian equivalent as the means by which Daniel might avoid 'the dead anatomy of culture'. According to Geoffrey Hartman, the apostle Paul's use of a spirit/letter dichotomy to help reread the Jewish law and explain the relationship between the Hebrew Bible and Christianity was restated by Early Church fathers such as Augustine to the effect that 'Christian freedom is freedom from the literalism of Jewish ritual law and, generally, from a literal interpretation of what has come to be known as the Old (superseded) Testament. Freedom and spirituality are contrasted with Jewish slavery, that is, with the carnal or literal interpretation of Old Testament commandments, rituals, and narratives.'[23] In the rest of his essay 'The Letter as Revenant' Hartman considers the limitations of this binary and exposes Christianity's misreading of the Jewish tradition. While Hartman may be accused of underestimating the important contribution of materialist thought to the history of Christian theology, there can be little doubt that a privileging of the spiritual over the material was popular in many of the Evangelical circles that Eliot came to reject. Hartman's claim that the materiality ascribed to Jewish thought contains within it a greater interpretative freedom than Christians have often alleged, is borne out by the use to which Eliot puts it in *Daniel Deronda*. At several points in the novel, the hope and vitality offered by the prophetic depends on the sustenance of the material world that it mediates, as the following observation by Mordecai illustrates:

I said, let my body dwell in poverty, and my hands be as the hands of the toiler; but let my soul be as a temple of remembrance where the treasures of knowledge enter and the inner sanctuary is hope. I knew what I chose. They said, 'He feeds himself on visions', and I denied not; for visions are the creators and feeders of the world. I see, I measure the world as it is, which the vision will create anew. You are not listening to one who raves aloof from the lives of his fellows.[24]

IMMANENT THEOLOGY AND THE RISE OF THE SOCIAL GOSPEL

In *The Age of Atonement* Boyd Hilton observes a theological transition in the nineteenth century between the age of Atonement and the age of Incarnation: the former, dominant in the first half of the century, is said to have been characterized by a pessimistic view of the world's fallen nature and emphasized the need for redemption to avoid the judgement of hell; the latter, which is alleged to have come to the fore in the second half of the century, brought with it a more optimistic focus on this world rather than the afterlife, believing it possible to bring about social transformation and see the kingdom of God manifested on earth. Hilton readily admits that this narrative involves broad brushstrokes (which are made to seem broader by their brief summary here) but he is far from alone in pointing to a fundamental theological shift around the middle of the nineteenth century. He writes: 'By 1870 it was commonplace for Anglicans to assert that a theological transformation had recently taken place, whereby a worldly Christian compassion, inspired by the life of Jesus, had alleviated such stark Evangelical doctrines as those of eternal and vicarious punishment.'[25] Tracing the Victorians' self-awareness of a shift in theological attitudes, Hilton tells us that '[t]he *coup de grâce* came with the publication of *Lux Mundi: A Series of Studies in the Religion of the Incarnation* by a posse of High Churchmen in 1889'.[26]

Hilton's focus on Evangelicalism encourages him to use the categories of Atonement and Incarnation; other commentators, however, have utilized other vocabulary to convey their sense of a theological shift. Philip Davis, for example, employs terms used by the theologian Aubrey Moore, who 'suggested that throughout the ages the emphasis in the religious temper had oscillated between two doctrines of God — God as transcendent, the Creator separate from the world; and God as immanent within His creation. The second half of the nineteenth century was, he said, the age of the Incarnation rather than of the Fall, and, especially with the rise of evolutionary theory, an age of immanence rather than of transcendence.'[27] While this schema runs the risk of erecting a false divide between immanence and transcendence, two categories that have been intrinsically linked throughout the history of Christian theology, it relates to some of the broader philosophical trends of the period (e.g. the growth of materialism and the influence of Hegel), as well as helping to contextualize the important theological dispute between F. D. Maurice and Henry L. Mansel in the late 1850s.

In 1858 Mansel published the Bampton theology lectures he had given at Oxford in a book entitled *The Limits of Religious Thought*. His opening lecture began by considering the conflict between dogmatism and rationalism, before locating the dichotomy with reference to the traditional theological distinction between revelation and reason. Though recognizing the importance of reason for philosophical thought, Mansel's Kantian understanding of the synthetic and limited nature of knowledge encouraged him to reject all attempts at a theology based on human rationality and, instead, to privilege revelation as the only means of positive knowledge about God. To illustrate his belief that God was beyond all finite, rational thought, Mansel distinguished the apostle Paul's recourse in Corinthians to the 'limits of human knowledge'[28] from Hegel's claim that '[t]he logical conception is the absolute divine conception'.[29] Mansel's distrust of Hegelian pantheism and his preference for a uniquely Christian transcendent theology was reflected in the second lecture of *The Limits of Religious Thought*: 'so far is human reason from being able to construct a scientific Theology, independent of and superior to Revelation, that it cannot even read the alphabet out of which that Theology must be framed.'[30]

The importance that Mansel attached to 'separating, as far as it can be effected, the language of prayer and praise from the definitions and distinctions of philosophy' was rejected by Maurice, who detailed his objections in *What is Revelation?* (1859).[31] Given the veracity and extensiveness of Maurice's critique, it was unsurprising that Mansel should respond aggressively in *An Examination of the Rev. F. D. Maurice's Strictures on the Bampton Lectures of 1858* (1859). Maurice then penned a further, shorter response entitled *Sequel to the Inquiry, What is Revelation?* (1860). The core of Maurice's critique was Mansel's elevation of mystery and emphasis on transcendence. Not only did Maurice think that elevating mystery ran counter to the central message of the New Testament—the revelation of God made known in the person of Jesus—he feared that Mansel's theological method encouraged a static dogma, dislocated from and lacking engagement with contemporary thought. Maurice did not share the view of those in the Church who claimed that Mansel's argument undermined the role of a rational Christian apologetic; instead, Maurice argued that Mansel was constructing an alternative apologetic, one that arrogantly sought to place itself beyond criticism by insisting that God's understanding is radically different from our own. The consequence—private dogma over public truth—was a position Maurice believed to be antithetical to Christian faith. Claude Welch succinctly captures Maurice's desire to eschew any sort of theological abstraction when he explains that, for Maurice, 'the root of the matter is "facts" and "reality", not doctrines'.[32] Nowhere was the difference between the two theologians more apparent than in the different approaches they took to the Bible, a text that both saw as being of prime importance. Maurice criticized Mansel's abstract defence of the divine authority of the Bible, for insisting that one must 'receive the Bible as a whole or not at all; so leading many to place it on their shelves as a book which it was safe to accept without any careful study of its contents; so driving others who felt doubts about particular passages, to cast it aside altogether'.[33] Rather than seeking to place the Bible beyond criticism or argue endlessly about its theoretical authority, Maurice encouraged people to read scriptural narratives and reflect upon them in the light of their own experience:

I fancied the Scripture language, instead of shrinking into a little corner of its own, and declining all comparison with any other, was capable of being tested by the metaphysical inquiries and beliefs of all peoples and ages. I could not doubt that it was, at the same time, the popular language, that it would go straight home to the very heart and spirit of our people—of the poor, to whom the Gospel was first preached—because it addressed itself, not to that which is superficial and accidental, but to that which is deepest in all, and common to all.[34]

While critics have rightly noted the difficulty of labelling Maurice's theological position, there can be little doubt that its immanent orientation was intimately linked to his desire for social justice. Indeed, the best known feature of Maurice's legacy is the role he played in the emergence of the Christian Socialists and what became known as the social Gospel. Proponents of the social Gospel construed the good news of the Christian message primarily in terms of its response to contemporary social problems and inequality. At the start of *The Victorian Christian Socialists* (1987) Edward Norman demarcates the unique contribution of early Christian Socialists such as Maurice, Charles Kingsley, Thomas Hughes, and J. M. Ludlow, explaining that their beliefs differed from the political revolutionaries associated with either Chartism or late nineteenth-century socialism. Christian Socialists were not, as Norman goes on to admit, alone in their desire to alleviate poverty and address social problems (as the history of Evangelicalism makes clear); nevertheless, they 'dared to contemplate, if not a transformed political structure, at any rate the vision of a humanity emancipated from the thrall of custom and the existing ties of social deference'.[35] Many of the formal bodies of Christian socialism did not emerge until the latter part of the nineteenth century (e.g. the Guild of St Matthew, founded in 1877, the Christian Social Union, founded in 1889, and the Christian Socialist League of 1894) but the theological foundation of the orientation towards the immediate, social implications of the Gospel were laid down by Maurice and popularized through the fiction of Kingsley, '*the* disseminator of the ideals of the Christian Socialists [italics added]'.[36]

The vision of Christianity proposed by Christian Socialists has been the subject of extensive critique over the years, and for good reason. Donald E. Hall tells us that: 'even though it was short-lived and some of its members are better remembered for their subsequent manifestations as muscular Christians, we are right to ask if Christian socialism itself was an abject failure.'[37] According to its detractors, Christian socialism was inadequate in terms of both its theology and its radical credentials. Before examining the former, it is worth interrogating briefly the charge that figures such as Maurice and Kingsley were ideologically conservative. It is easy to see why the best known Christian Socialists have been accused of masking a commitment to the status quo in their call for social change: their promotion of the virtues encouraged in the Sermon of the Mount (e.g. obedience, sacrifice, and forgiveness) appear to encourage acquiescence to the inequality of the day, while Maurice's suggestion 'that Domestic Morality is not only an integral portion of Social Morality, but should be the starting point of all discussions respecting it'[38] seems to fall short of the radical revolutionary rhetoric we find in Karl Marx and Frederick Engels. Through a careful examination of the language used in works such as *Politics for the People*, a Christian Socialist weekly that appeared briefly in 1848, Hall detects an inherent conservatism in the metaphors used by Maurice and his circle: 'The Christian Socialists and muscular Christians manipulated language as a pedagogical tool, one that they used to repudiate demands that they found uncomfortable and irreconcilable with their own class-bound view of the proper constitution of the body of the nation.'[39] While Hall's reading of texts by Christian Socialists is astute and persuasive, the implication that all references to ordered bodies have to be read as conservative needs to be questioned. Hall's conclusion—that 'when words are made flesh, they often form the bodies of soldiers'—may identify accurately the conservative usages to be found in much of the material written by the Christian Socialists, but it also anticipates, inadvertently, the militant radicalism of the next generation of adherents to the social Gospel; figures such as William and Catherine Booth, the founders of the Salvation Army, whose authoritarian impulses somehow found expression in a revolutionary movement that might better be described as paramilitary.[40] Many of the next generation of writers, including Eliza Lynn Linton, author of *Joshua Davidson, Christian and Communist* (1872), were far more radical than Kingsley's tailor and poet, Alton Locke, in their vision of a prophetic biblical call for social transformation.[41]

Although more radical Christian expressions of socialism suggested that the conservatism of Anglicans like Kingsley was not inherent to Christianity, they did little to answer the other major concern: namely, whether the focus on the material world was intrinsically secular.

Not everyone was certain that the social Gospel was still the Gospel. Conservative Evangelical publications frequently denounced 'broad-church perversions' of the Christian message, and even Evangelical factions with a clear commitment to responding to the material needs of the poor, such as the Salvation Army, displayed considerable unease regarding the theological relation between preaching the Gospel and addressing social need.[42] For some, the risk exemplified in *A Christmas Carol*'s translation of religion was one that threatened to culminate in the atheistic religion of humanity articulated by Ludwig Feuerbach in *The Essence of Christianity* (1841). Feuerbach argued that God was a projection of all that humanity aspired to be: 'The personality of God is thus the means by which man converts the quality of his own nature into the qualities of another being,—of a being external to himself. The personality of God is nothing else than the projected personality of man.'[43] However, instead of viewing atheism as antithetical to religion, Feuerbach thought it provided the means of appreciating the essence of religion: humanity.

Feuerbach's ideas about the religion of humanity were explored by the first English translator of *The Essence of Christianity*, George Eliot, in her novel *Silas Marner* (1861). Like the biblical character of Job, Silas experiences a series of tragic events, and these cause him to question his faith. However, in a text that frequently reflects upon the meaning of words that remain after their initial meaning has been lost—at one point Dolly declares 'I can never rightly know the meaning o' what I hear at church, only a bit here and there, but I know it's good words'—the allusion to Job becomes the means by which Eliot replaces the content of Christian thought with Feuerbach's ideas.[44] Whereas the Book of Job answers Job's questions about his suffering through the intervention of God, who speaks out of the whirlwind and inspires worship, Silas discovers a child called Eppie; his subsequent conversion to a new sense of hope and purpose is said to have reawakened a 'strong feeling ready to vibrate with sympathy'.[45] The key term here, as for some of the earlier nonconformists, is sympathy: in place of God, conspicuously absent from the religious language that permeates the latter stages of the novel, human companionship answers Silas's despair. Having observed that Silas 'was quite unable, by means of anything he heard or saw, to identify the Raveloe religion with his old faith', the narrator goes on to explain: 'He had no distinct idea about the baptism [of Eppie] and the church-going, except that Dolly had said it was for the good of the child; and in this way, as the weeks grew to months, the child created fresh and fresh links between his life and the lives from which he had hitherto shrunk continually into narrower isolation.'[46]

Owen Chadwick famously warned in *The Secularization of the European Mind in the Nineteenth Century* against convenient narratives of intellectual history that ignored the reality of social history. His warning is a useful reminder that, despite the influence of Eliot in mediating and exploring the religion of humanity, relatively few Victorians reached the same atheistic conclusion as Feuerbach. Callum Brown is right to insist that Christian discourse continued to dominate British culture well into the twentieth century, and the historian Hugh McLeod has carefully documented the persistence of religion among the working classes throughout the second half of the nineteenth century.[47] At the same time, the question underlying Feuerbach's work—how one should understand the essence of Christianity—was the concern of many Victorians. The extensive cultural transformations of the period forced people to reinterpret exactly what it was they believed and reconsider how those beliefs related to the world in which they found themselves. Such matters were, of course, extremely complex: even the reductive answer offered by Feuerbach acknowledges the broader difficulty of quantifying and objectifying the essence of faith. The chapters of *The Essence of Christianity* all reach slightly different conclusions about the question posed by the title, alerting readers to the polyphonic nature of the Christian narrative. Perhaps this explains Feuerbach's confusion in determining his own relation to the Christian tradition. In the space of one sentence, found in the preface to the second edition (published in the same year as *A Christmas Carol* and translated by Eliot in 1854), Feuerbach seems incapable of deciding whether his work is 'a close translation', a 'historical-philosophical analysis', or 'a solution of the enigma of the Christian religion'.[48]

Christianity's historic resistance to being distilled into a set formula reminds us of the need to remain alert to the mutability and plurality of belief as we (re)construct our own narratives of nineteenth-century secularization and religion. Rarely, if ever, does it help to characterize people's beliefs as either religious or secular. Much of the time, one encounters lines of thought that encompass both, and this is the case with the social Gospel. Religion does not have to rely on transcendence to secure its identity: interpreting belief in terms of material concern may run the risk of eroding a realist view of God but this is not the only possible outcome.[49] As the doctrine of the Incarnation makes clear, Christianity is committed to the possibility of thinking about the supernatural within the context of the material world and, for all its faults, Maurice's advocacy of the social Gospel engages with and explores this possibility. Contrary to the picture painted by some of his critics, Maurice was seeking to work within the Christian tradition. Bernard Reardon reminds us: 'For it was primarily as a theologian that Maurice saw himself, and such he claimed to be. His social reformism, for which he has usually been remembered, is really an aspect of his theology and an expression of one of its fundamental principles.'[50] In the admiring (and perhaps insufficiently critical) words of Edward Norman, it was the theological orientation of their engagement with the material world that enabled the Christian Socialists to be 'prophets of their times … [who] discerned ultimate meanings and moral lessons in the conditions of their day'.[51]

URBAN PROPHETS

Given the dramatic growth of cities in the nineteenth century, it is to be expected that commentators with an interest in religion should have sought to discern the spiritual impact of the new urban environment. The conclusion of many proponents of secularization is that urban growth was a catalyst for religious decline; less well known, however, is the extent to which the data used to support this comes from Christian sources.[52] Especially in the second half of the nineteenth century, Christians were at the forefront of those positing the city as a secular void with which the Church was failing to engage. Infamous in this regard was William Booth, whose *In Darkest England and the Way Out* (1890) borrowed the leading metaphor used by Henry Morton Stanley in his account of David Livingstone's mission to Africa, and applied it to London. Although Booth's narrow Evangelical beliefs did not incline him to view the religious dimension of the city positively, his dramatic invective against the city was not so much a cynical rhetorical ploy as the product of a mode of thought—the man who instructed his officers that their first aim was to attract attention was practically incapable of speaking in a measured, impartial tone.[53] Admitting the analogical dimension of his writing in the opening chapter of *In Darkest England* did not stop Booth from constantly implying that he was describing the city as it really was. The false claim for unmediated reportage is evident early on in the book when Booth likens the scenes he has seen to Dante's picture of hell, only then to declare that '[t]he man who walks with open eyes and with bleeding heart through the shambles of our civilisation needs no such fantastic images of the poet to teach him horror'.[54] But Booth's account of the city was far from being that of the neutral observer; as Joseph McLaughlin notes, Booth's belief that 'all the misery of modern existence could be traced to the migration of agricultural laborers from the countryside into the city' strongly influenced the picture he created.[55]

Booth's view of the city was one that he inherited from other nineteenth-century Evangelical urban commentators. Earlier in the century the more circumspect Thomas Chalmers had reached the negative conclusion that:

there is no denying of the fact, that were churches to be built at this moment, up to the full accommodation of all our city families, it would have almost no perceptible influence on the habit into which they have degenerated. It is not at the sound of a bell, that they will consent to relinquish the sordid or profane gratifications wherewith they fill up that day of rest, which they have turned into a day of rioting and lawless indulgence.[56]

The tendency among Evangelicals (and other Christian commentators) to presume the worst about the city has a long history and resists easy explanation. London's dramatic growth, around 1800, leading to the first city of modern times with over a million inhabitants, explains why commentators were keen to comment on urbanization, but it does not explain why the city was frequently seen as antipathetic to religious belief. Some critics have argued that the roots of this antipathy are to be found in the Bible's hostility to the city, yet, as Graham Ward explains, the biblical writers are more equivocal:

In the Bible, then, a complex weave of myth, fact, fear, hope and history circulates about cities. The utopian dreams of city-builders wishing to construct paradise within their boundaries, is crossed by a dark sense of judgement by God on 'all the lofty towers and all the sheer walls' (Isaiah 2: 12), and both these strains are filtered through stories of a heavenly archetypal city, the eschatological city of divine manufacture and perfection.[57]

Despite the complexity of the biblical narratives, the symbolic value of the city—epitomizing the height of humanity's achievement—combined with a largely Protestant tendency to emphasize humanity's sinfulness, go some way to accounting for the overly negative accounts found among many religious urban commentators in the nineteenth century. Moreover, as critics have pointed out, it was in the interests of religious groups seeking money and support for the missionary work they were undertaking in the city to exaggerate its heathen characteristics. In the case of *In Darkest England*, the book was a polemic designed to raise awareness of, and money for, the relief of poverty in England. This is not to deny the reality of much of what Booth described; rather, it reminds us of the need to read contemporary urban accounts from the nineteenth century, whether Christian, atheistic, or otherwise, with their mediated quality in view.

The effect of the sensational language used by writers like Booth compelled observers to reach dramatic conclusions which lacked nuance and minimized the complexities involved. All too often there was a distorted focus on whether or not the missionary work in the city was successful: in the face of alleged urban crises, it was inevitable that Victorians should seek anxiously for measurable signs of improvement. This framing of religious analysis in terms of success/failure, or growth/decline, was further encouraged by the nineteenth-century drive towards measurement and quantification, a tendency illustrated by the emergence of the social sciences and one to which Michel Foucault has alerted a whole generation of Victorian scholars.[58] Callum Brown points out that nineteenth-century Christians were caught up in the cultural obsession with quantification: 'In the 1840s and 1850s, churches were infected as much as other branches of the nation's life by the mania for statistics.'[59] The 1851 census and the furore that followed its findings highlight this mania: endless discussions about the methodological validity of the 1851 census, both at the time and ever since, are of limited value, and not simply because there is no earlier religious census with which to compare the 1851 data.[60] Interpreting religion primarily in terms of church attendance is limited and reductive, despite the convenience of the measurement.

While the obsession with quantification may not always have been helpful for Victorian analysts seeking to describe their culture, it played an important role in constructing nineteenth-century urban life. George Simmel's observation in 'The Metropolis and Mental Life' (1903) is perceptive: 'Punctuality, calculability, exactness are forced upon life by the complexity and extension of metropolitan existence ... These traits ... colour the contents of life and favour the exclusion of those irrational, instinctive, sovereign traits and impulses which aim at determining the mode of life from within, instead of receiving the general and precisely schematized form of life from without.'[61] The city's attempts to regulate its own activity are frustrated by the complexity and multiplicity of the social relations within it; the resulting disjuncture, between the fragmentation one experiences and the systemic impulse that motivates the idea of the city, explains why so many Victorians move endlessly between a bewildering encounter with the disorder of London to descriptions of the city that utilize epic and apocalyptic vocabulary. In a recent article entitled ' "And I saw the Holy City": London Prophecies in Charles Dickens and George Eliot', Elena Petrova considers how the London novels of Dickens and Eliot locate themselves in a Christian mythological tradition dating back to St Augustine's *City of God* and John's Book of Revelation.[62] Whereas Dickens and Eliot sought, in different ways, to use this tradition for the purposes of prophesying a renewal of the city, the next generation of writers were often less hopeful. Adrian Poole tells us in *Gissing in Context* that '[t]he major shift in consciousness between Dickens and later Victorian writers is in the recession of this confidence in the "blest morning" '.[63]

George Gissing's *The Nether World* (1889) imagines a London that is far closer to Babylon than it is to the New Jerusalem. The novel's lack of clergymen, its depiction of working-class characters who reject formal religion, and its insistence on conditions of poverty that are not relieved by the forces of providence, have led Stephen Gill to conclude, in his introduction to the Oxford World's Classics edition of the novel, that: 'Christianity ... is notably absent'.[64] Gill continues: 'During the latter third of the century a number of heroic clergymen attempted to revivify the Church as a force within working-class communities in London, and alongside them, inspired by Christian ideals, worked the volunteers for the university settlements. This limited but positive action is not even glanced at in *The Nether World*.'[65] Yet the novel is not as secular as Gill suggests. The work of Christian organizations among London's working-class communities is glanced at, albeit via a passing reference to a 'promenade of the Salvation Army',[66] whose work, as the narrator goes on to point out, 'half-puzzled, half-amused her [Jane Snowdon]; she spoke of it altogether without intolerance, as did her grandfather, but never dreamt that it was a phenomenon which could gravely concern her'.[67] While the reference to 'gravely concern' denotes a religion that is dying, the use of the word 'phenomenon' reminds readers that it is the temporal forms and expressions of religion that are in urgent need of renewal. The religious failure to address people's daily concerns is evident elsewhere in the novel: the bells of a church playing 'There is a happy land, far, far away' are still heard, but, as the narrator explicitly states, 'that hymn makes too great a demand upon the imagination to soothe amid instant miseries'.[68] At the start of the novel there is an insistence that religious forms in current usage no longer have anything to offer: Jane's anguish is said to have 'uttered itself, not in a mere sound of terror, but in a broken word or two of a prayer she knew by heart'.[69]

Although *The Nether World* offers glimpses of secularization, perhaps most apparent in Michael Snowdon selectively excising material from the Gospels when he teaches his granddaughter, there is more to the novel's religious orientation. For a start, the dark vision of London's nether region is contingent upon a Christian framework. At several points, beginning with the arrival of the mysterious benefactor Michael Snowdon, the narrative repeatedly holds out the hope of eschatological renewal, only to return to misery and hardship. The reliance upon a specifically Christian vision of a place where all hope is abandoned, is clear from the allusion to hell in the title. While the allusion is evident throughout the novel, particularly in the vocabulary used, it remains implicit until the intervention of the Christian prophet, Mad Jack. Towards the end of the novel, Mad Jack relates to the crowd a vision he claims to have received from an angelic being: 'This life you are now leading is that of the damned; this place to which you are confined is Hell! There is no escape for you.'[70] Mad Jack retains the dramatic language of sin and damnation common to apocalyptic accounts of hell and judgement, but the wording of the vision and its location at the climax of the novel make it clear that it is the whole of society that is being addressed. Commenting on this strange scene, in which Mad Jack shifts from praise to judgement and does not appear himself, Kirsten Hertel writes:

Even though Mad Jack only appears sporadically and has no influence whatsoever on the plot, his psalm singing and his soliloquizing speeches are reminiscent of the choir in ancient Greek tragedies, which functions mainly as the author's mouthpiece. Similarly, Mad Jack can be seen as Gissing's mouthpiece ... Mad Jack's dream at the end of the novel can be understood as giving voice to the author's own personal disappointment in, and dissatisfaction with, the political and social conditions not only in London, the capital, but also in a highly developed world on the threshold of the twentieth century.[71]

One might go even further and argue that Mad Jack articulates a reality that the narrator is incapable of admitting directly. In other words, Mad Jack is more than a vestige of Christianity, ridiculed by those around him and given limited space in the narrative; he is the prophetic voice the narrator aspires to during the rest of the novel. Up until this point, the narrator cannot stop himself from making condescending remarks about the nature of working-class characters and holding out an illusory hope for their future happiness.

Mad Jack is not the only urban prophet of the late nineteenth century. He bears a notable resemblance to William and Catherine Booth, despite viewing alcohol rather differently, and the novel's passing reference to the Salvation Army may be intended to suggest this. Like Mad Jack, the Booths were eccentric Christian prophets who frequently employed apocalyptic language to describe their experience of urban life. For W. T. Stead, who enlisted the Booths' help in producing his 1885 exposé of child prostitution, *The Maiden Tribute of Modern Babylon*, and then ghost-wrote William Booth's *In Darkest England*, the willingness to speak publicly and boldly was a major part of the Booths' appeal. Commenting on Catherine in his biography of her, published in 1900, Stead praised the 'whole-hearted zeal, a thoroughgoing earnestness, a flaming passion of indignation, that cheered one like the sound of trumpet ... Her utterances blazed with the sacred wrath of the Hebrew prophets.'[72] Stead's admiration of the public prophet, attributable in part to his own aspirations to be a voice to the nation, is mirrored in the role of his namesake, W. F. Stead, in recovering the work of another Christian prophet, Christopher Smart, who, as we discussed in Chapter 1, was committed to a lunatic asylum for praying in public places.[73] W. F. Stead's description of Smart's eccentricities—'such as saying his prayers in public; he insisted upon his friends praying with him, and he would fall upon his knees in the street to pour forth his prayers, in spite of the jeers of small boys and the curious glances of the passers-by'—is uncannily close to Gissing's description of Mad Jack's reception in *The Nether World*.[74]

Interpreting the return of the Christian prophet in the late nineteenth century is too complex a task for the interpretative framework offered by secularization theory. In *Queer Fish: Christian Unreason from Darwin to Derrida*, John Schad assesses the place of 'the Christian [who] emerges from the crowd as truly other, truly marginal' positively, recognizing that where mainstream culture and Christianity become too entwined, the latter loses its radical dimension and risks becoming a synonym for conservative bourgeois respectability.[75] If Schad is right, and the appearance of the marginalized Christian marks a potential return to a subversive religion that is truly prophetic, then one might read the figures of Mad Jack and the Booths in a manner that does not simply focus on their marginal status. By definition, prophets stand outside the mainstream; to interpret them solely as signifiers of religious demise fails to allow for their ability to renew religion. The role of the prophet is to break with the cultural conformity of their religious contemporaries in order to proclaim a radical message. By undertaking this role in such a public manner, the Christian prophets of the late nineteenth century break with privatized notions of faith in order to 'proclaim it [the Gospel] as part of the continuing conversation which shapes public doctrine'.[76]

RELIGION, MODERNITY, AND THE PUBLIC SPHERE

It is no coincidence that the reappearance of the Christian prophet occurs in the city. To appreciate the reasons for this, one needs to start by recognizing the substantial impact of modernity on public life. Jurgen Habermas's claim that modernity collapses society's public sphere is evident in the city.[77] Although critics have been quick to point out both the limitations of the public sphere of which Habermas mourns the loss, and the dynamic emergence of a nexus of social groups in its place, they have not always given sufficient weight to the negative impact of the city on public life. For example, Judith Walkowitz's claim in *City of Dreadful Delight* that the ' "dreadfully delightful city" [London in the 1880s] became a contested terrain, where new commercial spaces, new journalistic practices, and a range of public spectacles and reform activities inspired a different set of social actors to assert their own claims to self-creation in the public domain',[78] though true, runs the risk of failing to acknowledge how the fragmented nature of urban life simultaneously militates against the cohesive public space required by a new set of 'social actors'. The loss of the public sphere is evident in chapter XXI of *The Nether World* when the narrator describes people gathering at Clerkenwell Green to exchange ideas: 'From the doctrine of the Trinity to the question of cabbage *versus* beef; from Neo-Malthusianism to the grievance of compulsory vaccination; not a subject which modernism has thrown out to the multitude but here received its sufficient mauling.'[79] Ostensibly, this passage appears to foreshadow the line of thought that Walter Benjamin later developed in his famous essay 'The Work of Art in the Mechanical Age of Reproduction', and promotes the modernity of the city as a democratizing power. But read more closely, and interpreted in the context of a novel that insists on the stultifying environmental forces at work in the city, the passage not only reveals how complex ideas are 'mauled'; it hints at the collapse of public dialogue. In the preceding sentence we read: 'Innumerable were the little groups which had broken away from the larger ones to hold semi-private debate.'[80] The fragmentation of ideas and the fracturing of the public sphere become so great under the force of modernity that individual voices are in danger of becoming inaudible, as their particularity struggles to locate itself within a meaningful set of universal relations. It is significant that whereas the Trinity provides a model within Christian theology for relations between the particular and the universal, the scene Gissing describes relegates the Trinitarian ideal to another disconnected particular of semi-private interest.[81] At the end of the paragraph where these debates are described, the narrator emphasizes the death of the public sphere and the emptiness of modernity's public gesture with the comment: 'Above the crowd floated wreaths of rank tobacco smoke.'[82]

It would be a mistake to blame the privatization of religion on the growth of the modern city. What the new urban environment did in the late nineteenth century was to make explicit a trajectory that had been gathering pace since the advent of the Reformation and Modernity, two movements which, as Max Weber argued in *The Protestant Ethic and the Spirit of Capitalism*, have much in common.[83] While there can be no doubt that a number of religious commentators held the city responsible for the decline of Christian Britain, the growth of the metropolis did not always *encourage* secularization By exaggerating the privatizing trend of modernity, the city revealed a process of isolation that had been underway for some time. The stories of anonymous, forgotten people, and remote, detached *flâneurs* found in many urban narratives compelled some religious figures to recover the public dimension of their faith. Life in the city exposed the dangers of a religion that was too private and too isolated, thereby providing a context in which prophetic figures, such as Mad Jack, might once again find a place. Though the message Mad Jack proclaims is, for much of the novel, culturally disengaged and in need of translation—he is only heard when he speaks of hell; the rest of what he says 'sounded as gibberish'—it symbolizes a renewal of Christianity in the public sphere and, in turn, marks a recovery of Christianity's distinctive voice.[84]

On one level, Mad Jack's public proclamation of faith is a continuation of earlier religious activity. The turn of the nineteenth century saw the birth of several missionary organizations, such as the Baptist Missionary Society (1792), the London Missionary Society (1795), and the Church Missionary Society (1799). Moreover, as the century unfolded, Evangelical activism expressed itself through a multitude of philanthropic and religious organizations, many of which were located in, or focused on, the city. Indeed, long before Christianity showed signs of leaking away in the sense outlined by secularization theory, one finds it employing a deliberate strategy of leaking its message. Throughout the century Christianity sought ways of infiltrating mainstream culture with its reading of the Gospel, using a variety of means such as educational reform, charitable endeavours, and direct political action. Booth's *In Darkest England*, with its attempt to articulate a vision of social transformation, offers one example of such leakage, while the efforts of nonconformist Christians to prosecute Edward John Eyre, the Governor of Jamaica who imposed martial law in 1865 and brutally suppressed the indigenous people, provides another.[85] Instead of seeing instances of socio-political involvement as signs of secularization, one might argue that they demonstrate the opposite and reveal the extent to which Christian ideals and beliefs infused nineteenth-century culture. But if the leaking of Christianity was, at least in part, a deliberate and successful strategy, it also ran the risk of capitulating to other cultural pressures that, ultimately, threatened to silence the Christian voice. By the time one gets to Robert Louis Stevenson's *The Strange Case of Dr Jekyll and Mr Hyde* (1886), religion has been translated into a veneer of bourgeois respectability that can no longer offer a meaningful distinction between the morality of Jekyll and his alter ego.

What figures like Mad Jack offer is an alternative to those who, having exchanged the Christian prophetic vocation for too high a degree of cultural assimilation, have lost sight of the radical message they originally intended to proclaim. While Mad Jack's 'wild, discordant voice' may upset theorists of secularization who cannot account for his continuing presence and insight, it also upsets versions of the Christian faith that, in their drive for cultural respectability, are happy to ignore the harsh realities of the nether world.[86] A striking example of a respectable Christianity that is no longer respectable or effectual can be found in Gissing's novel when Pennyloaf walks past Mad Jack and enters the house of her alcoholic mother. The scene that confronts Pennyloaf is described by the narrator as follows:

There were five coloured cards, such as are signed by one who takes a pledge of total abstinence; each presented the signature, 'Maria Candy', and it was noticeable that at each progressive date the handwriting had become more unsteady. Yes, five times had Maria Candy promised, with the help of God, to abstain ... But it appeared that the help of God availed little against the views of one Mrs. Green, who kept the beer-shop ... [87]

As the narrator goes on to conclude: 'The struggle was too unequal between Mrs. Candy with her appeal to Providence, and Mrs. Green with the forces of civilisation at her back.'[88] By translating its message into an ineffectual but culturally respectable form—in this case the middle-class temperance movement—Christianity forfeits both its power and its distinctiveness. Ironically, it is the fragmentation of the city that helped expose this trend, thereby providing the impetus for Christianity to find a means of renewing itself and thus recover a prophetic public voice. In the context of Gissing's bleak narrative, Mad Jack is no more able to effect change or offer solutions than his respectable Christian counterparts, but whereas the former manages to retain a distinctive public voice that is capable, on occasion, of diagnosing society's ills, the latter, having allowed itself to be seduced by the pervading culture, has nothing to say and can no longer be heard.

FREETHINKING, BLASPHEMY, AND THE REWRITING OF RELIGION

State religion declined towards the end of the nineteenth century as its privileged position was rendered increasingly untenable by modernity. The decline of Christianity's privileged cultural status did not result in a decline of religion per se—as we have seen, space was created for the re-emergence of the prophet—but it was significant nevertheless. A corollary of this transformation was the growing power of Dissent, which, like the secular voices of figures such as Eliot and Huxley, benefited from the diminishing influence of the Anglican Church.[89] One of the many motifs used by writers to convey the change taking place was church bells. In *The Nether World* the narrator tellingly observes: 'The sound of church bells—most depressing of all sounds that mingle in the voice of London—intimated that it was nearly eleven o'clock, but neither of our friends had in view the attendance of public worship.'[90] It is an account that captures the ongoing presence of state religion while also introducing the possibility that the voice of established religion is not as compelling or influential as it once was. While question marks hang over the notion that the working class at the centre of Gissing's narrative previously experienced a golden age of religious engagement to the established Church, it is clear that those seeking to revive religion in the late nineteenth century were forced to do so amid changed cultural conditions. In place of the melodious sound of Anglican church bells one finds a cacophony of voices (including that of the prophet) seeking to attract people's attention. The resulting noise is conveyed throughout *In The Year of Jubilee* (1894): at one point the narrator describes how '[a]t Camberwell Green they mingled with a confused rush of hilarious crowds, amid a clattering of cabs and omnibuses, a jingling of tram-car bells'.[91] Modernity's noise necessitates media awareness and expertise on the part of those who wish to be heard, hence the fact that the physical noise of the city in *In The Year of Jubilee* is accompanied by an excess of advertisements competing for people's attention and drowning out individuals' ability (or willingness) to listen to the 'still small voice' (1 Kings 19: 11–13) of religious instruction: Ada Peachey's refusal to listen to her husband's admonitions leads him to conclude that 'living when she did … only a John Knox could have impressed her with this menace [hell]—to be forgotten when the echoes of his voice had failed'.[92] Aside from anything else, this insistence on the power of contemporary advertising, an important theme in a number of Gissing's novels, challenges the privileged position of the prophet who speaks with the unmediated and uncontested voice of divine authority.

Understanding the new material conditions in which the figure of the prophet re-emerged during the late nineteenth century is crucial. Among other things, fictional descriptions of the reception of prophetic voices insist that the space entered by prophets was not explicitly sacred. And with so many different voices contesting the role of prophet, it was difficult to decide who the true Christian prophets were. Prophets are heterodox by definition, and the declining influence of the Anglican Church in the second half of the nineteenth century removed any vestige of ecclesial authority to which Protestants might appeal when deciding to which prophets they should listen. Like Dissent, the role of the prophet exploited the blurred and permeable boundaries between orthodoxy and heresy, boundaries that were being stretched by many freethinkers in the second half of the nineteenth century to include heterodox, even atheistic messages. Perhaps the most famous of these irreligious prophets is the madman that embraces the prophetic mantel in Frederick Nietzsche's *The Gay Science* (1882; 1887) and announces God's death. Before Nietzsche, however, one finds a number of secularists rereading religious language in order to articulate opposition to what they see as the blindness and oppression caused by Christian religion. Some of the best known freethinkers of the period—including Charles Bradlaugh, G. W. Foote, and Annie Besant—regularly styled themselves as prophets and made use of associated rhetoric in an effort to proclaim an (ir)religious message they thought others needed to hear. In this context Joss Marsh's observation of the parallel between Foote's attempts to promote secularism and the work of the Booths is both fascinating and suggestive: 'Street speaking and meetings in open spaces were techniques Salvationists shared with Secularists, and which in an age of increasing advertisement and commercial display clearly provoked ... anxiety over public space and publicity.'[93]

Another freethinker who can be said to have situated himself within the prophetic tradition was the poet James Thomson. If William Blake was right and poets were the new prophets, then Thomson's *The City of Dreadful Night* (1874) can be read as a secular, poetic antecedent to *In Darkest England*. In her groundbreaking reading of Thomson's work Isobel Armstrong argues that:

Its Nietzschean project is to deconstruct the symbolic language of the western Christian tradition, not destroying these symbols ... but demonstrating that their language and imagery can *only* be used to adumbrate a quite different and systematically opposed account of experience. And so Thomson's black epistemological epic rigorously redefines terminology—'dream', 'real' and 'hope' are examples in the first poem. When the inhabitant of the city becomes aware of subliminal sound in the vast, oppressive silence, it is concealed, muffled and indistinct (III), as of 'hidden life asleep', the throbs of passion and 'Far murmurs, speech of pity and derision', the language of death-in-life, not the true language of death. Bradlaugh argued not simply that theistic terminology is inaccurate and misleading but that Christian antinomies constitute a nonsense language which has no basis in experience. (And so [Henry] Mansel's idealist propositions turn up in a strange context.) That is why the sounds of the city are incoherent. The atheist project was to change the meaning of the sign and to obliterate its customary distinctions.[94]

The sound of church bells is transformed by the double movement of Thomson's poem, which 'uses the language of hell and of Christian despair to enter fully into that condition, and at the same time withdraws from it to expose it as mystified mythology which collapses under an antagonistic alternative materialist mythology'.[95] Rather than undertaking the impossible task of replacing the language of Christianity with a new atheistic language, Thomson seeks '[t]o show the bitter old and wrinkled truth | Stripped naked of all vesture that beguiles'.[96] *The City of Dreadful Night* exemplifies the work of Jacques Derrida's *bricoleur*, who recognizes that rewriting is the only option available to revolutionary writers.[97] By thinking about the secular in terms of its attempts to rewrite religion (and vice versa), we end up with a more constructive paradigm for thinking about the position of religion in modernity than that offered by secularization theory. The flux of modernity and its distrust of authority encourage the process of rewriting, creating opportunities and difficulties for freethinker and believer alike. As the next chapter will note, the fluidity and contingency built into the idea of rewriting explains how a prominent freethinker like Annie Besant could move between Christianity, atheism, and theosophy, frustrating every attempt to theorize any teleology that insists on modernity's linear turn from (or to) religion.

Despite the continuity implicit in the idea of rewriting, it would be wrong to ignore the violent ruptures that often resulted from attempts to rewrite religion and/or the secular in the late nineteenth century. In *Word Crimes* Joss Marsh focuses on the alarm caused by alleged instances of blasphemy. Working on the assumption that '[t]here is little to learn from a naked and reductive formula, shorn of historical context' that describes blasphemy as *'the speaking of the unspeakable'*, Marsh shows how charges of blasphemy frequently slide into charges of obscenity and/or attempts through language to undermine the authority of the establishment.[98] Chapter 6 of Marsh's work turns its attention to Thomas Hardy's *Jude the Obscure* (1895), a novel that some early reviewers thought of as blasphemous. Marsh observes that 'the hysterical chorus was not without motivation. Blasphemy is both subject and willed effect of Hardy's swan song to fiction.'[99] She goes on: 'Structured around a sequence of blasphemous scenes, surprisingly innocent of commentary, *Jude* works across the historical registers to invoke blasphemy both in traditional religious terms and as the class crime of language and offense against literary values that the debacle of 1883 [Foote's trial for blasphemy] had made of it.'[100] Sacred texts and ideas are parodied throughout Hardy's novel: Sue's purchases of two pagan statuettes early on sets out the novel's rejection of the hopeful conclusion to tragedy found in the Book of Job; Jude idealizes a town pointedly called Christminster only to discover, in a scene echoing the nativity story, that no rooms are available for him and his family in their hour of need; and Sue's grief at the death of her children is met by the sound of the organist at the College chapel playing 'the anthem from the seventy-third Psalm; "Truly God is loving unto Israel"'.[101] Highlighting another example of Hardy's attempts to parody religion, Marsh reflects upon Jude's death at the end of the novel and the accompanying liturgical-style references to the Book of Job. She writes: 'There is an element of blasphemous *imitatio* in Jude's intoning of biblical text, while the disconnected "responses" of the holiday crowd outside, watching the boat races, turn the scene into an anti-church service.'[102]

There is, however, more than one way of interpreting *Jude the Obscure*'s blasphemous subtext. Hardy's novel may rewrite religion but the important scene in which Sue and Jude are sacked from their job of 'relettering' the Ten Commandments in the church may not be as dismissive of the biblical text as Marsh implies when she explains how 'this kind of manhandling of sacred text was a job for "militant" Secularists'.[103] Instead, *Jude the Obscure* suggests that the 'relettering' Sue and Jude are asked to undertake is a process intrinsic to the Bible. When Jude returns to the church the day after being given the contract to restore the Ten Commandments, the narrator describes how: 'He found that what the contractor's clerk had said was true. The tables of the Jewish law towered sternly over the utensils of Christian grace.'[104] By implicitly acknowledging the way in which the New Testament writers rewrite the Mosaic Law, Hardy indicates that the novel's religious revisions are a continuation of the rewriting of the Christian tradition. Significantly, when Sue and Jude flee to Melchester, Sue asks Jude: 'will you let me make you a *new* New Testament, like the one I made for myself at Christminster?'[105] While Sue's desire to remould the Bible may have appeared blasphemous to some readers, she goes on to describe her work as expressive of a freedom to interpret the Sacred Text without constraint. Sue views her action of 'cutting up all the Epistles and Gospels into separate *brochures*, and re-arranging them in chronological order as written', as preferable to the way in which ecclesial authorities have framed and canonized Sacred Texts, exclaiming passionately: 'I won't say any more, except that people have no right to falsify the Bible!'[106] The possibility that Sue's rewriting of the Bible continues an interpretative tradition common to Protestantism in general and Dissent in particular modifies the meaning we ascribe to the so-called blasphemy of Hardy's novel. Although blasphemy remains a helpful term for describing the ruptures created by this text, it does not have to be read exclusively within the Secularist paradigm detailed by Marsh. Nor does the novel's blasphemous content provide evidence for the abstract account of religious decline presented by some advocates of secularization theory. Christianity was certainly rewritten in the nineteenth century, largely in response to major cultural changes brought about by modernity, but whether, as in the case of Dickens's reworking of the Christmas story, the result is best described as religious or secular is a difficult, perhaps impossible question to answer.

NOTES

1. S. Bruce, *God is Dead: Secularization in the West* (Oxford: Blackwell Publishers, 2002), 2.
2. See, for example, historical work such as H. McLeod and W. Ustorf (eds.), *The Decline of Christendom in Western Europe, 1750–2000* (Cambridge: Cambridge University Press, 2003), and H. McLeod, *Religion and Society in England, 1850–1914* (Basingstoke: Macmillan, 1996); sociological work such as C. G. Brown, *The Death of Christian Britain: Understanding Secularisation, 1800–2000* (London: Routledge, 2001); literary and cultural theory such as Slavoj Žižek, *On Belief* (London: Routledge, 2001), and J. Derrida and G. Vattimo (eds.), *Religion* (Cambridge: Polity Press, 1998), and nineteenth-century cultural history such as R. Luckhurst, *The Invention of Telepathy* (Oxford: Oxford University Press, 2002), and A. Owen, *The Place of Enchantment: British Occultism and the Culture of the Modern* (Chicago: University of Chicago Press, 2004).
3. Owen, *The Place of Enchantment*, 10.
4. J. L. Larson, *Dickens and the Broken Scripture* (Athens, Ga.: University of Georgia Press, 1985).
5. C. Dickens, *A Christmas Carol* (1843), in *Christmas Books*, ed. E. Farjeon (Oxford: Oxford Illustrated Dickens, 1994), 37.
6. Ibid. 21, 10.
7. The parasitic relation of the secular to religion is theorized at length in G. Vattimo, *End of Modernity: Nihilism and Hermeneutics in Postmodern Culture*, trans. J. Snyder (Baltimore: Johns Hopkins University Press, 1988) and G. Vattimo, *Belief*, trans. L. D'Isanto and D. Webb (Oxford: Polity, 1999).
8. P. Davis, *The Oxford English Literary History*, viii. *1830–1880: The Victorians* (Oxford: Oxford University Press, 2002), 141.
9. For further information on the reception of Darwin see J. Moore, *The Post-Darwinian Controversies: A Study of the Protestant Struggles to Come to Terms with Darwin in Great Britain and America, 1870–1900* (Cambridge: Cambridge University Press, 1979), and R. L. Numbers and J. Stenhouse (eds.), *Disseminating Darwinism: The Role of Place, Race, Religion and Gender* (Cambridge: Cambridge University Press, 1999).
10. See A. Fyfe, *Science and Salvation: Evangelical Popular Science Publishing in Victorian Britain* (Chicago: University of Chicago Press, 2004). For

further discussions of the encounter between religion and science in the nineteenth century, see D. Knight, *Science and Spirituality: The Volatile Connection* (London: Routledge, 2003), and D. Knight and M. D. Eddy (eds.), *Science and Beliefs: From Natural Philosophy to Natural Science, 1700–1900* (Aldershot: Ashgate, 2005).

11. S. Prickett, *Narrative, Religion and Science: Fundamentalism versus Irony, 1700–1999* (Cambridge: Cambridge University Press, 2002), 76.

12. Ibid. 79.

13. See A. Desmond, *Huxley: From Devil's Disciple to Evolution's High Priest* (Harmondsworth: Penguin Books, 1997).

14. T. H. Huxley, 'On The Physical Basis of Life' (1868), in *Collected Essays*, i (London: Macmillan and Co., 1894), 130–65 (164).

15. E. Bulwer Lytton, 'The Haunted and the Haunters', *Blackwood's Edinburgh Magazine*, 86 (Aug. 1859), 224–45 (230–1).

16. S. Le Fanu, *In A Glass Darkly* (1872), ed. R. Tracy (Oxford: Oxford World's Classics, 1993), 30.

17. G. Eliot, *The Lifted Veil and Brother Jacob*, ed. S. Shuttleworth (Harmondsworth: Penguin Classics, 2001), 18.

18. Ibid. 38.

19. Ibid. 41.

20. S. Le Fanu, 'An Account of Some Strange Disturbances in an Old House in Aungier Street', *Dublin University Magazine*, 42 (Dec. 1853), 721–31 (721).

21. G. Eliot, *Daniel Deronda* (1876), ed. G. Handley (Oxford: Oxford World's Classics, 1988), 308.

22. Ibid. 451.

23. G. Hartman, *Scars of the Spirit: The Struggle Against Inauthenticity* (Basingstoke: Palgrave, 2002), 109.

24. Eliot, *Daniel Deronda*, 426.

25. B. Hilton, *The Age of Atonement* (Oxford: Clarendon Press, 1988), 5.

26. Ibid. Also, see C. Gore (ed.), *Lux Mundi: A Series of Studies in the Religion of the Incarnation* (London: John Murray, 1889).

27. Davis, *The Oxford English Literary History*, viii. 139.

28. H. Mansel, *The Limits of Religious Thought* (Oxford: John Murray, 1858), 29–30.

29. Ibid. 30.

30. Ibid. 61.

31. Ibid. 65. One of the most interesting readings of the debate between Maurice and Mansel can be found in ch. 5 of S. Prickett, *Romanticism and Religion: The Tradition of Coleridge and Wordsworth in the Victorian Church* (Cambridge: Cambridge University Press, 1976). Prickett rejects the standard account of the disagreement between Maurice and Mansel and argues that the 'apparent similarity with Mansel was to drive Maurice

to attack him with a fervour unusual even for himself in controversy. Mansel's position is far too close for comfort: it is like a heavy-footed parody of the very subtle structure that Maurice was struggling to expound in *The Kingdom of Christ*' (137–8).

32. C. Welch, *Protestant Thought in the Nineteenth Century*, i. *1799–1870* (New Haven: Yale University Press, 1972), 255.

33. F. D. Maurice, *Sequel to the Inquiry, What is Revelation?* (Cambridge: Macmillan and Co., 1860), 279.

34. Ibid. 15. Maurice's desire to read Scripture in the light of human experience helps explain the parallels between his Christian socialism and the Liberation Theology of the late twentieth century.

35. E. Norman, *The Victorian Christian Socialists* (Cambridge: Cambridge University Press, 1987), 2.

36. Ibid. 36.

37. D. E. Hall, 'On the Making and Unmaking of Monsters: Christian Socialism, Muscular Christianity, and the Metaphorization of Class Conflict', in D. E. Hall (ed.), *Muscular Christianity: Embodying the Victorian Age* (Cambridge: Cambridge University Press, 1994), 63.

38. F. D. Maurice, *Social Morality* (London: Macmillan and Co., 1869), 13.

39. Hall, 'On the Making and Unmaking of Monsters', 64.

40. Ibid.

41. Although Alton Locke claims that 'those old Jewish heroes did fill my whole heart and soul', the 'lessons' he claims to have learnt from 'Moses leading his people out of Egypt; Gideon, Barak, and Samson, slaying their oppressors ... [and] Jehu, executing God's vengeance on the kings' seem to have lost their radical edge in translation. See C. Kingsley, *Alton Locke, Tailor and Poet: An Autobiography* (1850), 2 vols. (London: Chapman and Hall, 1851), i. 13.

42. The Salvation Army's anxiety regarding the relationship between social action and preaching the Gospel manifested itself in a number of internal debates in the 1880s: having previously argued that the Gospel alone could transform the lives of the destitute, William Booth found himself increasingly drawn to the potential for social schemes to alleviate poverty, culminating in the publication of *In Darkest England and the Way Out* (1890). For a helpful discussion of the factors that gave rise to this change of emphasis, see K. Inglis, *Churches and the Working Classes in Victorian England* (London: Routledge and K. Paul, 1963).

43. L. Feuerbach, *The Essence of Christianity*, 2nd edn. (1843), trans. M. Evans (London: John Chapman, 1854), 224.

44. G. Eliot, *Silas Marner* (1861), ed. D. Carroll (Harmondsworth: Penguin Classics, 1996), 143.

45. Ibid. 125.

46. Ibid.

47. See Brown, *The Death of Christian Britain*, and McLeod, *Religion and Society in England, 1850–1914*.

48. Feuerbach, *The Essence of Christianity*, p. v.

49. Slavoj Žižek argues otherwise when he claims that Christianity revises the Old Testament's transcendent understanding of God to reveal the deity as 'one of us'. Žižek concludes his argument by inviting Christianity to complete the undoing of its essentialist roots: 'That is the ultimate heroic gesture that awaits Christianity: in order to save its treasure, it has to sacrifice itself...' See S. Žižek, *The Puppet and the Dwarf: The Perverse Core of Christianity* (Cambridge, Mass.: MIT Press, 2003), 171.

50. B. M. G. Reardon, *Religious Thought in the Victorian Age: A Survey from Coleridge to Gore* (London: Longman, 1980), 166.

51. Norman, *The Victorian Christian Socialists*, 182.

52. For further discussion on the relation between urbanization and secularization, see H. McLeod, *Class and Religion in the Late Victorian City* (London: Croom Helm, 1974), and H. McLeod (ed.), *European Religion in the Age of the Great Cities 1830–1930* (London: Routledge, 1995).

53. Booth explained that 'the first necessity of the movement' is 'TO ATTRACT ATTENTION'. See W. Booth, *All About the Salvation Army* (London: Salvation Army Book Stores, 1883), 11.

54. W. Booth, *In Darkest England and the Way Out* (London: International Headquarters of The Salvation Army, 1890), 13. Commenting on this analogical link between hell and poverty in London, Alison Milbank writes: 'Booth's answer to this diurnal inferno was literal removal by emigration to the colonies, as well as a purged Britain. The protestant conception of the afterlife as an extension of this earthly existence ... has become actual. Booth's Salvation Army, as it became, was in itself a literalisation but in some ways also a secularisation of the Christian doctrine of the Church Militant. The relations between its rescue work and its message of redemption remains problematic to this day.' See A. Milbank, *Dante and the Victorians* (Manchester: Manchester University Press, 1998), 201.

55. J. McLaughlin, *Writing the Urban Jungle: Reading Empire in London from Doyle to Eliot* (Charlottesville, Va.: University Press of Virginia, 2000), 98.

56. T. Chalmers, *The Christian and Civic Economy of Large Towns*, ii (Glasgow: Chalmers & Collins, 1823), 2–3.

57. G. Ward, *Cities of God* (London: Routledge, 2000), 33.

58. See M. Foucault, *Discipline and Punish: The Birth of the Prison*, trans. A. Sheridan (Harmondsworth: Penguin Books, 1979).

59. Brown, *The Death of Christian Britain*, 25.

60. For a thoughtful statistical analysis of the data gathered by the 1851 religious census, see K. D. M. Snell and P. S. Ell, *Rival Jerusalems: The Geography of Victorian Religion* (Cambridge: Cambridge University Press, 2000).

61. G. Simmel, 'The Metropolis and Mental Life' (1903), in *Simmel on Culture: Selected Writings*, ed. D. Frisby and M. Featherstone (London: Sage Publications, 1997), 177–8.

62. E. Petrova, ' "And I saw the Holy City": London Prophecies in Charles Dickens and George Eliot,' *Literary London: Interdisciplinary Studies in the Representation of London*, 2: 2 (2004).

63. A. Poole, *Gissing in Context* (Basingstoke: Macmillan, 1975), 38.

64. S. Gill, 'Introduction', to G. Gissing, *The Nether World* (1889), ed. S. Gill (Oxford: Oxford World's Classics, 1992), p. xv.

65. Ibid.

66. Gissing, *The Nether World*, 152.

67. Ibid. 152.

68. Ibid. 120.

69. Ibid. 7.

70. Ibid. 345.

71. K. Hertel, 'In Darkest London: George Gissing's *The Nether World* as Urban Novel', *The Gissing Journal*, 40: 1 (2004), 12–34 (32).

72. W. T. Stead, *Mrs Booth of the Salvation Army* (London: James Nisbet & Co. Ltd., 1900), 200–1.

73. W. F. Stead published a version of Smart's *Jubilate Agno* under the title *Rejoice in the Lamb: A Song from Bedlam*.

74. W. F. Stead, 'Introduction', to C. Smart, *Rejoice in the Lamb: A Song from Bedlam* (London: Jonathan Cape, 1939), 27.

75. J. Schad, *Queer Fish: Christian Unreason from Darwin to Derrida* (Brighton: Sussex Academic Press, 2004), 107.

76. L. Newbigin, *Truth to Tell: The Gospel as Public Truth* (Grand Rapids, Mich.: William B. Eerdmans Publishing Company, 1991), 64.

77. See J. Habermas, *The Structural Transformation of the Public Sphere*, trans. T. Burger and F. Lawrence (Cambridge: Polity Press, 1989), and J. Habermas, *Between Facts and Norms: Contributions to a Discourse Theory of Law and Democracy*, trans. W. Rehg (Cambridge, Mass.: MIT Press, 1996). For a useful collection of essays on literature and the public sphere, see S. VanZanten Gallagher and M. Walhout (eds.), *Literature and the Renewal of the Public Sphere* (Basingstoke: Macmillan Press, 2000. Also, see C. Calhoun (ed.), *Habermas and the Public Sphere* (Cambridge, Mass.: MIT Press, 1992).

78. J. Walkowitz, *City of Dreadful Delight: Narratives of Sexual Danger in Late-Victorian London* (London: Virago Press, 1992), 18.

79. Gissing, *The Nether World*, 181.

80. Ibid.

81. See C. Gunton, *The One, The Three & The Many* (Cambridge: Cambridge University Press, 1993).

82. Gissing, *The Nether World*, 181.

83. While Weber's idea that the Protestant work ethic was the primary motivation for the development of capitalism has rightly been critiqued as too simplistic, the observation of a vital and significant link between the emergence of Protestantism and the rise of western capitalism remains instructive.

84. Gissing, *The Nether World*, 337.

85. While a number of religious figures from the Anglican Church sought to defend Governor Eyre, missionary leaders from nonconformist organizations were instrumental in fighting for him to be prosecuted. See T. Larsen, *Contested Christianity: The Political and Social Contexts of Victorian Theology* (Waco, Tex.: Baylor University Press, 2004), ch. 12.

86. Gissing, *The Nether World*, 75.

87. Ibid. 75–6.

88. Ibid. 76.

89. See Chapter 1 of this book for a more detailed discussion of Dissent.

90. Gissing, *The Nether World*, 319.

91. G. Gissing, *In the Year of Jubilee* (1894), ed. J. Halperin (London: The Hogarth Press, 1987), 60.

92. Ibid. 244.

93. J. Marsh, *Word Crimes: Blasphemy, Culture, and Literature in Nineteenth-Century England* (Chicago: University of Chicago Press, 1998), 163.

94. I. Armstrong, *Victorian Poetry: Poetry, Poetics and Politics* (London: Routledge, 1993), 469.

95. Ibid. 463.

96. J. Thomson, *The City of Dreadful Night and Other Poems* (London: Reeves and Turner, 1888), 2.

97. Jacques Derrida, 'Structure, Sign and Play in the Discourse of the Human Sciences,' in *Writing and Difference*, trans. A. Bass (London: Routledge, 2003).

98. Marsh, *Word Crimes*, 7.

99. Ibid. 269.

100. Ibid. 270.

101. T. Hardy, *Jude the Obscure* (1894–5), ed. C. H. Sisson (Harmondsworth: Penguin Classics, 1985), 411.

102. Marsh, *Word Crimes*, 276.
103. Hardy, *Jude the Obscure*, 369; Marsh, *Word Crimes*, 277.
104. Hardy, *Jude the Obscure*, 369.
105. Ibid. 206.
106. Ibid. 206, 207.

6

Catholicism and Mysticism: Huysmans to Chesterton

ONE of the most surprising converts to Roman Catholicism in the late nineteenth century was the Decadent writer, J. K. Huysmans. Well before his conversion in 1892 and the subsequent 'Catholic phase' of his writing, Huysmans's writing had signalled an interest in Catholicism. As Ellis Hanson observes in *Decadence and Catholicism*: 'In fact, both *A Rebours* [*Against Nature*] and *Là-Bas* [*The Damned*] are Christian conversion narratives, replete with the sort of scholarly disquisitions on mysticism, the liturgy, and Church architecture that are character-istic of his post-conversion work.'[1] *Against Nature*'s engagement with Catholicism is far from straightforward, however, as Hanson goes on to explain, and the parallel of the novel with a conversion narrative is not without its limitations: 'The final passionate prayer of *A Rebours* is by no means a resolution to Des Esseintes's oscillations. It is, rather, an inconclusive repetition in a circular narrative that rearticulates over and over the same eccentric sensibility in different words.'[2] By reminding us that the narrative does not culminate in a clear and unambiguous reli-gious resolution, Hanson points towards the way in which Huysmans's text exemplifies the complex and difficult place of Catholicism in late nineteenth-century literature. Catholicism proves incapable of answer-ing Des Esseintes's spiritual questions and explorations: the ending of the novel may continue to use Catholic discourse but it does so in an inconclusive, even hopeless, manner. Yet Hanson's insightful focus on the novel's circularity is in danger of missing the transformation that does take place in the religious discourse embraced by Des Esseintes. It is a transformation, or development, that hints at the broader appeal of Catholicism for a range of writers who, like Huysmans, converted to the Catholic faith at the end of the nineteenth century.

At an early stage of *Against Nature*, Des Esseintes's eccentricity and elitism are made clear through the narrator's description of the protagonist acting out the role of a priest:

His final caprice had been to fit up a lofty hall in which to receive his tradesmen. They used to troop in and take their places side by side in a row of church stalls; then he would ascend an imposing pulpit and preach them a sermon on dandyism, adjuring his bootmakers and tailors to conform strictly to his encyclicals on matters of cut, and threatening them with pecuniary excommunication if they did not follow to the letter the instructions contained in his monitories and bulls.[3]

The French context in which Huysmans is writing encourages us to align the vocabulary and imagery used to describe the religious instruction with Catholicism; however, the centrality of preaching in this scene owes more to Protestantism than it does to Catholicism. In Protestant ecclesiology, particularly nonconformist Protestant ecclesiology, the emphasis on the proclamation of the Word of God shows itself in both the time given to preaching in church meetings and the architectural design used to facilitate those meetings. Unlike Catholic churches, in which the pulpit is one feature among many in their architectural make-up, Protestant churches typically locate the pulpit centre stage. The Protestant mode of religious address that Des Esseintes embraces during the early stages of the novel quickly gives way to other forms of religious expression that allow for greater mystery. Des Esseintes rejects the linear, direct dynamic of preaching in favour of new modes of religious expression that offer a greater capacity for handling the complexity and subtlety of religious reflection. In doing so, Des Esseintes provides the reader with a parable of the search among Huysmans's contemporaries for new ways of mediating religious thought and addressing their own spiritual restlessness. Des Esseintes's disillusion with simplistic religious expression does not culminate in a rejection of all religion; instead, he comes to admire writers who recognize the difficulty language has when talking about God and dealing with humanity's spiritual dimension: Baudelaire is praised for 'expressing the inexpressible' and using his poetry to make out the 'hieroglyphics of the soul'; Ernest Hello is admired for recognizing that 'extraordinary things can only be stammered out'; and Paul Verlaine is acknowledged for his 'ability to communicate deliciously vague confidences in a whisper in the twilight. He alone had possessed the secret of hinting at certain strange spiritual aspirations, of whispering

certain thoughts, of murmuring certain confessions, so softly, so quietly,
so haltingly, that the ear that caught them was left hesitating.'[4] Although
Against Nature does not always make the Catholicity of these writers'
technique explicit, the novel continually associates mysterious language
and expression with the 'poetic and poignant atmosphere of Catholicism
in which he [Des Esseintes] had been steeped as a boy, and whose essence
he had absorbed through every pore'.[5] In this respect Des Esseintes anticipates Oscar Wilde, a writer greatly influenced by Huysmans, who also
converted to Catholicism. Like Huysmans, Wilde thought that the complexity of modern life required 'atmosphere with its subtlety of *nuances*,
of suggestion, of strange perspectives', and his decision to forsake his
Protestant upbringing in favour of Catholicism was partly motivated by
the ability of the latter to mediate a 'Love that dare not tell its name'.[6]

A number of critics have expressed doubt as to how seriously we are to
take the Catholicism of Huysmans, Wilde, and their peers. The Catholicism of the Decadents is rejected by some as a mere pose; others ignore
the religious ideas espoused in the belief that they are merely a symptom
of more profound intellectual and cultural forces, such as sexuality, aestheticism, and symbolism. This chapter will suggest otherwise, arguing
that many of the aspersions cast on Decadent Catholicism take their cue
from the sort of prejudicial anti-Catholicism displayed by Bram Stoker's
Dracula (1897). The caricature of Catholic belief evident in *Dracula* is
part of a long tradition of British anti-Catholicism, which, as we shall
see, blinded Protestant readers to the diversity, nuance, and intellectual
vitality of Catholic thought. This becomes evident when we consider
the poetry of Michael Field (the pseudonym of Edith Cooper and Katherine Bradley), in which Catholic theology is of primary importance,
despite its surprising and unusual formulation. To insist on the unique
contribution of Catholic theology to literary and cultural developments
in the period does not entail privileging theology as the only cultural
determinant, nor does it require the claim that Catholic theology is in-
violate and distinct from other cultural forces. It does, however, insist on
acknowledging a religious element that has sometimes been ignored by
critics. Among other things, taking the religion of the period seriously
is a prerequisite for appreciating the contribution of Catholicism to the
growth of publishing and for exploring the space that was opened up by
Catholic publishers. This will be considered in the second section of the
chapter alongside a central tenet of Catholic theology—nature and the

doctrine of creation. In the aftermath of Vatican I and with the renewal of interest in the theology of Thomas Aquinas, nature was reinterpreted by Catholic writers in the light of claims made by aestheticism. Several Catholic writers turned to the trope of a book as a means of thinking about nature, and this chapter will focus on two of them: Alice Meynell and Oscar Wilde. Wilde's *The Picture of Dorian Gray* highlights different perspectives regarding the public nature of the sacramental, as the chapter will discuss. Although sacramental theology provided a means of holding together a number of apparently divergent ideas at the end of the nineteenth century, it brought with it certain difficulties, including an openness to eclecticism, heterodoxy, and mysticism. This brings us to the final section of the chapter. After surveying some of the mystical perspectives that were popular during the period, especially Theosophy, the chapter will use Meynell's distinction between mysticism and religion as a means of structuring a final comparison between the attitudes toward religious authority in the work of two important and iconic writers: W. B. Yeats and G. K. Chesterton.

TAKING CATHOLICISM SERIOUSLY

Evidence of typical attitudes to Catholicism among British Protestants at the end of the nineteenth century can be found in Bram Stoker's *Dracula*. When Professor Van Helsing leads a small group of men to the tomb of the Un-Dead figure of Lucy Westenra in an attempt to destroy her, the novel uses the diary of Dr John Seward to record the events that ensue:

As to Van Helsing, he was employed in a definite way. First he took from his bag a mass of what looked like thin, wafer-like biscuit, which was carefully rolled up in a white napkin; next he took out a double-handful of some whitish stuff, like dough or putty. He crumbled the wafer up fine and worked it into the mass between his hands. This he then took, and rolling it into thin strips, began to lay them into the crevices between the door and its setting in the tomb. I was somewhat puzzled at this, and being close, asked him what it was that he was doing. Arthur and Quincey drew near also, as they too were curious. He answered:—

'I am closing the tomb, so that the Un-Dead may not enter.'

'And is that stuff you have put there going to do it?' asked Quincey. 'Great Scott! Is this a game?'

'It is.'

'What is that which you are using?' This time the question was by Arthur. Van Helsing reverently lifted his hat as he answered:—

'The Host. I brought it from Amsterdam. I have an Indulgence.' It was an answer that appalled the most sceptical of us ... [7]

As Maud Ellmann points out in the notes to her edition of the novel, the reason Seward is appalled may well be Van Helsing's manipulation of a sacred Catholic practice. The remission of temporal punishments for sin provided by Indulgences are not meant to be used in this way; nor is the Host, the body of Christ, said to be transubstantiated into wafers during communion, intended for the sort of manipulation to which Van Helsing subjects it. But given the scepticism of Seward and his companions towards any manifestation of religion or the supernatural—at one point Seward refers scathingly to the 'religious mania' of his patient[8]—the appalled reaction described by the text may also be read as a reaction to the way in which Catholic practice pervades this scene. Throughout the novel Stoker associates certain tenets of Catholic theology with superstition, horrible occurrences, and the demonic (at one point Dracula is referred to as 'Count de Ville'[9]), in an effort to register in Stoker's predominantly Protestant readership the same abhorrence and distaste felt by Seward. The religious practices employed by Van Helsing are clearly marked as foreign and superstitious in the text, and, even in the scene just described, the foregrounding of the Catholic mass and the acknowledgement of its potential power is undermined by Van Helsing's ability to manipulate it. Not only is Catholic theology treated as no more than a 'game', consisting of a set of arbitrary rules capable of being endlessly reworked and reinterpreted, but Van Helsing's ability to alter the elements of the mass symbolizes the novel's efforts to strip away the superstition and supernaturalism alleged to be at the heart of the Catholic faith. The redefinition of the word 'mass' in this scene, from a signifier of Catholic communion to a descriptor of physical space within the hands of Van Helsing, the consummate professional with an ability to manage everything, is significant.

Dracula is far from being the only text to make a link between Catholicism and superstition. As Victor Sage has argued in *Horror Fiction in the Protestant Tradition*, the gothic genre has, from its origins in the eighteenth century, frequently manifested Protestant anxieties and fears about Catholicism, and this goes some way to explaining the popular appeal of gothic fiction among British audiences throughout the nineteenth century. In the same way that alarm at the French Revolution reinvigorated a long tradition of British anti-Catholicism at the end of the eighteenth century, other events, including, as Susan Griffin reminds us, 'the heavy Irish immigration to England and the United States following the 1845 failure of the potato crop', 'revivified them in the nineteenth century'.[10] Among the myriad of reasons behind this prejudicial attitude was the perception of Catholicism in the British imagination as a threat to national identity (which had come to be understood as Protestant). Combined with the popular assumption that Protestant missionary activity was compatible with the civilizing purposes of a divinely inspired British Empire, the perception of Catholicism as a threat to the imperial project explains why the 'reverse colonization' threatened by Dracula includes the possible return to a superstition marked as Catholic.[11] One of the Count's early observations to the quintessentially English Jonathan Harker—'[o]ur ways are not your ways, and there shall be to you many strange things'—parodies Isaiah 55: 8 and constructs a radical separation between superstitious Catholicism and rational Protestantism.[12] Harker cements the link between foreign superstition and Catholicism when he describes his experience of the crucifix in Transylvania, and evokes the distinction between the Protestant belief in communion as a symbolic event remembering the work of Christ on the Cross, and the Catholic belief that it is a sign in which the body and blood of Christ are really manifest and present: 'It is odd that a thing which I have been taught to regard with disfavour and as idolatrous should in a time of loneliness and trouble be of help. Is it that there is something in the essence of the thing itself, or that it is a medium, a tangible help, in conveying memories of sympathy and comfort?'[13]

The pressure on Protestant religion in the late nineteenth century, most evident, perhaps, in the scientific advances that were increasingly able to explain phenomena previously considered a mystery, meant that the superstition associated with Catholicism was seen as retrograde.[14] If Count Dracula symbolizes an ancient Catholic mentality, then Van Helsing and his company, who, for all their gestures towards the superstitious, work on a professional, collective, and scientific basis, are seen as thoroughly modern.[15] The sense of a Catholicism that was out of place because of its inherent superstition caused many to view it as deviant. And because the philosophical tradition of nineteenth-century rational thought in Britain tended to eschew the complexities of continental epistemology in favour of a belief in a truth that was self-evident and natural, any belief-system relying on a set of mysterious symbols (from garlic to Indulgences) was viewed as a threat to received wisdom, and dismissed as abnormal. The suggestion that an allegedly superstitious Catholicism might not only be primitive but also deviant and unnecessary, explains why in the late nineteenth century we find frequent descriptions of Catholic converts as perverts; it also explains the equation of Catholic attitudes to transubstantiation with vampirism, the allegation that the ethics or casuistry of the Jesuits are counter-intuitive and false, and the frequent reading of Catholicism as 'a religion which is theatrically performed'.[16]

Among the multiplicity of Protestant constructions and misreadings that pervade the critical reading of late nineteenth-century Catholicism, the suggestion that Catholic theology is false by virtue of its performativity (and thus insincerity) is perhaps the most troubling. It is troubling because it is so engrained, revealing itself, for instance, in the continuing debates among scholars of the late nineteenth century regarding the extent to which the Catholicism professed by Wilde and company can be taken seriously. For many, the Catholicism of the Decadents is inherently false, a pose that exemplifies the Decadent fascination for the exotic and bizarre, and one that should not be mistaken for a sincerely held belief. In some ways such readings are understandable given the obvious difficulty of reading Wilde's religious pronouncements. Wilde's references to religion are complex, full of contradiction, and frequently accompanied by disclaimers. As Hilary Fraser rightly observes in *Beauty and Belief: Aesthetics and Religion in Victorian Literature*: '[I]t is extremely difficult to tie down Wilde's religious attitudes with any certainty. For every acquaintance or critic who dismisses him as an impostor, there is one who, taking Wilde at his own word, compares him with Christ.'[17] Fraser's response to this predicament is to read Wilde in terms of his 'dual sympathies for Catholicism and what we may loosely call Hellenism', which are said to have 'pulled him in two different directions throughout much of his life'.[18] Her reading is productive and sensitive to the vital interaction between these intellectual currents in the late nineteenth century, but it is not, as she admits, the only way of interpreting Wilde's apparent religious ambivalence. Another response, and the one which will inform the subsequent discussion of Wilde in this chapter, is to expand our understanding of the term Catholicism, recognizing that the constructed and performed elements of a belief-system do not render that system inherently false.

No belief-system is entirely consistent, and no one, however pious, is always able to *act* consistently. Of course, some nineteenth-century Evangelicals insisted that religion be read as a black-and-white issue, in which there was a clear demarcation between the theatrical and the essential, and in which religious beliefs were viewed as either false or straightforward. Leaving aside the difficulty of such readings, it is ironic that this rigid mindset has been perpetuated by aspects of our contemporary, largely secular, academic discourse, which frequently insists on choosing between sincerity and pretence when assessing the Catholicism of the Decadents. As Oscar Wilde came to discover, the theological complexity of religion in general and Catholicism in particular, a theological range that the open-ended nature of symbolism tended to encourage, allows for a belief-system that is mutable, performative, and yet capable of being held genuinely. The theatricality of Catholic religion emerges in *De Profundis*, Wilde's extended letter to Lord Alfred Douglas. In the same way that the performative aspect of the letter does not make Wilde's confession inherently false, as though one could ever hope to discover an essential Wilde behind the confession through which we read him, the insistence that '[r]eligion does not help me' does not stop Wilde from choosing to utilize and be influenced by religious categories of forgiveness and suffering throughout the letter; nor does it stop him from making a decision to interpret his own experiences in the light of the Incarnation.[19] Despite his stringent criticisms of the Church—visible, for example, in his complaint about 'Clergymen and people who use phrases without wisdom'—Wilde turns to a confessional form in this letter to help him with his reflections.[20] Just because the religious turn of the letter is not to be equated with a narrow, unambiguous statement of faith, it does not follow that the religion espoused has to be declared false and thus ignored. Indeed, it is the resistance of the Catholic theological tradition to doctrinal closure (a resistance that Wilde and others were familiar with through their reading of religious history), as well as its capacity to find space for a range of sometimes contradictory emotions, that seem to have attracted Wilde. As he writes towards the end of his letter to Douglas: 'I have grown tired of the articulate utterances of men and things. The Mystical in Art, the Mystical in Life, the Mystical in Nature—this is what I am looking for.'[21]

Huysmans and Wilde were not the only writers of the late nineteenth century to recognize the theological resources of Catholicism. Another writer displaying acute awareness of the ways in which theological writing might contribute to artistic form and content, was Michael Field. In a chapter entitled 'Lesbian Trinitarianism, Canine Catholicism', Frederick Roden focuses on the interplay between the body, identity, and Trinitarian thought in the sexualized poetry of Michael Field, telling us that 'Field actively used Catholic symbol, sacrament, and story as vehicles for articulating their longing for one another'.[22] While this comment is indicative of the helpful way in which his discussion remains alert to the

real contribution of Catholic sacramentalism and Trinitarian theology
to the poetry of Michael Field, the language through which Roden's
thoughts are expressed is problematic: it is in danger of inadvertently
relegating Catholic theology to a secondary tool which narrates a desire
that is essentially non-theological. Roden's later reference to the way
in which 'Bradley desexualizes the heteronormativity of the patriarchal
God by feminizing Christ and attributing desire to Mary' runs a similar
risk of failing to foreground fully the potential contribution of Catholic
theology to Bradley's intellectual project and her rejection of a patriarchal
concept of God.[23] What Michael Field and others discovered in the
extended Christian tradition, especially in some of the mystical Christian
writers they read at length, was a range of theological ideas that helped
shape their thinking. Of course, these theological ideas were formed in
the context of earlier cultures (rather than being essential ideas handed
down by unmediated divine fiat), and contemporary cultural trends
helped to shape Field's theological perspective, but it is important
to avoid a framework in which the contribution of religion is seen
necessarily as secondary. Even if theology is understood as non-essential,
as it is for Ellis Hanson, it can still provide a primary category for thinking
about the writing of late nineteenth-century writers.[24] With this in mind,
Hanson is keen to remind us that the Decadents were 'ardent scholars
of Church history, and they reproduced in their own work the obscure
debates of theologians, the sublime eroticism of the mystics, the very
leap of faith that every Christian genre ultimately demands. Martyrdom
and hagiography were cause for considerable speculation.'[25]

One of the most distinctive theological ideas informing Michael Field's
poetry is the Christian doctrine of the Trinity, which claims an eternal
unity, integrity, and relationality between Father, Son, and Holy Spirit.
Unlike the Unitarians, who rejected the doctrine of the Trinity as
an obscure mathematical formula imposed on Christianity by Greek
philosophy, Field found in the mysterious doctrine of the Trinity a thoroughly Christian way of thinking about love and the interrelatedness
of living beings (human and non-human). Recent critics have drawn
attention to this aspect of Field's poetry, showing how Field utilizes
the concept of the Trinity to refigure a divine and eternal relationship
of love between Katherine, Edith, and their dog, Whym Chow.[26] The
poem 'Whym Chow', for example, employs a Trinitarian vocabulary,
describing the dog as 'my eternal attribute', '[t]he very essence of the
thing I am'.[27] In addition to framing and elevating Field's personal
relations, the doctrine of the Trinity provided Field with a means of

coming to terms with contemporary changes in the understanding of metaphysics. Up until the second half of the nineteenth century, the Hellenistic inheritance of western culture meant that the temporal world was often seen as an inadequate echo of perfect, immutable, and timeless forms. Through his famous analogy of a cave, Plato had explained the temporal world as a flawed copy or imitation of the divine. The influence of this Hellenistic perspective on much of the Christian tradition in the west was a key factor behind Frederick Nietzsche's extensive and vehement critique of religion. Nietzsche was not alone in questioning the metaphysical assumptions common to Christian religion in the nineteenth century, and others, such as Walter Pater, helped develop new modes of thought, such as aestheticism, which viewed the arts as a mode of expression necessary for realizing the world's fundamental fluidity. In the doctrine of the Trinity, Field discovered a metaphysical framework capable of acknowledging the flux of the universe without collapsing into intellectual chaos. The possibilities of the doctrine of the Trinity for metaphysics are explored by Field in the first stanza of the poem 'Old and New':

> The Motions of the Trinity
>   When the old ways God used toward men
>   Were over earth,
> Before the Word stooped into mortal birth:—
> Elijah heard a wind, he heard a flame and then
> A still, small voice, and 'mid the three
> God only dwelt within the little girth
> Of silence in its thrilled profundity.[28]

Rather than treating the progressive revelation of the books of the Bible as a concession by God to the needs of a temporal world that can only understand things in linear fashion, the gradual nature of revelation is seen as continuous with the very person of God, whose 'Motions' are fundamental to his being and whose activity is orientated 'towards' others. Having established a Triune view of God as a being who has always existed in movement and relation, Field goes on to observe the link to the Incarnation, finding continuity in the understanding of Jesus as one who became flesh and 'stooped into mortal birth'. As well as providing a means of thinking about metaphysics without returning to older ideas of fixity and stasis, the doctrine of the Trinity equipped Field with the theological resources needed for fluid and imaginative artistic exploration.

THE BOOK OF NATURE AND THE SACRAMENTAL UNIVERSE

Appreciating the potential of theology to make a serious contribution to the arts allows us to realize the integrity and richness of the work produced by another famous late nineteenth-century Catholic poet and writer, Alice Meynell. Meynell's understanding of a sacramental universe, in which the whole of the created order is seen as a sign of the presence of God, provided a means of integrating Impressionism with her religious beliefs. While references to a sacramental universe are to be found across the Christian denominations, they are most pervasive in Catholic theology, partly because of the extensive use of symbolism within Catholic practice and partly because, unlike Protestantism, which typically emphasizes the world's fallenness, Catholic theology tends to hold a higher view of the created order and is more likely to seek God's revelation in the natural world. The importance of creation in Catholic theology, and the related interest in sacramental theology, was given fresh impetus in the latter part of the nineteenth century by Vatican I and a revival of interest in the work of Thomas Aquinas. Convoked by Pope Pius IX in 1868, the first Vatican Council was held in Rome between 1869 and 1870. Originally it was intended to cover a wide range of subjects but the outbreak of war between France and Prussia in July 1870 cut short the discussions and ensured that only certain issues were addressed. In addition to pronouncing in favour of Papal Infallibility, the first Vatican Council produced a revised constitution on faith, 'Dei Filius', which attacked the materialism and atheism of the day and offered chapters on God as Creator, revelation, faith, and the relationship between faith and reason. In focusing on questions of faith and reason, it was inevitable that the discussions of the Council should draw upon the medieval theologian Thomas Aquinas, who wrote extensively on the subject and explored ways in which language and creation might reveal God. The interest in medieval figures such as Aquinas was part of a broader interest among the Victorians in the medieval period, and the Decadents read a variety of works by assorted theologians and saints. After Pope Leo XIII's bull *Aeterni Patris* (1879), Aquinas became especially important to Catholic thinkers and the school of theology known as Thomism enjoyed a new period of ascendancy at the turn of the century. Leo XIII called upon all students of theology to read Aquinas and the medieval theologian was subsequently made patron of all Catholic universities.

It is difficult to assess the precise impact of Thomistic theology on British Catholicism in the late nineteenth century; one can, however, see clear traces of Aquinas in the work of Alice Meynell, a writer who, as one of the best known literary celebrities of the 1890s, was referred to by Wilde as the 'new Sibyl of style'.[29] Meynell produced an extensive range of poetry, journalism, and essays up until her death in 1922 but it is probably her work of the 1890s that is most deserving of renewed attention, primarily because of its engagement with literary Impressionism.[30] Whereas some Catholic thinkers, such as Chesterton, noted the tendency of Impressionism towards illusion, and thought that this made it the polar opposite of Aquinas's bold affirmation of existence, other Catholics presented more positive readings of Impressionism and managed to reconcile it with their theology. Meynell was among the latter: she wrote extensively about Impressionism in the 1890s and was a vital figure in encouraging fellow writers to realize the importance of Impressionism for literature. The arts were seen as mimetic for much of the nineteenth century and, by the mid-Victorian period, the realist novel was the dominant literary form. The position of the realist novel was further consolidated in the 1870s and 1880s through the burgeoning interest in naturalism. But as the century drew to a close, the rise of aestheticism, encouraged by Impressionism's emphasis on the subjectivity of art, called the basis of mimetic realism into question. The challenge to earlier views of the purpose of literature was epitomized by Wilde's provocative reversal of the accepted subservience of art to nature in his preface to *The Picture of Dorian Gray* (1891). Although Meynell thought mimetic realism inadequate, she did not think that the answer was to reverse older notions and claim, like Wilde, that life imitated art. Instead, Meynell conceived of the relation between art and nature in dynamic terms, refusing to flatten the difference between them and refusing to prioritize one over the other. Meynell's understanding of the arts emerges in 'Rain', an essay published in *The Spirit of Place and Other Essays* (1899). Reflecting on the phenomenon of rain, she observes that 'there is nothing in nature that so outstrips our unready eyes'.[31] The comment reveals something of her debt to Impressionism in its interest in the observer and their subjective perception of the world; however, the idea of nature outstripping our perception ensures that the focus on the role of the writer or artist does not undermine the contingency of the arts on the world in which they undertake their imaginative activity.

One of the most striking aspects of 'Rain' is the way in which Meynell reconfigures the trope of nature as a book to be read. While the Calvinism of Reformed Protestantism, with its emphasis on total depravity and the sinfulness of the world, suggested that the natural world yielded virtually no information about God, the majority of British Protestants thought that the natural world was a self-evident and self-interpreting book, one which, though much less important than Scripture, complemented the Bible as a source of revelation. Yet viewing nature as an alternative source of revelation that might be understood in a similar textual fashion to the Divine Word was problematic: either it tended to reduce the material world to an inadequate echo of God or, conversely, it subverted the need for the Special Revelation of Scripture by promoting a naturalistic Deism in which, as our chapter on Unitarianism shows, God became increasingly absent and unnecessary. As a Catholic Meynell was less anxious about the inviolability of Sacred Texts, and in an attempt to avoid the dilemma described above, she reconfigured the book of nature as a dynamic text that informs our reading and yet is also added to by our perception of it:

The visible world is etched and engraved with the signs and records of our halting apprehension; and the pause between the distant woodman's stroke with the axe and its sound upon our ears is repeated in the impression of our clinging sight. The round wheel dazzles it, and the stroke of the bird's wing shakes it off like a captivity evaded. Everywhere the natural haste is impatient of these timid senses; and their perception, outrun by the shower, shaken by the light, denied by the shadow, eluded by the distance, makes the lingering picture that is all our art. One of the most constant causes of all the mystery and beauty of that art is surely not that we see by flashes, but that nature flashes on our meditative eyes.[32]

Meynell is careful to emphasize the movement of the natural world and to locate our acts of perception as part of the world's essential relatedness: 'signs' and 'records' are, in her words, 'engraved' or written into the visible world. Her suggestion that nature answers the 'meditative eyes' turned towards it implies that the dynamic hermeneutic she envisages is deliberate rather than accidental, and by replacing the glass through which Paul claims to see darkly (1 Corinthians 13) with rain, Meynell makes her notion of dynamic, fluid reading integral to our perception of the universe. As with Field's Trinitarian conception of metaphysics, the world is seen to be constituted by its inherent relatedness. This organic understanding of the natural world not only invites readers to participate in it; it also points to a God behind it who is simultaneously present and involved.

The resulting theological sacramentalism, with its understanding of a God who is really present (rather than just echoed) in the material world, is sustained by Meynell's regard for the doctrine of the Incarnation. In the poem 'Unto us a Son is Given' Meynell begins: 'GIVEN not lent | And not withdrawn—once sent'.[33] The play of the word 'lent' on the period of abstinence that Christian tradition practises in the period immediately prior to Easter Sunday suggests that Meynell views the Incarnation as a more useful starting-point for theology than the focus on the Cross favoured by Protestantism. In her emphasis on the Incarnation, Meynell continues the work of Gerard Manley Hopkins, who, as Hilary Fraser points out, turned to the Incarnation to help him overcome the 'problem with sacramental views of nature … that … did not seem to offer a specifically Christian concept of nature'.[34] For both Hopkins and Meynell, the continuing presence of Christ in the natural world ensured a text that could only be read by way of a dynamic hermeneutic that was specifically Christian. Meynell's idea that 'Art and Nature are separate, complementary; in relation, not in confusion with one another', provided her art with a means of social engagement, an emphasis central to Catholic social teaching and evident in her journalism.[35] It also enabled a theological openness to, and awareness of, the power of language, an openness that found support in Aquinas's decision to open his *Summa Theologica* with an affirmation of the capacity of finite language to refer to God. In a period where authors with a Protestant heritage frequently exhibited considerable anxiety about the world of publishing—one thinks of Gissing railing against the injustice of commercial publishing in *Old Grub Street* (1891) and Marie Corelli associating publishing with the Devil in *The Sorrows of Satan* (1895)—it is striking that Meynell should be at the forefront of a growth in Catholic writing. In contrast to John Henry Newman's gloomy prediction that English literature was essentially Protestant and destined to remain so, Alice Meynell and her husband Wilfred were at the forefront of a revival in Catholic literary publication at the turn of the century.[36] As well as writing regularly for leading newspapers and periodicals such as the *Spectator*, the *Pall Mall Gazette*, and the *Illustrated London News*, publications that another prominent Catholic, Chesterton, would also write for, Meynell and her husband edited *Merry England*, 'a nursing place where young Catholic genius might be planted and become full of growing. The established writers of the faith, Coventry Patmore, and Aubrey de Vere, gave it their support ... and many more' contributed, including Katherine Tynan, Francis Thompson, Lionel Johnson, and Hilaire Belloc.[37] The publishing activity of the Meynells, along with other Catholic presses such as Sheed and Ward, and Burns and Oates, did much to strengthen the position of Catholic writers in the literary market at the start of the twentieth century, and may be seen as paving the way for the next generation of Catholic writers, including Graham Greene, Evelyn Waugh, and Muriel Spark.[38]

Meynell's confidence in the power of the written word and its capacity to mediate religious belief is evident throughout her writing in the numerous claims she makes about words and language. Despite complaining in an essay entitled 'Pocket Vocabularies' about the way in which '[c]ertain poets, a certain time ago, ransacked the language for words full of life and beauty, made a vocabulary of them, and out of wantonness wrote them to death', and despite expressing concern at the way in which some of her contemporaries had taken the 'very word that lives, "new every morning"', and 'killed' it, she remained confident that language was capable of resisting death and closure.[39] Unlike some of her Protestant predecessors and contemporaries, who wanted to fix the meaning of words, Meynell admired the independence of a language she saw as related to, but not entirely under the control of, its authors. In her essay 'Composure' she writes of the essential harmony between language and author: 'Every language, by counter-change, replies to the writer's touch or breath his own intention, articulate: this is his note.'[40] Meynell's confidence in language is intrinsic to her understanding of the relationality at the centre of life, and is underlined by a belief that words mediate rather than distort the divine, albeit in an incomplete fashion. Describing Meynell's critical perspective on language, Anne Tuell tells us that: 'To regard it [language] as the dress of thought in the time-honoured way is the fallacy of those who "separate a building from its architecture". The true poet must see in poetry the incarnate word, "the organic articulation of means in which metre, diction, pause, rhyme, phrase, are not accidental but essential".'[41]

Where Decadent Catholic contemporaries differed from Meynell was over the extent to which the sacramentalism of language might be seen as public. For Meynell, the doctrine of the Incarnation meant that the religious referent of all writing, whether journalism or poetry, was public. This belief helps explain her prolific publishing activity, as well as her insistence in 'The Point of Honour' that Impressionism was 'doubly bound' to record its subjective impressions honestly.[42] Meynell attacked fellow writers who used the shadowy world of Impressionism to pretend that they had 'a word worth hearing—nay, worth overhearing—a word that seeks to withdraw even while it is uttered'.[43] Her public reading of sacraments stands in contrast to writers such as Ernest Dowson and Oscar Wilde, who conceived the sacramental realm of language as private and described it in terms of silence and secrecy. In his short poem 'A Valediction', for instance, Dowson signals a loss of belief in the ability of divine words to speak publicly: 'Words are so weak | When love hath been so strong: | Let silence speak'.[44] The communication offered by silence is real but it is also intensely private; although this claim appears unproblematic, theological questions emerge when Dowson carries over the same line of thought to his evocative poem 'Benedictio Domini':

> Without, the sullen noises of the street!
>   The voice of London, inarticulate,
> Hoarse and blaspheming, surges in to meet
>   The silent blessing of the Immaculate.
>
> Dark is the church, and dim the worshippers,
>   Hushed with bowed heads as though by some old
>   spell,
> While through the incense-laden airs there stirs
>   The admonition of a silver bell.
>
> Dark is the church, save where the altar stands,
>   Dressed like a bride, illustrious with light,
> Where one old priest exalts with tremulous hands
>   The one true solace of man's fallen plight.
>
> Strange silence here: without, the sounding street
>   Heralds the world's swift passage to the fire:
> O Benediction, perfect and complete!
>   When shall men cease to suffer and desire?[45]

Although the 'silent blessing' of the Church communicates more than '[t]he voice of London, inarticulate', a voice said to have grown 'hoarse' through its noise, and although the unspoken message of the Church is beautiful, it no longer speaks publicly. Two of the stanzas open by insisting that the church is 'Dark' and the absence of light is also manifest in the shadowy worshippers. The reference to a 'Strange silence' in the last stanza of the poem acknowledges that the message of the Church is not meant to be private, but neither the culturally anachronistic priest or the altar, with its 'illustrious' light, are capable of dispelling the pervading darkness and allowing the masses to experience divine revelation.

Like Dowson, Wilde struggles to comprehend the sacramental quality of language as public. Nowhere is this more evident than in the secrecy of the '[s]acramental theology' that 'infuses' *The Picture of Dorian Gray*.[46] Lord Henry reflects that although 'the body had its moments of spirituality … Who could say where the fleshly impulse ceased.'[47] Similarly, Dorian thinks that religious readings should remain subjective and private: despite thinking that his portrait, a 'visible symbol of the degradation of sin', will 'reveal to him his own soul', he refuses to allow anyone else to share in the revelation.[48] When Basil Hallward suggests exhibiting the picture, Dorian feels 'a strange sense of terror creeping over him. Was the world going to be shown his secret? Were people to gape at the mystery of his life? That was impossible.'[49] Dorian's perpetual fear that his secret might be discovered is shown as unnecessary in a narrative that is mysterious, indirect, and far from the straightforward moral allegory that some readers suggested upon the book's publication. While the possibility of a public confession is continually held out to the reader, Dorian's final laughter at this 'monstrous' idea underlines the impossibility of confession being anything other than private.[50] His death takes place behind closed doors, and although the reader is allowed to hear Dorian's last meditations and read about his tragic demise, the ambiguity of the concluding pages stops them from being an equivalent to the sort of public confession that one finds at the end of Stevenson's *Dr Jekyll and Mr Hyde*. By continually making reference to confession but refusing to admit its public dimension, the novel revises a well-known Christian sacrament. Hence at the same time that we are told in chapter 11 of Dorian's attraction to the Roman Catholic communion, we are left with an image of a private, hidden confessional: 'As he passed out, he used to look with wonder at the black confessionals, and long to sit in the dim shadow of one of them and listen to men and women whispering through the worn grating the true story of their lives.'[51] Dorian's view that language speaks of religion but does so privately, is also evident in Basil's reflections. After confessing how Dorian has shaped his art, Basil explains himself: 'It was not intended as a compliment. It was a confession. Now that I have made it, something seems to have gone out of me. Perhaps one should never put one's worship into words.'[52]

MYSTICISM VERSUS RELIGION

If the sacramental language offered by both nature and the arts is essentially private, it is difficult to see a limit to the referent of that language. As a consequence, when several authors at the turn of the century grew disillusioned with a strictly materialist philosophy and sought to revisit spirituality, they turned to a dramatically eclectic range of esoteric beliefs extending well beyond the broad parameters of the Christian faith. Perhaps the most prominent expression of this renewed interest in mystical spirituality during the late nineteenth century was the Theosophical Movement, founded by the charismatic Helene Petrovna Blavatsky in 1875. Theosophy fused spiritualism with oriental religious beliefs and sought to promote the study of comparative religion alongside investigation of the occult and the pursuit of hidden knowledge. The eclecticism of Theosophical thought is illustrated through the conversion of Annie Besant to Theosophy in the late 1880s: before her conversion, Besant had been a leading freethinker and a powerful advocate of socialism; afterwards, she applied her forceful personality to Theosophy and succeeded Blavatsky as the movement's leader.[53] Among the numerous books and pamphlets produced by Besant to explain the ideals of Theosophy, *Mysticism* (1912) provides some of the firmest evidence of the movement's broad, and typically vague, use of spiritual terminology: 'Theosophy is the reassertion of Mysticism within the bosom of every living religion, the affirmation of the reality of the mystic state of consciousness and of the value of its products. In the midst of a scholarly and critical generation, it reproclaims the superiority of the knowledge which is drawn from the direct experience of the spiritual world.'[54]

Theosophy provides a useful starting-point for examining the interest in mysticism at the turn of the century; its trace can be found in the work of a number of writers, from Rider Haggard to Marie Corelli. In an essay on Rider Haggard, Carolyn Burdett notes the symbolic importance of the journey to Tibet in *Ayesha: The Return of She* (1905) and explains:

The importance of Tibet as a centre for occult philosophy and practice had been widely popularised, both through the notoriety of Helene Petrovna

Blavatsky and by Alfred Sinnet's influential books, *The Occult World* and *Esoteric Buddhism*, published in the early 1880s. These works set out the tenets of Theosophy and, in part, chart Sinnet's relations with Madame Blavatsky and the 'Masters' with whom she communed.[55]

Burdett goes on to argue that, like Theosophy, Haggard's novel encourages the study of comparative religion, challenges the 'exceptionalism of Christian doctrine', and concludes that truth is found in a religious hybrid.[56] A similar preference for religious eclecticism can be found in the work of Corelli, whose popularity among the reading public suggests that interest in esoteric spirituality was not confined to a select group of writers. Different expressions of spirituality are present throughout Corelli's work—*A Romance of Two Worlds* (1886) is centred around the occult and *Ardath* (1889) explores reincarnation, to give just two examples—but the willingness to rework central aspects of the Christian narrative are most apparent in Corelli's trilogy of novels: *Barabbas* (1893), *The Sorrows of Satan* (1895), and *The Master Christian* (1900). Given the ease with which all three books throw off the constraints of theological orthodoxy, it is no surprise that ecclesial authorities are the subject of extensive critique in these narratives. Prince Rimânez, the devil who comes to London in *The Sorrows of Satan*, seems to reflect his author's prejudice when he observes: 'Many of the clergy are doing their utmost best to *destroy* religion—by cant, by hypocrisy, by sensuality, by shams of every description.'[57] While the main ecclesial target of Corelli's novels is the Roman Catholic Church, an Anglican reviewer of her work, writing for *The Church Quarterly Review* in January 1901, felt the need of 'protesting somewhat indignantly against the vilification of a Church which, in spite of many shortcomings, is, and ever has been, a source of blessing and not a curse to humanity'.[58]

Like Corelli, Besant's writing displays a repeated hostility to Roman Catholicism. In her biography of Besant, Anne Taylor reads the 'antipathy to the Christian Church' that pervades Besant's writing on Theosophy as a vestige of her earlier atheism and involvement with the National Secular Society. Taylor rightly points out that Besant had 'to force herself—not always successfully—to observe the central tenet of Theosophy: that all religious were equally entitled to respect'.[59] In a number of her works Besant ends up distinguishing true religion from the corruption of it by the Roman Catholic Church, and Catholicism is often situated as the polar opposite of the inclusivity and openness said to be embodied by Theosophy. In *The Spirit of the Age* (1908), for example,

Besant complains that: 'Rome's matchless organisation is to be used to discover and to crush every professor who will not teach along the lines that she lays down ... There is something magnificent in the audacity which rears its haughty head against the modern world, and seeks to throw across the stream of thought a dam constructed out of mediaeval theology.'[60] The reference to medieval theology reflects the direction of Roman Catholic theology after Vatican I and the analogy of a dam underlines Besant's concern about the rigid imperialism of the Catholic Church; at the same time, elsewhere, Besant inadvertently reinscribes the religious imperialism to which she objects. In *Theosophy and Christianity* (1914) Besant describes Theosophy as the final arbiter of religious difference: 'To-day the religious field is a field of combat; rival Churches, rival war-cries, rival Religions, and if Theosophy be but one more combatant, one more rival sect, the world could well enough do without it. But the stately figure of the ancient Wisdom Religion does not enter the field as a combatant but as a peace-maker, not as a rival but as an explainer.'[61]

Besant's inconsistent talk of a universal religion highlights the failure of Theosophy to recognize the numerous differences of different belief-systems: indeed, some expressions of *fin-de-siècle* spirituality embraced esoteric ideas antithetical to the Christian faith. Writers who aligned themselves with orthodox Christianity often pointed this out: for example, Alice Meynell insisted on distinguishing religion from mysticism in her introduction to Adeline Cashmore's *The Mount of Vision: A Book of English Mystical Verse* (1910):

I have used the word religious rather than mystical, not because the terms are precisely equivalent, but because the first is the safer. It is ominous to hear the name of mysticism so easily used, given and taken, without a thought of its cost. It is not long since an interesting novel appeared of which the motive and the whole subject was Mysticism. Visions were easy to come by; and revelations, and such extreme things as 'the unitive life'—things for which the Saints thought fifty years of self-conquest and self-abandonment a paltry price—were discussed as incidents of well-read aspiration. There was no mention of the first step, there was much chatter of the last.[62]

Although Meynell avoids constructing a strict dichotomy between the religious and the mystical, she does warn against critical schemas that treat Huysmans's conversion to Catholicism and Besant's turn to Theosophy as equivalent and interchangeable expressions of spiritual intent. Whatever the limitations of Meynell's distinction, it is worth giving serious consideration to the terms she employs. Reviewing Viola Meynell's memoir of her mother, Chesterton remarked that Alice

Meynell 'was in a sense fastidious about selecting or rejecting words; but she selected them because they were fresh, or rejected them because they were not fresh enough'.[63] Recognizing that the renewal of spiritual interest at the turn of the century ran the risk of becoming tired and outdated (a risk epitomized in *Against Nature* by Des Esseintes's short-lived fascination with particular Catholic writers), Meynell urges her readers to think again about what terms such as 'religion' and 'mysticism' refer to. Her preference for the term religion, because of its historic acknowledgement of the discipline, cost, and continuity of faith, is an attempt to address the ephemeralization and commodification of belief at the end of the nineteenth century. Meynell felt that some of her contemporaries were picking different aspects of broader belief-systems at random and mixing them together to suit their immediate wants, a tendency that revealed the extent to which modern consumerism had infiltrated religion by the *fin de siècle*. Meynell's use of the term 'chatter' to describe the mystical discourse of her day points to a banality that sometimes accompanied spiritual talk, and the word offers a marked contrast to the whispered, elevated, and inexpressible language admired by Des Esseintes.

Like Meynell, Chesterton thought it problematic to use the words religion and mysticism interchangeably: whereas the Catholic religion affirmed the value of the material world by insisting on its ongoing relation to the God who created it; mysticism tended to downplay the material world by collapsing any distinction between Creator and creation and suggesting that material particularity was merely an illusion, the uncovering of which would reveal an essential unity. In the chapter of his autobiography discussing the intellectual currents he experienced in the suburb of Bedford Park during the 1890s, Chesterton draws upon this distinction to offer a critique of Yeats's spirituality: 'Yeats affected me strongly, but in two opposite ways; like the positive and negative poles of a magnet.'[64] On the one hand, Chesterton admired the way in which, against a 'drab background of dreary modern materialism, Willie Yeats was calmly walking about as the Man Who Knew the Fairies. Yeats stood for enchantment ... He was the real original rationalist who said that the fairies stand to reason'; on the other hand, Chesterton noted that '[i]n the scheme of mysticism to which he more and more tended after his first more fortunate adventures among farmers and fairies, the ancient religions stood more and more for the idea that the secret of the sphinx is that she has no secret'.[65] Despite its polemical and exaggerated tone, Chesterton's observation is perceptive: Yeats's desire to find the 'secret of the sphinx' is evident in his movement between different occult groups (in the late 1880s, for instance, Yeats participated in both the Esoteric Section of the Theosophical Society and the Hermetic Order of the Golden Dawn), and his ongoing attempts to validate the occult through experimentation and investigation. Yeats never gave up on spirituality, however. In 1914 he became interested in the work of Emanuel Swedenborg, and during the latter part of his life he expended considerable energy on *A Vision* (1925, 1937), a book outlining a mystical philosophy of history allegedly revealed through the help of automatic writing. Yeats's understanding of what mysticism entailed became ever more distant from the theistic beliefs central to the Christian faith.[66]

Reflecting on the 'manifold' uses of occultism for Yeats, Roy Foster speculates how '[t]he world of the Golden Dawn provided a compensation for the daily struggle in Bedford Park: a sign that, somewhere, a world might exist where reality could echo and confirm his magnificent imagination'.[67] This reading of Yeats as understanding mysticism and the occult in relation to the imagination, is supported by the recollection of Yeats's admission that 'magic gave him metaphors for his poetry'.[68] Although Yeats's reliance on symbolism and his wide-ranging engagement with diverse beliefs make it almost impossible to condense his thought into a clear philosophical system, his writing bears strong traces of an esoteric idealism akin to pantheism, with its rejection of any distinction between God and the world. In an essay on the famous Idealist philosopher, George Berkeley, Yeats describes 'the movement of philosophy from Spinoza to Hegel' as 'the greatest of all works of intellect'.[69] Everything in existence, from everyday material objects to the land of fairies and alleged instances of supernatural phenomena, are to be seen as manifestations of a universal thought, one that Hegel described in terms of an Absolute Spirit and one that Yeats conceived of, perhaps more flexibly, in terms of the imagination. Yeats articulates his thinking on this matter at the conclusion to his essay 'Magic' (1901), where he insists that 'surely, at whatever risk, we must cry out that imagination is always seeking to remake the world according to the impulses and the patterns in that Great Mind, and that Great Memory?'[70] At the time of 'Magic' Yeats still appears to have contemplated the possibility that the 'supreme Enchanter, or some one in His councils' is the source of our imaginative activity, but, as Chesterton later realized, he became less and less convinced by the idea that an Enchanter lay behind the imagination.[71] Symbols were not, for Yeats, a sign of the presence of the divine, as Chesterton and other sacramental theologians claimed; instead, they were themselves intrinsically divine, mysterious signifiers of an infinite series of associations. In his essay 'The Symbolism of Poetry' (1900) Yeats explained:

All sounds, all colours, all forms, either because of their preordained energies or because of long association, evoke indefinable and yet precise emotions, or, as I prefer to think, call down among us certain disembodied powers, whose footsteps over our hearts we call emotions; and when sound, and colour, and form are in a musical relation, a beautiful relation to one another, they become, as it were, one sound, one colour, one form, and evoke an emotion that is made out of their distinct evocations and yet is one emotion. The same relation exists between all portions of every work of art, whether it be an epic or a song, and the more perfect it is, and the more various and numerous the elements that have flowed into its perfection, the more powerful will be the emotion, the power, the god it calls among us.[72]

Ultimately, symbolism allowed Yeats to explicate his belief in the unity of all things, a unity that eschewed any distinction between God and the world, and sought instead to discover the god within.

The critique of Yeats proffered by Chesterton reminds us of the danger of conflating the interest in mysticism and Catholicism during the *fin de siècle*: Chesterton may have 'preferred the Celtic Twilight to the materialistic midnight' but he rejected Yeats's implicit pantheism in favour of a Catholicism that maintained a distinction between the Creator and the created.[73] To understand the extent of the difference between these positions, it is helpful to turn to Chesterton's novel *The Man who was Thursday: A Nightmare* (1908), a surreal tale reflecting Chesterton's struggles with contemporary pessimism in the 1890s and his 'inward impulse to revolt; to dislodge this incubus or throw off this nightmare'.[74] In the novel the protagonist, Gabriel Syme, comes to realize that the world is not as bad as it seems and that not everyone is in a conspiracy against him. Syme's growing realization culminates in a climactic encounter with the godlike figure of Sunday, which leads to the conclusion that the world is somehow infused with the divine. But a world infused with the divine is not the same as a world created and sustained by the divine. Responding to the suggestion that 'the pantomime ogre who was called Sunday ... was meant for a blasphemous

version of the Creator', Chesterton offered the following gloss on his
novel: 'But the point is that the whole story is a nightmare of things,
not as they are, but as they seemed to the young half-pessimist of the
'90s; and the ogre who appears brutal but is also cryptically benevolent
is not so much God, in the sense of religion or irreligion, but rather
Nature as it appears to the pantheist, whose pantheism is struggling out
of pessimism.'[75] Here, and elsewhere in his autobiography, Chesterton
treats pantheism as a stepping stone to theism; unlike theism, however,
it has no doctrine of Creation by which one might express gratitude
to the author of existence. Chesterton's preference for pantheism over
materialism should not obscure his considerable hostility to both. It is an
objection that emerges clearly in *Orthodoxy* (1908), where Chesterton
turns his attention to Annie Besant's announcement that 'there was only
one religion in the world' and details his concern at her 'thoughtful
and suggestive description of the religion in which all men must
find themselves in agreement'.[76] Having linked Besant's mysticism to
Buddhist thought, Chesterton proceeds to explain the conflicting claim
made by the Christian faith:

It is just here that Buddhism is on the side of modern pantheism and immanence. And it is just here that Christianity is on the side of humanity and liberty
and love. Love desires personality; therefore love desires division. It is the
instinct of Christianity to be glad that God has broken the universe into little
pieces, because they are living pieces. ... This is the intellectual abyss between
Buddhism and Christianity; that for the Buddhist or Theosophist personality
is the fall of man, for the Christian it is the purpose of God, the whole point of
his cosmic idea. The world-soul of the Theosophists asks man to love it only in
order that man may throw himself into it. But the divine centre of Christianity
actually threw man out of it in order that he might love it. ... No other philosophy makes God actually rejoice in the separation of the universe into living
souls. But according to orthodox Christianity this separation between God and
man is sacred, because this is eternal.[77]

By celebrating difference in this manner, Chesterton offers a reading of
Christian theology that affirms the particularity of the material world
and refuses to narrow the sphere of religious concern to a discrete
spiritual realm. Moreover, the suggestion that there might be something
sacred about the way in which the universe is deliberately broken
into little, living pieces, encourages us to explore further the multiple
controversies and debates surrounding religion and literature in the long
nineteenth century.

NOTES

1. E. Hanson, *Decadence and Catholicism* (Cambridge, Mass.: Harvard University Press, 1997), 110.
2. Ibid. 133.
3. J. K. Huysmans, *Against Nature*, ed. R. Baldick (Harmondsworth: Penguin Classics, 1959), 26–7.
4. Ibid. 148, 191, 159, and 186.
5. Ibid. 93.
6. O. Wilde, *De Profundis and Other Writings*, ed. H. Pearson (London: Penguin Classics, 1986), 144, 121. The phrase 'Love that dare not tell its name' is taken from Alfred Douglas's poem 'Two Loves', the last two lines of which are: 'Then sighing said the other, "Have thy will, | I am the Love that dare not speak its name".' Our reading of the Love referred to by Wilde deliberately slips between religion and sexuality, echoing the broader slippage between these two subjects in *De Profundis*. For an intriguing and suggestive discussion of the relationship between religion and sexuality in Wilde, see chapter 5 of J. Schad, *Queer Fish: Christian Unreason from Darwin to Derrida* (Brighton: Sussex Academic Press, 2004).
7. B. Stoker, *Dracula*, ed. M. Ellmann (Oxford: Oxford World's Classics, 1998), 209–10.
8. Ibid. 100.
9. Ibid. 273.
10. S. M. Griffin, *Anti-Catholicism and Nineteenth-Century Fiction* (Cambridge: Cambridge University Press, 2004), 3. Thomas Woodman identifies two other main factors contributing to the development of Catholicism in the second half of the nineteenth century: the restoration of the hierarchy in 1850, in which the Pope appointed a hierarchy of bishops to govern the Catholic Church, and the Oxford Movement. See T. Woodman, *Faithful Fictions: The Catholic Novel in British Literature* (Milton Keynes: Open University Press, 1991), 5.
11. The term 'reverse colonization' is used by Stephen Arata in his well-known essay on *Dracula*. See S. Arata, 'The Occidental Tourist: Dracula and the Anxiety of Reverse Colonization', *Victorian Studies*, 33 (1990), 621–45.
12. Stoker, *Dracula*, 21.
13. Ibid. 28.
14. Science and superstition were not considered polar opposites by everyone, however. As Roger Luckhurst argues: 'Spiritualism and Theosophy were often defined as belief systems in opposition to the orthodoxies of science, but psychical research often sought as many legitimating interconnections to scientific modernity as possible.' See R. Luckhurst, 'Knowledge, Belief and the Supernatural at the Imperial Margin', in N. Bown, C. Burdett, and

P. Thurschwell (eds.), *The Victorian Supernatural* (Cambridge: Cambridge University Press, 2004), 203. Chapter 5 of our book discusses further the way in which ghosts stories and a range of strange phenomena foregrounded questions of scientific epistemology during the nineteenth century. For an interesting anthropological account of strange phenomena at the close of the nineteenth century, in which the author does his best to describe unusual experiences without determining whether or not their supernatural elements are real, see A. Lang, *Cock Lane and Common-Sense* (London: Longmans, Green, & Co., 1894).

15. See the discussion of professionalism in *Dracula* in N. Daly, *Modernism, Romance, and the Fin de Siècle: Popular Fiction and British Culture, 1880–1914* (Cambridge: Cambridge University Press, 1999).

16. Griffin, *Anti-Catholicism and Nineteenth-Century Fiction*, 5.

17. H. Fraser, *Beauty and Belief: Aesthetics and Religion in Victorian Literature* (Cambridge: Cambridge University Press, 1986), 209.

18. Ibid.

19. Wilde, *De Profundis*, 154.

20. Ibid. 160.

21. Ibid. 207.

22. F. Roden, *Same-Sex Desire in Victorian Religious Culture* (Basingstoke: Palgrave, 2002), 198.

23. Ibid. 210.

24. See Hanson, *Decadence and Catholicism*, 19.

25. Ibid. 6.

26. See Roden, *Same-Sex Desire*, ch. 7.

27. In M. Field, *Wild Honey from Various Thyme* (London: T. Fisher Unwin, 1908).

28. In M. Field, *The Wattlefold: Unpublished Poems by Michael Field*, collected by E. C. Fortey and with a preface by Father V. McNabb (Oxford: Basil Blackwell, 1930).

29. Wilde, *De Profundis*, 147.

30. An excellent reading of Meynell's impressionist poetics can be found in chapter 2 of A. Vadillo, *Women Poets and Urban Aestheticism: Passengers of Modernity* (Basingstoke: Palgrave, 2005).

31. A. Meynell, *The Spirit of Place and Other Essays* (London: John Lane, 1899), 77.

32. Ibid. 78.

33. A. Meynell, *The Poems of Alice Meynell: Complete Edition* (London: Oxford University Press, 1940).

34. Fraser, *Beauty and Belief: Aesthetics and Religion in Victorian Literature*, 69.

35. A. Meynell, 'Pathos', in *The Rhythm of Life and Other Essays* (London: Elkin Matthews and John Lane, 1893), 47.

36. John Henry Newman discusses this in his essay on 'Catholic Literature in the English Tongue, 1854–8'. For a useful discussion of this perspective, see the introductory chapter of I. Ker, *The Catholic Revival in English Literature, 1845–1961* (Notre Dame, Ind.: University of Notre Dame Press, 2003).

37. A. K. Tuell, *Mrs. Meynell and Her Literary Generation* (New York: E. P. Dutton and Company, 1925), 68. Of course, Chesterton did not formally convert to Catholicism until 1922, long after he had written extensively for many of London's leading newspapers and journals, but, as most critics acknowledge, his theological position was Catholic long before he formally joined the Church.

38. For a helpful reading of Catholic writers in the twentieth century, see Woodman, *Faithful Fictions*.

39. Meynell, 'Pocket Vocabularies', in *The Rhythm of Life*, 41–2.

40. Meynell, 'Composure', in *The Rhythm of Life*, 55.

41. Tuell, *Mrs. Meynell and Her Literary Generation*, 181.

42. Meynell, 'The Point of Honour', in *The Rhythm of Life*, 51.

43. Ibid. 53.

44. In E. Dowson, *Verses* (London: Leonard Smithers, 1896).

45. Ibid.

46. Roden, *Same-Sex Desire in Victorian Religious Culture*, 141.

47. O. Wilde, *The Picture of Dorian Gray* (1891), ed. D. Lawler (New York: W. W. Norton and Co., 1988), 50.

48. Ibid. 76, 84.

49. Ibid. 88.

50. Ibid. 169

51. Ibid. 103.

52. Ibid. 91.

53. For a more detailed account of the change in Besant's thought, see A. Taylor, *Annie Besant: A Biography* (Oxford: Oxford University Press, 1992).

54. A. Besant, *Mysticism* (Madras: The Theosophist Office, 1912), 6.

55. C. Burdett, 'Romance, Reincarnation and Rider Haggard', in Bown, Burdett, and Thurschwell (eds.), *The Victorian Supernatural*, 220.

56. Ibid. 228.

57. M. Corelli, *The Sorrows of Satan* (1895), ed. P. Keating (Oxford: Oxford World's Classics, 1998), 57.

58. Anon., 'The Theological Works of Marie Corelli', *The Church Quarterly Review*, 51 (Jan. 1901), 369–79 (379).

59. Taylor, *Annie Besant*, 263.

60. A. Besant, *The Spirit of the Age* (Madras: Theosophist Office, 1908), 12.

61. A. Besant, *Theosophy and Christianity* (Madras: The Theosophical Publishing House, 1914), 4.

62. A. Meynell, 'Introduction', to Adeline Cashmore (ed.), *The Mount of Vision: A Book of English Mystical Verse* (London: Chapman and Hall, Limited, 1910), p. x.

63. G. K. Chesterton, *A Handful of Authors*, ed. D. Collins (London: Sheed and Ward, 1953), 175–6. Chesterton and Meynell shared a considerable admiration for one another and collaborated on an edition of selected work by Samuel Johnson. In her memoir of her mother, Viola Meynell commented that: 'The chief enthusiasm in the contemporary reading of all her later years was this for Chesterton. She found him to be at once the wittiest and the most serious of living writers.' See V. Meynell, *Alice Meynell: A Memoir* (London: Jonathan Cape, 1929), 259. Chesterton was similarly complimentary in his autobiography. His chapter on literary celebrities of the *fin de siècle* ends with a few words on Meynell: 'But among these literary figures, there was one figure whom I shall put last because I ought to put first... though she passed through my own life fitfully, and far more rarely than I could wish.' See G. K. Chesterton, *Autobiography* (1936) (Sevenoaks: Fisher Press, 1992) 294–5.

64. Chesterton, *Autobiography*, 143.

65. Ibid. 147, 150.

66. For a useful introduction to Yeats's mystical beliefs, see G. Hough, *The Mystery Religion of W. B. Yeats* (Sussex: The Harvester Press, 1984).

67. R. F. Foster, *W. B. Yeats: A Life*, i. *The Apprentice Mage, 1865–1914* (Oxford: Oxford University Press, 1997), 106.

68. Ibid.

69. W. B. Yeats, 'Bishop Berkeley' (1931), in *Essays and Introductions* (London: Macmillan and Co. Ltd., 1961), 396–411 (396).

70. Yeats, 'Magic' (1901), in *Essays and Introductions*, 28–52 (52).

71. Ibid. 52.

72. Yeats, 'The Symbolism of Poetry', in *Essays and Introductions*, 153–64 (156–7)

73. Chesterton, *Autobiography*, 152.

74. Ibid. 91. For an extended reading of pessimism and evil in *The Man who was Thursday: A Nightmare*, see M. Knight, *Chesterton and Evil* (New York: Fordham University Press, 2004).

75. Chesterton, *Autobiography*, 99.

76. G. K. Chesterton, *Orthodoxy* (1908) (London: John Lane, 1927), 242.

77. Ibid. 243–4.

Bibliography

ADELPHOS, 'Modern Spurious Revivals', in *The Revival: An Advocate of Evangelical Truth*, 14 (6 Feb. 1866), 71–3.

AIKIN, L., *Memoir of Mrs Barbauld including Letters and Notices of her Family and Friends* (London: George Bell and Sons, 1874).

ALLEN, R. C., *David Hartley on Human Nature* (New York: State University of New York, 1999).

ALTHOLZ, J. L., *Anatomy of a Controversy: The Debate over Essays and Reviews 1860–1864* (Aldershot: Scholar Press, 1994).

ALTHUSSER, L., *Lenin and Philosophy* (London: New Left Books, 1971).

ANDREWS, S., *Methodism and Society* (London: Seminar Studies in History, Longman, 1970).

—— *Unitarian Radicalism: Political Rhetoric 1770–1814* (Basingstoke: Palgrave, 2003).

—— 'Review of Thomas Bowdler's *The Family Shakespeare; in which nothing is added to the original text, but those words and expressions are omitted which cannot with propriety be read in a family*', *The Christian Observer*, 60 (May 1860), 360–1.

—— 'Theodore Parker and the Oxford Essayists', *The Christian Observer*, 60 (July 1860), 467–87.

—— *Good Words: The Theology of its Editor and of Some of its Contributors*, 2nd edn. (London: The Record Offices, 1863).

ANON., 'Cleaving to the Dust', *The Evangelical Magazine*, 6 (Dec. 1864), 791–4.

—— 'The Defects of Broad Church Theology', *Evangelical Christendom*, 6 (1 May 1865), 211–16.

—— 'Sensational Literature', *The Christian Observer,* 65 (Nov. 1865), 809–13.

—— 'Unity of Creed: The Union of the Christian Church', *The Revival: An Advocate of Evangelical Truth,* 15 (1866), 71–3.

—— 'The Theological Works of Marie Corelli', *The Church Quarterly Review*, 51 (Jan. 1901), 369–79.

ARATA, S., 'The Occidental Tourist: Dracula and the Anxiety of Reverse Colonization', *Victorian Studies*, 33 (1990), 621–45.

ARMSTRONG, I., *Victorian Poetry: Poetry, Poetics and Politics* (London: Routledge, 1993).

ARNOLD, M., *Literature and Dogma; an essay towards a better apprehension of the Bible* (London: Smith, Elder and Co., 1873).

—— *Culture and Anarchy* (1869), ed. J. Dover Wilson (Cambridge: Cambridge University Press, 1990).

ASHFIELD, A., and de BOLLA, P. (eds.), *The Sublime: A Reader in British Eighteenth-Century Aesthetic Theory* (Cambridge: Cambridge University Press, 1996).

BAKER, F., *William Grimshaw: 1708–1763* (London: The Epworth Press, 1963).

BALLEINE, G. R., *A History of the Evangelical Party in the Church of England* (London: Church Book Room Press, 1908).

—— *Devotional Pieces, compiled from the Psalms and the Book of Job: to which are prefixed, Thoughts on the Devotional Taste, on Sects, and on Establishments* (London: J. Johnson, 1775).

—— *Remarks on Mr Gilbert Wakefield's Enquiry into the Expediency and Propriety of Public or Social Worship* (London: Johnson, 1792).

—— *Pastoral Lessons and Parental Conversations, intended as a Companion to Hymns in Prose*, 3rd edn. (London: Darton and Harvey, 1803).

BARBAULD, A. L., *Anna Letitia Barbauld: Selected Poetry and Prose*, ed. W. McCarthy and E. Kraft (Peterborough, Ontario: Broadview, 2002).

BARKER, J., *Wordsworth: A Life* (London: Viking, 2000).

BEBBINGTON, D. W., *Evangelicalism in Modern Britain: A History From the 1730s to the 1980s* (London: Unwin Hyman, 1989).

BENJAMIN, W., *Illuminations*, ed. H. Arendt (London: Pimlico, 1999).

BENTLEY, J., *Ritualism and Politics in Victorian Britain: The Attempt to Legislate for Belief* (Oxford: Oxford University Press, 1978).

BERNSTEIN, S. D., *Confessional Subjects: Revelations of Gender and Power in Victorian Literature and Culture* (Chapel Hill, NC, and London: University of North Carolina Press, 1997).

BESANT, A., *The Spirit of the Age* (Madras: The Theosophist Office, 1908).

—— *Mysticism* (Madras: The Theosophist Office, 1912).

—— *Theosophy and Christianity* (Madras: The Theosophical Publishing House, 1914).

BLACK, A., *Political Thought in Europe 1250–1450* (Cambridge: Cambridge University Press, 1992).

BLAIR, K. (ed.), *John Keble and his Contexts* (London: AMS, 2004).

BLAKE, W., *The Poetry and Prose of William Blake*, ed. David V. Erdman (New York: Doubleday, 1965).

BOLAM, C. G., *et al.*, *The English Presbyterians: From Elizabethan Puritanism to Modern Unitarianism* (London: Allen and Unwin, 1968).

BOOTH, W., *All About the Salvation Army* (London: Salvation Army Book Stores, 1885).

—— *In Darkest England and the Way Out* (London: International Headquarters of The Salvation Army, 1890).

BOWN, N., BURDETT C., and THURSCHWELL, P. (eds.), *The Victorian Supernatural* (Cambridge: Cambridge University Press, 2004).

BRADLEY, I., *The Call to Seriousness: The Evangelical Impact on the Victorians* (London: Cape, 1976).

Breton, A. L. Le, *Memoir of Mrs Barbauld including Letters and Notices of her Family and Friends by her great niece* (London: George Bell and Sons, 1874).

Bright, M. H., 'English Literary Romanticism and the Oxford Movement', *Journal of the History of Ideas*, 40: 3 (1979), 385–404.

Brontë, C., *Jane Eyre* (1847), ed. M. Smith (Oxford: Oxford World's Classics, 2000).

Brontë, E., *The Poems of Emily Brontë*, ed. D. Roper and E. Chitham (Oxford: Clarendon Press, 1995).

Brown, A. W., *Recollections of the Conversation Parties of the Rev. Charles Simeon* (London, 1862).

Brown, C. G., *The Death of Christian Britain: Understanding Secularisation, 1800–2000* (London: Routledge, 2001).

Brown, M., and Behler, E. (eds.), *The Cambridge History of Literary Criticism: Romanticism* (Cambridge: Cambridge University Press, 2000).

Bruce, S., *God is Dead: Secularization in the West* (Oxford: Blackwell Publishers, 2002).

Bulwer Lytton, E., 'The Haunted and the Haunters', *Blackwood's Edinburgh Magazine*, 86 (Aug. 1859), 224–45.

Burke, E., *Edmund Burke: On Taste, On the Sublime and Beautiful, Reflections on the French Revolution, A Letter to a Noble Lord*, ed. C. W. Eliot (New York: P. F. Collier, 1909).

Burrows, H. W., *The Half-Century of Christ Church, Albany Street, St. Pancras* (London: Skeffington and Son, 1887).

Burrows, K. C., 'Some Remembered Strain: Methodism and the Anti-Hymns of Emily Brontë', *West Virginia University Philological Papers*, 24 (1977), 48–61.

Calhoun, C. (ed.), *Habermas and the Public Sphere* (Cambridge, Mass.: MIT Press, 1992).

Cashmore, A. (ed.), *The Mount of Vision: A Book of English Mystical Verse* (London: Chapman and Hall, Limited, 1910).

Chadwick, O., *The Mind of the Oxford Movement* (London: A. & C. Black, 1960).

—— *The Victorian Church*, 2 vols. (London: A. & C. Black, 1966).

—— *The Secularization of the European Mind in the Nineteenth Century* (Cambridge: Cambridge University Press, 1975).

Chalmers, T., *The Christian and Civic Economy of Large Towns*, ii (Glasgow: Chalmers & Collins, 1823).

—— et al., *Essays on Christian Union* (London: Hamilton, Adams and Co., 1845).

Chapple, J. A. V., and Pollard, A. (eds.), *The Letters of Mrs. Gaskell* (Manchester: Manchester University Press, 1966).

—— *Orthodoxy* (1908) (London: John Lane, 1927).

—— *A Handful of Authors*, ed. D. Collins (London: Sheed and Ward, 1953).

CHESTERTON, G. K., *Autobiography* (1936) (Sevenoaks: Fisher Press, 1992).

CHESTERTON, G. K., *The Man who was Thursday: A Nightmare* (1908), ed. S. Medcalf (Oxford: Oxford, World's Classics, 1996).

CHORLEY, H. F., *Memorials of Mrs Hemans: with illustrations of her literary character from her private correspondence,* 2 vols. (London: Saunders and Otley, 1836).

Christian Union, *A Full Report of the Proceedings of the Great Meeting Held at Exeter Hall, 1st June 1843 to promote and extend Christian Union* (London: D. Stroud, 1843).

CLARE, J., *John Clare: A Critical Edition of the Major Works,* ed. E. Robinson and D. Powell (Oxford: Oxford University Press, 1984).

CLERY, E. J., *The Rise of Supernatural Fiction 1762–1800* (Cambridge: Cambridge University Press, 1995).

CLIFFORD, D., and ROUSSILLON, L. (eds.), *Outsiders Looking In: The Rossettis Then and Now* (London: Anthem, 2003).

COLERIDGE, J. T. (ed.), *Memoir of the Rev. John Keble* (Oxford and London: James Parker, 1869).

COLERIDGE, S. T., *The Collected Letters of Samuel Taylor Coleridge,* ed. E. L. Griggs, 6 vols. (Oxford: Oxford University Press, 1956–71).

—— *The Friend,* ed. Barbara E. Rooke, 2 vols. (London: Routledge, 1969).

—— *The Collected Works of Samuel Taylor Coleridge,* ed. K. Coburn, 16 vols. (Princeton: Princeton University Press, 1969–2002).

—— *Table Talk, recorded by Henry Nelson Coleridge and John Taylor Coleridge,* ed. Carl Woodring (London: Routledge, 1990).

COLERIDGE, S., *Memoir and Letters of Sara Coleridge,* 2 vols. (London: Henry S. King and Co., 1873).

COLLINS, W., *The Moonstone* (1868), ed. J. Stewart (Harmondsworth: Penguin Classics, 1986).

—— *Armadale* (1864–6), ed. J. Sutherland (Harmondsworth: Penguin Books, 1995).

CORELLI, M., *The Sorrows of Satan* (1895), ed. P. Keating (Oxford: Oxford World's Classics, 1998).

COTTLE, J., *Early Recollections chiefly relating to … Samuel Taylor Coleridge during his long residence in Bristol,* 2 vols. (London, 1837).

COWPER, W., *Cowper: Selected Poems and Letters,* ed. A. N. Jeffares (Oxford: Oxford University Press, 1963).

COX, J., *Imperial Fault Lines: Christianity and Colonial Power in India, 1818–1940* (Stanford, Calif.: Stanford University Press, 2002).

CRONIN, R., CHAPMAN, A., and HARRISON, A. H. (eds.), *A Companion to Victorian Poetry* (Oxford: Blackwell, 2002).

CUNEO, T., and VAN WOUDENBERG, R. (eds.), *The Cambridge Companion to Thomas Reid* (Cambridge: Cambridge University Press, 2004).

CUNNINGHAM, V., *Everywhere Spoken Against: Dissent in the Victorian Novel* (Oxford: Clarendon Press, 1975).

CUPPLES, C., 'Pious Ladies and Methodist Madams: Sex and Gender in Anti-Methodist Writings of Eighteenth-Century England', *Critical Matrix*, 5 (1990), 30–60.

DALY, N., *Modernism, Romance, and the Fin de Siècle: Popular Fiction and British Culture, 1880–1914* (Cambridge: Cambridge University Press, 1999).

DAVIDOFF, L., and HALL, C., *Family Fortunes: Men and Women of the English Middle Class, 1780–1850*, 2nd edn. (London: Routledge, 2002).

DAVIE, D., *The Eighteenth-Century Hymn in England* (Cambridge: Cambridge University Press, 1993).

DAVIES, A., *The Quakers in English Society 1655–1725* (Oxford: Clarendon Press, 2000).

DAVIES, C. M., *Philip Paternoster: A Tractarian Love Story by an Ex-Puseyite*, 2 vols. (London: Richard Bentley, 1858).

DAVIES, H., *Worship and Theology in England: From Watts to Wesley to Martineau 1690–1900* (Cambridge: W. B. Erdmans, 1996).

DAVIS, P., *The Oxford English Literary History*, viii. *1830–1880: The Victorians* (Oxford: Oxford University Press, 2002).

DEFOE, D., *Fortunes and Misfortunes of the Famous Moll Flanders*, ed. G. A. Starr (Oxford: Oxford University Press, 1998).

DELAURA, D. J., *Hebrew and Hellene in Victorian England: Newman, Arnold, Pater* (Austin, Tex.: University of Texas Press, 1969).

DERRIDA, J., *Writing and Difference*, trans. A. Bass (London: Routledge, 2003).

—— and VATTIMO, G. (eds.), *Religion* (Cambridge: Polity Press, 1998).

DESMOND, A., *Huxley: From Devil's Disciple to Evolution's High Priest* (Harmondsworth: Penguin Books, 1997).

DICKENS, C., *Bleak House* (1852–3), ed. O. Sitwell (Oxford: Oxford Illustrated Dickens, 1991).

—— *A Christmas Carol* (1843), in *Christmas Books*, ed. E. Farjeon (Oxford: Oxford Illustrated Dickens, 1994).

—— *David Copperfield* (1849–50), ed. R. H. Malden (Oxford: Oxford Illustrated Dickens, 1996).

DORLING, W., *Memoirs of Dora Greenwell* (London: James Clarke and Co., 1885).

DOWSON, E., *Verses* (London: Leonard Smithers, 1896).

DREW, S., *The Life of Thomas Coke* (London, 1817).

DREYER, F., 'A "Religious Society Under Heaven": John Wesley and the Identity of Methodism', *Journal of British Studies*, 25 (1986), 62–83.

ELIOT, G., 'Evangelical Teaching: Dr Cumming', *Westminster Review*, 16 (Oct. 1855), 436–62.

—— 'Worldliness and Otherworldliness', *Westminster Review*, 67 (Jan. 1857).

ELIOT, G., *Daniel Deronda* (1876), ed. G. Handley (Oxford: Oxford World's Classics, 1988).

—— *Silas Marner* (1861), ed. D. Carroll (Harmondsworth: Penguin Classics, 1996).

—— *Middlemarch* (1871–2), ed. D. Carroll (Oxford: Oxford World's Classics, 1998).

—— *The Lifted Veil and Brother Jacob*, ed. S. Shuttleworth (Harmondsworth: Penguin Classics, 2001).

ELLIS, G. A., *A Memoir of Mrs Anna Laetitia Barbauld, with many of her letters* (Boston: James R. Osgood and Company, 1874).

ELLIS, I., *Seven Against Christ: A Study of 'Essays and Reviews'* (Leiden: Brill, 1980).

EMERSON, R. W., *Ralph Waldo Emerson: Selected Essays*, ed. L. Ziff (London: Penguin, 1982).

ESTLIN, J. P., *Familiar Lectures on Moral Philosophy*, 2 vols. (London: Longman, Hurst, Rees, Orne, and Brown, 1818).

FABER, F. W., *The Cherwell Water-Lily and Other Poems* (London, 1840).

FAY, E. (ed.), 'Romantic Passions', Romantic Circles Praxis Series, Apr. 1998 http://www.rc.umd.edu/praxis/

FEUERBACH, L., *The Essence of Christianity*, 2nd edn. (1843), trans. M. Evans (London: John Chapman, 1854).

FIELD, M., *Wild Honey from Various Thyme* (London: T. Fisher Unwin, 1908).

—— *The Wattlefold: Unpublished Poems by Michael Field*, collected by E. C. Fortey and with a preface by Father V. McNabb (Oxford: Basil Blackwell, 1930).

FISCH, H., *New Stories for Old: Biblical Patterns in the Novel* (New York: Macmillan Press, 1988).

FLEW, A., *David Hume: Writings on Religion* (Chicago: Open Court, 1992).

FOSTER, R. F., *W. B. Yeats: A Life*, i. *The Apprentice Mage, 1865–1914* (Oxford: Oxford University Press, 1997).

FOUCAULT, M., *Discipline and Punish: The Birth of the Prison*, trans. A. Sheridan (Harmondsworth: Penguin Books, 1979).

—— *The History of Sexuality: An Introduction* (1976), trans. Robert Hurley (London: Penguin, 1990).

FRASER, H., *Beauty and Belief: Aesthetics and Religion in Victorian Literature* (Cambridge: Cambridge University Press, 1986).

FULLER, A., *The Calvinistic and Socinian Systems Examined and Compared, as to their Moral Tendency* (London, 1802).

FYFE, A., *Science and Salvation: Evangelical Popular Science Publishing in Victorian Britain* (Chicago: University of Chicago Press, 2004).

GASKELL, E., *North and South* (1854–5), ed. Angus Easson (Oxford: Oxford University Press, 1998).

—— *Wives and Daughters* (1864–6), ed. Angus Easson (Oxford: Oxford University Press, 2000).

GAY, J., *The Beggar's Opera* (London: W. Heinemann, 1921).

GILL, S., *William Wordsworth: A Life* (Oxford: Oxford University Press, 1989).

—— *Wordsworth and the Victorians* (Oxford: Clarendon Press, 1998).

GILLEY, S., and SHEILS, W. J. (eds.), *A History of Religion in Britain: Practice and Belief from Pre-Roman Times to the Present* (Oxford: Blackwell, 1994).

GISSING, G., *In the Year of Jubilee* (1894), ed. J. Halperin (London: The Hogarth Press, 1987).

—— *The Nether World* (1889), ed. S. Gill (Oxford: Oxford World's Classics, 1992).

GLEADLE, K., *The Early Feminists: Radical Unitarians and the Emergence of the Women's Rights Movement 1831–51* (Basingstoke: Macmillan, 1995).

—— and RICHARDSON, S. (eds.), *Women in British Politics 1760–1860: The Power of the Petticoat* (Basingstoke: Macmillan Press, 2000).

—— (ed.), *Radical Writing on Women, 1800–1850: An Anthology* (Basingstoke: Palgrave, 2002).

GODWIN, W., *Memoirs of the Author of* A Vindication of the Rights of Woman (1798) (London: Penguin, 1987).

GORE, C. (ed.), *Lux Mundi: A Series of Studies in the Religion of the Incarnation* (London: John Murray, 1889).

GORDON, A., *Heads of English Unitarian History* (1895) (Bath: Cedric Chivers, 1970).

GOSLEE, D., *Romanticism and the Anglican Newman* (Athens, Oh.: Ohio University Press, 1996).

GRAY, J., 'Dora Greenwell's Commonplace Book', *Princeton University Library Chronicle*, 57: 1 (1995), 47–74.

GREEN, V. H. H., *The Young Mr Wesley: A Study of John Wesley and Oxford* (London: Edward Arnold, 1961).

—— *John Wesley* (London: Thomas Nelson and Sons, 1964).

GREENWELL, D., *John Woolman* (London: F. B. Kitto, 1871).

—— *Liber Humanitatis: A Series of Essays on Various Aspects of Spiritual and Social Life* (London: Daldy, Isbister and Co., 1875).

GRIFFIN, S. M., *Anti-Catholicism and Nineteenth-Century Fiction* (Cambridge: Cambridge University Press, 2004).

GUNTON, C., *The One, The Three & The Many* (Cambridge: Cambridge University Press, 1993).

HABERMAS, J., *The Structural Transformation of the Public Sphere*, trans. T. Burger and F. Lawrence (Cambridge: Polity Press, 1989).

—— *Between Facts and Norms: Contributions to a Discourse Theory of Law and Democracy*, trans. W. Rehg (Cambridge, Mass.: MIT Press, 1996).

HACKABOUT, M., *The Harlot's Progress, ingraved from Mr Hogarth's Originals*, 6th edn. (London: R. Montagu, 1740).

HAIGHT, G. S. (ed.), *The George Eliot Letters*, 7 vols. (New Haven: Yale University Press, 1954–6).

HALL, D. E. (ed.), *Muscular Christianity: Embodying the Victorian Age* (Cambridge: Cambridge University Press, 1994).

HANSON, E., *Decadence and Catholicism* (Cambridge, Mass.: Harvard University Press, 1997).

HARDY, T., *Jude the Obscure* (1894–5), ed. C. H. Sisson (Harmondsworth: Penguin Classics, 1984).

—— *Tess of the D'Urbervilles* (1891), ed. D. Skilton (Harmondsworth: Penguin Classics, 1985).

HARTMAN, G., *Scars of the Spirit: The Struggle Against Inauthenticity* (Basingstoke: Palgrave, 2002).

—— and O'HARA, D. T., *The Geoffrey Hartman Reader* (Edinburgh: Edinburgh University Press, 2004).

HEDLEY, D., *Coleridge, Philosophy and Religion: Aids to Reflection and the Mirror of the Spirit* (Cambridge: Cambridge University Press, 2000).

HEITZENRATER, R. P., *Wesley and the People called Methodists* (Nashville, Tenn.: Abingdon Press, 1995).

—— *Songs of the Affections, with Other Poems* (Edinburgh: Blackwood, 1830).

—— *Hymns on the Works of Nature, for the Use of Children* (London: John Mardon, 1833).

—— *Scenes and Hymns of Life, with Other Religious Poems* (Edinburgh: William Blackwood; London: T. Cadell, 1834).

—— *The Works of Mrs Hemans with a Memoir by Her Sister*, ed. H. Hughes, 7 vols. (Edinburgh: William Blackwood and Sons, 1839).

HEMANS, F., *Felicia Hemans: Selected Poems, Prose and Letters*, ed. G. Kelly Peterborough, (Ontario: Broadview Press, 2002).

HEMPTON, D., *Methodism and Politics in British Society 1750–1850* (London: Hutchinson, 1984).

HERRING, G., *What was the Oxford Movement?* (London: Continuum, 2002).

HERTEL, K., 'In Darkest London: George Gissing's *The Nether World* as Urban Novel', *The Gissing Journal*, 40: 1 (2004), 12–34.

HILLIARD, D., 'UnEnglish and UnManly: Anglo-Catholicism and Homosexuality', *Victorian Studies*, 25: 2 (1982), 181–210.

HILLIS MILLER, J., 'Introduction', in C. Dickens, *Bleak House* (Harmondsworth: Penguin Classics, 1971).

HILTON, B., *The Age of Atonement* (Oxford: Clarendon Press, 1988).

HODDER, E., *The Life and Work of the Seventh Earl of Shaftesbury, K.G.*, 3 vols. (London: Cassell, 1886).

HOLMES, F. M., *Exeter Hall and its Associations* (London: Hodder & Stoughton, 1881).

HOPKINS, G. M., *The Correspondence of Gerard Manley Hopkins and Richard Watson Dixon*, ed. Claude Colleer Abbott (Oxford and London: Oxford University Press, 1935).

—— *Poems and Prose of Gerard Manley Hopkins*, ed. W. H. Gardner (London: Penguin, 1953).

HOUGH, G., *The Mystery Religion of W. B. Yeats* (Sussex: The Harvester Press, 1984).

HOUSE, H., and STOREY, G. (eds.), *The Journals and Papers of Gerard Manley Hopkins* (Oxford and London: Oxford University Press, 1959).

HUYSMANS, J. K., *Against Nature*, ed. R. Baldick (Harmondsworth: Penguin Classics, 1959).

HUXLEY, T. H., *Collected Essays*, i (London: Macmillan and Co., 1894).

—— *Science and Education: Essays by Thomas H. Huxley* (London: Macmillan and Co., 1899).

INGLIS, K., *Churches and the Working Classes in Victorian England* (London: Routledge and K. Paul, 1963).

JASPER, D., *The Sacred and Secular Canon in Romanticism: Preserving the Sacred Truths* (Basingstoke: Macmillan, 2000).

—— *A Short Introduction to Hermeneutics* (London: Westminster John Knox Press, 2004).

—— *Religion of the Heart: Anglican Evangelicalism and the Nineteenth-Century Novel* (Oxford: Clarendon Press, 1979).

—— (ed.), *The Evangelical and Oxford Movements* (Cambridge: Cambridge University Press, 1983).

JAY, E., *Faith and Doubt in Victorian Britain* (Basingstoke: Macmillan, 1986).

JOHNSON, D. A. (ed.), *Women in English Religion* (New York and Toronto: The Edwin Mellen Press, 1983).

JOHNSTON, A., *Missionary Writing and Empire, 1800–1860* (Cambridge: Cambridge University Press, 2003).

JONES, M. G., *Hannah More* (Cambridge: Cambridge University Press, 1952).

JORDAN, J. (ed.), *The Cambridge Companion to Charles Dickens* (Cambridge: Cambridge University Press, 2001).

KANT, I., *Kant's Political Writings*, ed. H. Reiss, trans. H. B. Nisbet (Cambridge: Cambridge University Press, 1996).

—— *The Assize Sermon on 'National Apostasy'*, Oxford Movement Centenary preached by the Rev. J. Keble in St Mary's Church at Oxford on 14 July 1833, *Bodleian Pamphlets on Church Finance 23* (1850–1935).

—— *Occasional Papers and Reviews* (Oxford and London: James Parker and Co., 1877).

KEBLE, J., *Lectures on Poetry 1832–41*, trans. E. K. Francis, 2 vols. (Oxford: Clarendon Press, 1912).

KELLY, J. N. D., *The Athanasian Creed* (London: A. & C. Black, 1964).

—— *Early Christian Creeds*, 3rd edn. (Harlow: Longman, 1972).

KENT, D. A., *The Achievement of Christina Rossetti* (Ithaca, NY, and London: Cornell University Press, 1987).

KER, I., *The Catholic Revival in English Literature, 1845–1961* (Notre Dame, Ind.: University of Notre Dame Press, 2003).

KINGSLEY, C., *Alton Locke, Tailor and Poet: An Autobiography* (1850), 2 vols. (London: Chapman and Hall, 1851).

KNIGHT, D., *Science and Spirituality: The Volatile Connection* (London: Routledge, 2003).

—— and Eddy, M. D. (eds.), *Science and Beliefs: From Natural Philosophy to Natural Science, 1700–1900* (Aldershot: Ashgate, 2005).

KNIGHT, M., *Chesterton and Evil* (New York: Fordham University Press, 2004).

KNOX, E. A., *The Tractarian Movement: 1833–1845* (London: Putnam, 1934).

KNOX, R. A., *Enthusiasm: A Chapter in the History of Religion* (Oxford: Clarendon Press, 1950).

KRAMNICK, I. (ed.), *The Portable Enlightenment Reader* (London: Penguin, 1995).

LAMB, C., *The Complete Works of Charles Lamb* (New York: The Modern Library, 1935).

LANG, A., *Cock Lane and Common-Sense* (London: Longmans, Green, & Co., 1894).

LANGFORD, P., *A Polite and Commercial People: England 1727–1783* (Oxford: Oxford University Press, 1989).

LARSEN, T., *Contested Christianity: The Political and Social Contexts of Victorian Theology* (Waco, Tex.: Baylor University Press, 2004).

LARSON, J. L., *Dickens and the Broken Scripture* (Athens, Ga.: University of Georgia Press, 1985).

LE FANU, S., 'An Account of Some Strange Disturbances in an Old House in Aungier Street', *Dublin University Magazine*, 42 (Dec. 1853), 721–31.

—— *In A Glass Darkly* (1872), ed. R. Tracy (Oxford: Oxford World's Classics, 1993).

LEVINE, G. (ed.), *The Cambridge Companion to George Eliot* (Cambridge: Cambridge University Press, 2001).

LIDDON, H. P., *Life of Edward Bouverie Pusey*, ed. Revd. J. O. Johnston and the Revd. R. J. Wilson, 4 vols. (London: Longmans and Co., 1893–7).

LINTON, W. J., *James Watson: A Memoir* (1880) (New York: A. M. Kelley, 1971).

LOCKHART, J. G., *Memoirs of the Life of Sir Walter Scott, Bart*, 7 vols. (London: Murray and Whittaker, 1838).

LOOTENS, T., *Lost Saints: Silence, Gender and Victorian Literary Canonisation* (Charlottesville, Va., and London: University Press of Virginia, 1996).

LUCKHURST, R., *The Invention of Telepathy* (Oxford: Oxford University Press, 2002).

McCALMAN, I., *Radical Underworld: Prophets, Revolutionaries, and Pornographers in London 1795–1840* (Oxford: Clarendon Press, 1988).

McCosh, J., 'The Ulster Revival and its Physiological Accidents', *Evangelical Christendom*, 13 (1 Oct. 1859).

McDonnell, W. M., *Exeter Hall: A Theological Romance*, 10th edn. (Boston: Colby & Rich Publishers, 1885).

McLaughlin, J., *Writing the Urban Jungle: Reading Empire in London from Doyle to Eliot* (Charlottesville, Va.: University Press of Virginia, 2000).

Macleod, D., *Memoir of Norman Macleod*, 2 vols. (London: Daldy, Isbister and Co., 1876).

McLeod, H., *Class and Religion in the Late Victorian City* (London: Croom Helm, 1974).

—— *European Religion in the Age of the Great Cities 1830–1930* (London: Routledge, 1995).

—— *Religion and Society in England, 1850–1914* (Basingstoke: Macmillan, 1996).

—— and Ustorf, W. (eds.), *The Decline of Christendom in Western Europe, 1750–2000* (Cambridge: Cambridge University Press, 2003).

Makdisi, S., *William Blake and the Impossible History of the 1790s* (Chicago: University of Chicago Press, 2003).

Mansel, H., *The Limits of Religious Thought* (Oxford: John Murray, 1858).

Marsh, Jan, *Christina Rossetti: A Literary Biography* (London: Pimlico, 1995).

Marsh, Joss, *Word Crimes: Blasphemy, Culture, and Literature in Nineteenth-Century England* (Chicago: Chicago University Press, 1998).

Martineau, J., *Hymns for the Christian Church and Home* (London: John Greenwell, 1840).

—— 'Christina Rossetti and the Doctrine of Reserve', *The Journal of Victorian Culture*, 7: 2 (2002), 196–219.

—— ' "Some god of wild enthusiast's dreams": Methodist Enthusiasm and the Poetry of Emily Brontë', *Victorian Literature and Culture*, 31: 1 (2003), 263–77.

Mason, E., *Women Poets of the Nineteenth Century*, Writers and their Work (Tavistock: Northcote House, 2006).

Maurice, F. D., *Sequel to the Inquiry, What is Revelation?* (Cambridge: Macmillan & Co., 1860).

—— *Social Morality* (London: Macmillan, 1869).

Mee, J., *Romanticism, Enthusiasm and Regulation: Poetics and the Policing of Culture in the Romantic Period* (Oxford: Oxford University Press, 2003).

Meynell, A., *The Rhythm of Life and Other Essays* (London: Elkin Matthews and John Lane, 1893).

—— *The Spirit of Place and Other Essays* (London: John Lane, 1899).

—— *The Poems of Alice Meynell: Complete Edition* (London: Oxford University Press, 1940).

Meynell, V., *Alice Meynell: A Memoir* (London: J. Cape, 1929).

MILBANK, A., *Dante and the Victorians* (Manchester: Manchester University Press, 1998).

MILLER, P. N., *Defining the Common Good: Empire, Religion and Philosophy in Eighteenth-Century Britain* (Cambridge: Cambridge University Press, 1994).

MITCHELL, S., *The Fallen Angel: Chastity, Class and Women's Reading, 1835– 1880* (Bowling Green, Oh.: Bowling Green University Popular Press, 1981).

MONRO, E., *Sermons Principally on the Responsibilities of the Ministerial Office* (London: J. H. Parker, 1850).

MOORE, J., *The Post-Darwinian Controversies: A Study of the Protestant Struggles to Come to Terms with Darwin in Great Britain and America, 1870–1900* (Cambridge: Cambridge University Press, 1979).

MORE, H., *Practical Piety; or, The Influence of the Religion of the Heart on the Conduct of Life*, 2 vols. (1811).

—— *Hannah More: Her Bible Dramas, Poems and Tragedies Complete*, 2 vols. (London: Thynne and Co., 1931).

MORLEY, E. J. (ed.), *Henry Crabb Robinson on Books and Their Writers*, 3 vols. (London: J. M. Dent, 1938).

MORRIS, D. B., *The Religious Sublime: Christian Poetry and Critical Tradition in Eighteenth-Century England* (Lexington, Ky.: The University Press of Kentucky, 1972).

MOTT, A. (ed.), *The Journal and Essays of John Woolman* (London: Macmillan, 1922).

NEWBIGIN, L., *Truth to Tell: The Gospel as Public Truth* (Grand Rapids, Mich.: William B. Eerdmans Publishing Company, 1991).

NEWMAN, J. H., *Discussions and Arguments on Various Subjects* (London: Longmans and Green, 1911).

—— *Apologia pro Vita Sua* (1864), ed. I. Ker (London: Penguin, 1994).

NEWSOME, D., *The Parting of Friends: A Study of the Wilberforces and Henry Manning* (London: John Murray, 1966).

NOCKLES, P. B., *The Oxford Movement in Context: Anglican High Churchmanship 1760–1857* (Cambridge: Cambridge University Press, 1994).

NORMAN, E., *The Victorian Christian Socialists* (Cambridge: Cambridge University Press, 1987).

NORTON, D., *A History of the English Bible as Literature* (Cambridge: Cambridge University Press, 2000).

NUMBERS, R. L., and STENHOUSE, J. (eds.), *Disseminating Darwinism: The Role of Place, Race, Religion and Gender* (Cambridge: Cambridge University Press, 1999).

OLIPHANT, M., *The Life of Edward Irving*, 2nd edn. (London: Hurst & Blackett, 1862).

OLLARD, S. L. (ed.), *A Dictionary of English Church History* (1912) (London and Oxford: A. R. Mowbray, 1948).

OWEN, A., *The Place of Enchantment: British Occultism and the Culture of the Modern* (Chicago: University of Chicago Press, 2004).

PAINE, T., *Political Writings*, ed. B. Kuklick (Cambridge: Cambridge University Press, 2000).

PALEY, M. D., 'Apocalypse and Millennium in the Poetry of Coleridge', *The Wordsworth Circle*, 23: 1 (1992), 24–34.

PATER, W., *The Renaissance* (1873), ed. Adam Phillips (Oxford: Oxford University Press, 1986).

——*Appreciations: With an Essay on Style* (London: Macmillan, 1889).

PEARCE, J., *Literary Converts: Spiritual Inspiration in an Age of Unbelief* (London: HarperCollins, 1999).

PERRY, S. (ed.), *Coleridge's Notebooks: A Selection* (Oxford: Oxford University Press, 2002).

PETROVNA, E. '"And I saw the Holy City": London Prophecies in Charles Dickens and George Eliot', *Literary London: Interdisciplinary Studies in the Representation of London*, 2: 2 (2004).

PICKERING, S., *The Moral Tradition in English Fiction, 1785–1850* (Hanover, NH: The University Press of New England, 1976).

POCOCK, J. G. A. (ed.), *Three British Revolutions: 1641, 1688, 1776* (Princeton: Princeton University Press, 1980).

POOLE, A., *Gissing in Context* (Basingstoke: Macmillan, 1975).

PORTER, A., *Religion versus Empire: British Protestant Missionaries and Overseas Expansion, 1700–1914* (Manchester: Manchester University Press, 2004)

PRICE, R., *Observations on the nature of civil liberty, the principles of government, and the justice and policy of the war with America. To which is added an appendix, containing a state of the national debt, an estimate of the money drawn from the public by the taxes, and an account of the national income and expenditure since the last war* (London: T. Cadell, 1776).

——*A Sermon, Delivered to a Congregation of Protestant Dissenters, at Hackney, On the 10th of February last*, 2nd edn. (London, 1779).

PRICKETT, S., *Romanticism and Religion: The Tradition of Coleridge and Wordsworth in the Victorian Church* (Cambridge: Cambridge University Press, 1976).

——*Narrative, Religion and Science: Fundamentalism versus Irony, 1700–1999* (Cambridge: Cambridge University Press, 2002).

——*An Examination of Dr Reid's Inquiry into the Human Mind on the Principles of Common Sense, Dr Beattie's Essay on the Nature and Immutability of Truth, and Dr Oswald's Appeal to Common Sense in Behalf of Religion* (London: J. Johnson, 1774).

——*The doctrine of philosophic necessity illustrated an appendix to the Disquisitions relating to matter and spirit. To which is added an answer to the Letters on materialism and on Hartley's Theory of the mind* (1777) (London, 1782).

PRIESTLEY, J., *Theological and Miscellaneous Works*, ed. J. T. Rutt, 25 vols. (London: George Smallfield, 1817–31).

PRIESTLEY, J., *Autobiography of Joseph Priestley. Contains Memoirs of Dr Joseph Priestley, written by himself* (1806), introd. J. Lindsay (Bath: Adams and Dart, 1970).

PUNSHON, J., *Portrait in Grey: A Short History of the Quakers* (London: QHS, 1986).

RADCLIFFE, A., *The Italian or the Confessional of the Black Penitents: A Romance*, introd. E. J. Clery, ed. F. Garber (Oxford: Oxford University Press, 1998).

RANDALL, I., and HILBORN, D., *One Body in Christ: The History and Significance of the Evangelical Alliance* (Carlisle: Paternoster Press, 2001).

REARDON, B. M. G., *Religious Thought in the Victorian Age: A Survey from Coleridge to Gore* (London: Longman, 1980).

REED, J. S., ' "Giddy Young Men": A Counter-Cultural Aspect of Victorian Anglo-Catholicism', *Comparative Social Research*, 11 (1989), 209–26.

—— *The Cultural Politics of Victorian Anglo-Catholicism* (Nashville, Tenn., and London: Vanderbilt University Press, 1996).

—— *Gorious Battle: The Cultural Politics of Victorian Anglo-Catholicism* (Nashvile, Tenn.: Vanderbilt University Press, 1996).

RIVERS, I., *Reason, Grace and Sentiment: A Study of the Language of Religion and Ethics in England 1660–1780*, 2 vols. (Cambridge: Cambridge University Press, 1991–2000).

ROBERTS, J., 'St Paul's Gifts to Blake's Aesthetic: "O Human Imagination, O Divine Body" ', *The Glass*, 15 (2003), 8–18.

RODEN, F., *Same-Sex Desire in Victorian Religious Culture* (Basingstoke: Palgrave, 2002).

ROE, N., *Wordsworth and Coleridge: The Radical Years* (Oxford: Clarendon Press, 1988).

ROSSETTI, C., *The Face of the Deep* (London: S.P.C.K., 1892).

—— *Christina Rossetti: The Complete Poems*, ed. R. W. Crump and B. S. Flowers (London: Penguin, 2001).

ROWELL, G., *Hell and the Victorians: A Study of the Nineteenth-Century Theological Controversies Concerning Eternal Punishment and the Future Life* (Oxford: Clarendon Press, 1974).

—— *The Vision Glorious: Themes and Personalities of the Catholic Revival in Anglicanism* (Oxford: Oxford University Press, 1983).

ROWLAND, C., (ed.), *Radical Christianity: A Reading of Recovery* (Oxford: Polity Press, 1988).

—— *The Cambridge Companion to Liberation Theology* (Cambridge: Cambridge University Press, 1999).

RUSSELL, G., and TUITE, C., (eds.), *Romantic Sociability: Social Networks and Literary Culture in Britain 1770–1840* (Cambridge: Cambridge University Press, 2002).

RYLE, J. C., 'Evangelical Religion: what it is, and what it is not', in *Truths for the Times* (London: William Hunt and Company, 1867).

SAGE, V., *Horror Fiction in the Protestant Tradition* (Basingstoke: Macmillan, 1988).

SAUNDERS, J., 'Putting the Reader Right: Reassessing Hannah More's *Cheap Repository Tracts*', *Romanticism on the Net*, 16 (Nov. 1999).

SCHAD, J., *Queer Fish: Christian Unreason from Darwin to Derrida* (Brighton: Sussex Academic Press, 2004).

SCHLEIERMACHER, F., *On Religion: Speeches to its Cultured Despisers* (1799), trans. and ed. R. Crouter (Cambridge: Cambridge University Press, 2003).

SCHOFIELD, R. E., *The Enlightenment of Joseph Priestley: A Study of his Life and Work from 1733 to 1773* (University Park, Pa.: Pennsylvania State University Press, 1997).

SCHRAMM, J. M., *Testimony and Advocacy in Victorian Law, Literature and Theology* (Cambridge: Cambridge University Press, 2000).

SEED, J., 'Gentlemen Dissenters: The Social and Political Meanings of Rational Dissent in the 1770s and 1780s', *The Historical Journal*, 28: 2 (1985), 299–325.

SEMLER, J. S., *D. J. S. Semlers Abfertigung der neuen Geister und alten Irtümer in der Lohmannischen Begeisterung ... nebst theologischen Untersicht von dem Ungrunde der gemeinen Meinung von leiblichen Besitzungen des Teufels und Bezauberungen der Christen* (Halle, 1760).

SHEA, V., and WHITLA, W. (eds.), *Essays and Reviews: The 1860 Text and its Reading* (Charlottesville, Va.: University Press of Virginia, 2000).

SHIPLEY, O. (ed.), *The Church and the World: Essays on Questions of the Day in 1868* (London: Longmans, Green, Reader and Dyer, 1868).

SIMMEL, G., *Simmel on Culture: Selected Writings*, ed. D. Frisby and M. Featherstone (London: Sage Publications, 1997).

SMART, C., *Rejoice in the Lamb: A Song from Bedlam*, ed. W. F. Stead (London: Jonathan Cape, 1939).

—— *The Poetical Works of Christopher Smart*, ed. K. Williamson (Oxford: Clarendon Press, 1980–96).

SMITH, A., *The Theory of Moral Sentiments* (1759), ed. K. Haakonssen (Cambridge: Cambridge University Press, 2002).

SNELL, K. D. M., and ELL, P. S., *Rival Jerusalems: The Geography of Victorian Religion* (Cambridge: Cambridge University Press, 2000).

SREBRNIK, P., *Alexander Strahan: Victorian Publisher* (Ann Arbor: University of Michigan Press, 1986).

STEAD, W. T., *Mrs Booth of the Salvation Army* (London: James Nisbet & Co. Ltd., 1900).

STOKER, B., *Dracula*, ed. M. Ellmann (Oxford: Oxford World's Classics, 1998).

STOUT, H., *The divine Dramatist: George Whitefield and the Rise of Modern Evangelicalism* (Grand Rapids, Mich.: Eerdmans, 1991).

TAYLOR, A., *Annie Besant: A Biography* (Oxford: Oxford University Press, 1992).

TAYLOR, B., *Eve and the New Jerusalem: Socialism and Feminism in the Nineteenth Century* (London: Virago, 1983).

TAYLOR, B., *Mary Wollstonecraft and the Feminist Imagination* (Cambridge: Cambridge University Press, 2003).

TENNYSON, G. B., *Victorian Devotional Poetry: The Tractarian Mode* (Cambridge, Mass.: Harvard University Press, 1981).

THISELTON, A. C., *New Horizons in Hermeneutics: The Theory and Practice of Transforming Biblical Reading* (Grand Rapids, Mich.: Zondervan, 1992).

THOMPSON, E. P., *The Making of the English Working Class* (New York: Pantheon, 1963).

—— *Witness Against the Beast: William Blake and Moral Law* (Cambridge: Cambridge University Press, 1993).

THOMSON, J., *The City of Dreadful Night and Other Poems* (London: Reeves and Turner, 1888).

TOLAND, J., *Socinianism truly stated; an example of fair dealing in all theological controversys; to which is prefixt, indifference in disputes: recommended by a pantheist to an orthodox friend* (London, 1705).

Tracts for the Times, by members of the University of Oxford, 6 vols. (London, 1838–41).

TROLLOPE, A., *Barchester Towers* (1857), ed. J. Sutherland (Oxford: Oxford University Press, 1998).

TUCKER, S., *Enthusiasm: A Study of Semantic Change* (Cambridge: Cambridge University Press, 1972).

TUELL, A. K., *Mrs. Meynell and Her Literary Generation* (New York: E. P. Dutton and Company, 1925).

TURNER, M., *Trollope and the Magazines: Gendered Issues in Mid-Victorian Britain* (Basingstoke: Palgrave, 2000).

VADILLO, A., *Women Poets and Urban Aestheticism: Passengers of Modernity* (Basingstoke: Palgrave, 2005).

VANZANTEN GALLAGHER, S., and WALHOUT, M. D., *Literature and the Renewal of the Public Sphere* (Basingstoke: Macmillan Press, 2000).

VARGO, L., 'The Case of Anna Laetitia Barbauld's "To Mr C(olerid)ge"', *Charles Lamb Bulletin*, 102 (1998), 55–63.

VATTIMO, G., *End of Modernity: Nihilism and Hermeneutics in Postmodern Culture*, trans. J. Snyder (Baltimore: Johns Hopkins University Press, 1988).

—— *Belief*, trans. L. D'Isanto and D. Webb (Oxford: Polity, 1999).

WAKEFIELD, G., *A General Reply to the Arguments Against the Enquiry into Public Worship* (London, 1792).

WALKER, G., *Sermons* (London, 1790).

WALKER, P. J., *Pulling the Devil's Kingdom Down: The Salvation Army in Victorian Britain* (Berkeley: University of California Press, 2001).

WALKOWITZ, J., *City of Dreadful Delight: Narratives of Sexual Danger in Late-Victorian London* (London: Virago Press, 1992).

WALSH, W., *The Secret History of the Oxford Movement*, 3rd edn. (London: Swan Sonnenschein and Co., 1898).

WARD, G., *Cities of God* (London: Routledge, 2000).

WARD, M. A., *A Writer's Recollections 1856–1900* (London: W. Collins Sons and Co. Ltd., 1918).

WARD, W. R., *Religion and Society in England 1790–1850* (London: B. T. Batsford, 1972).

WATSON, J. R., *The Poetry of Gerard Manley Hopkins* (London: Penguin, 1987).

—— *The English Hymn: A Critical and Historical Study* (Oxford: Clarendon Press, 1997).

WATTS, I., *The Doctrine of the Passions Explained and Improved, Or, A Brief and comprehensive scheme of the Natural Affections of Mankind, Attempted in a plain and easy Method. With an Account of their Names, Nature, Appearances, Effects and Different Uses in Human Life to which are subjoined Moral and Divine Rules for the Regulation or Government of them* (1729), 5th edn. (London: J. Buckland and T. Longman, 1770).

—— *The Works of the Rev. Isaac Watts D. D.*, ed. Edward Parsons, 7 vols. (Leeds: Edward Bains, 1800).

WEBER, M., *The Protestant Ethic and the Spirit of Capitalism*, trans. T. Parsons (London: Allen and Unwin, 1930).

WELCH, C., *Protestant Thought in the Nineteenth Century*, i. *1799–1870* (New Haven: Yale University Press, 1972).

WESLEY, C., *A Collection of Psalms and Hymns* (London: W. Strahan, 1744).

—— *Hymns for those that Seek and those that have Redemption in the Blood of Jesus Christ* (Bristol: Felix Farley, 1747).

WESLEY, J., *The Works of John Wesley*, ed. A. C. Outler, 26 vols. (Nashville, Tenn.: Abingdon Press; Oxford: Clarendon Press, 1975–).

WESLEY, S., Jr., *John Wesley's First Hymn-Book: A Collection of Psalms and Hymns* (1737), ed. F. Baker and G. W. Williams (Charleston, SC: Dalcho Historical Society, 1964).

WHEELER, M., *Heaven, Hell and the Victorians* (Cambridge: Cambridge University Press, 1994).

—— *Ruskin's God* (Cambridge: Cambridge University Press, 1999).

WHITE, D. E., 'Anna Barbauld and Dissenting Devotion: Extempore, Particular, Experimental', *Enlightenment, Gender and Religion Colloquium*, University of London (2004).

WHITE, N., *Hopkins: A Literary Biography* (Oxford: Clarendon Press, 1992).

WIGLEY, J., *The Rise and Fall of the Victorian Sunday* (Manchester: Manchester University Press, 1980).

WILDE, O., *De Profundis and Other Writings*, ed. H. Pearson (London: Penguin Classics, 1986).

—— *The Picture of Dorian Gray* (1891), ed. D. Lawler (New York: W. W. Norton and Co., 1988).

WILLIAMS, I., *The Cathedral, or the Catholic and Apostolic Church in England, in verse* (Oxford, 1838).

—— *The Altar: Or, Meditations in Verse on the Great Christian Sacrifice* (London: James Burns, 1847).

WILSON, J., 'Was Margaret a Christian?', *The Eclectic Review*, 12 (1842), 568–79.

WOLFFE, J., *The Protestant Crusade in Great Britain, 1829–1860* (Oxford: Clarendon Press, 1991).

WOLLSTONECRAFT, M., *The Works of Mary Wollstonecraft*, ed, J. Todd and M. Butler, 7 vols. (London: Pickering and Chatto, 1989).

WOLTERSTORFF, N., *Thomas Reid and the Story of Epistemology* (Cambridge: Cambridge University Press, 2001).

WOOD, E., *East Lynne* (1860–1), ed. A. Maunder (Peterborough, Ontario: Broadview, 2002).

WOODMAN, T., *Faithful Fictions: The Catholic Novel in British Literature* (Milton Keynes: Open University Press, 1991).

WORDSWORTH, W., *William Wordsworth: Poems*, ed. J. O. Hayden, 2 vols. (London: Penguin, 1977).

—— *The Prelude: 1799, 1805, 1850*, ed. J. Wordsworth, M. H. Abrams, and S. Gill (London: W. W. Norton, 1979).

YATES, N., *Buildings, Faith and Worship: The Liturgical Arrangement of Anglican Churches 1600–1900* (Oxford: Clarendon Press, 1991).

YEATS, W. B., *Essays and Introductions* (London: Macmillan and Co. Ltd., 1961).

YOUNG, E., *The Poetical Works of Edward Young*, 2 vols. (London: George Bell, 1906).

ZEMKA, S., *Victorian Testaments: The Bible, Christology, and Literary Authority in Early-Nineteenth-Century British Culture* (Stanford, Calif.: Stanford University Press, 1997).

ŽIŽEK, S., *On Belief* (London: Routledge, 2001)

—— *The Puppet and the Dwarf: The Perverse Core Of Christianity* (Cambridge, Mass.: MIT Press, 2003).

Index